BEHOLDING BEAUTY

BEHOLDING BEAUTY

Mary and the Song of Songs

By Gregory Cleveland, OMV

Pauline
BOOKS & MEDIA
Boston

Library of Congress Cataloging-in-Publication Data: 2020934873

ISBN 10: 0-8198-1245-5

ISBN 13: 978-0-8198-1245-2

Cover design by Rosanna Usselmann

Cover art: Batoni, Virgin of the Annunciation; istockphoto.com/©Fomalgaut

---

Published by Pauline Books & Media, 50 Saint Pauls Avenue, Boston, MA 02130-3491

Printed in the U.S.A.

www.pauline.org

Pauline Books & Media is the publishing house of the Daughters of St. Paul, an international congregation of women religious serving the Church with the communications media.

2 3 4 5 6 7 8 9 28 27 26 25 24 23

Contents

Foreword

I confess that my first tentative forays into the Song of Songs were confusing and even comical. The ancient love similes were difficult for me to relate to, such as: "Your hair is like a flock of goats moving down the slopes of Gilead. Your teeth are like a flock of shorn ewes that have come up from the washing" (Song 4:1–2). I wondered how far any amorous modern might get in wooing his sweetheart by inspecting her teeth and comparing her to farm animals.

Indeed, the Song of Songs is utterly unique among the sacred books of the Bible, almost daring one to take it seriously. Those who do are changed forever.

The Song of Songs occupies a central place in the Scriptures, both literally and figuratively. It stands alone, even within the wisdom genre where it is nestled, the whole category itself inherently lyrical and stylized. The Song has no references to the spiritual disciplines (liturgy, prayer, fasting, study of Scripture, evangelization, etc.); God is never mentioned directly in the entire text; and its sensual language and intimate marital context are impossible to ignore.

Add to that the obscure way the text is arranged—somewhat like a play—and the Song of Songs can intimidate and even put off the casual reader. But this is no casual book, and Father Gregory Cleveland, OMV is no casual observer. He has experienced what this sacred song is meant to communicate to humanity about God's love.

Notably, the ancient peoples of the Bible did not express the superlative adjectives the way we do: "good, better, best." Rather, they expressed something in triple repetition. For example: "Holy, holy, holy is the LORD of hosts" (Is 6:3); "This is the temple of the LORD, the temple of the LORD, the temple of the LORD" (Jer 7:4); "O land, land, land, hear the word of the LORD" (Jer 22:29); and "A ruin, a ruin, a ruin—I will make it" (Ezek 21:27).

Another prominent ancient Hebrew method for superlative expression was to declare something the X of all other X's: "Holy of holies"; King of kings"; "Lord of Lords"; "vanity of vanities." How utterly beautiful this phrase is, the *song of songs*.

In *Beholding Beauty*, Father Greg Cleveland invites us to contemplate the song of all songs with him. The Song of Songs in the Scriptures is the superlative song, the loveliest song ever composed. Passionate drama and delicate poetry about the richest king to ever rule Israel and a common girl combine in this sacred expression of intense passion and profound love.

As one who struggled with worthlessness and rage under the damaging effects of father wounds and early trauma that caused me to doubt God's love and care, I, too, have been satiated and eternally changed by the lover in this Song. I have never been so deeply touched, my spirit has never been so profoundly healed, my heart has never swelled so large, nor my spirit grown as fertile, as they have through my own slow, deliberate meditation on this book of the Bible.

How many of us are suspicious of God's motives? Or suspect he punishes with suffering? Or wonder: *Is this all there is? I thought Christianity was supposed to be more exciting. I expected* more.

I believe most of us are stuck in such ruminations. In my years of ministry as "Bible Study Evangelista," I have spoken with Catholic after Catholic who is more-or-less stagnant in his or her faith. Whether throughout a lifetime or simply a season, we long to be stunned with eternity. We ache for the beauty we glimpse in the weeping of violins; the silent, earthy creeping of dusk; and the bliss of sloppy kisses and gangly little boy arms around a tired, disillusioned neck.

Father Greg invites us to contemplate Our Lady as the ultimate subject of spiritual beauty and the icon of the Church in this soaring canticle. In *Beholding Beauty*, Father Greg explores Mary as the guide to that elusive *more* that the soul searches and longs for and calls us away from the sleep of complacency to an unimaginable eternal bliss in the final consummation—union with God.

He explores Mary's own yearnings, her pondering heart, her unique grace and humility that led to a supreme and incarnational generosity. He probes her terrible sorrow and guides us to follow her into and through our own terrible sorrows so that we, too, can experience the secret bliss of an incarnational faith that changes the world.

Masterfully, he breaks open the teachings of the Church and the observations of the saints on the Song of Songs. He leads us through the difficult imagery, the ancient language, and the comical superficiality into the riveting depths of a Reality so deep, so profound, and so transformative, that your faith will never be the same if you permit the message to penetrate.

So read this substantial labor of love with an open heart. Ask Mary to reveal herself more fully to you as you consider her from so many angles and titles. Savor every chapter and allow the Holy Spirit to enrapture you as he enraptured her, and other serious contemplatives of his Song for millennia. Implore him to impress upon your weary soul what Father Greg himself came to realize through the Song of Songs, "that God's heart had a place that only I could fill."

Sonja Corbitt

Bible Study Evangelista
Best-selling author, broadcaster, speaker,
and multi-media Bible study producer

Introduction

A New Perspective on Mary

One morning, I was praying with the words of the Song of Songs in the chapel of our rectory in Denver. My eyes were closed, and an image from our stained glass window in the sanctuary came to mind. The image is of the Woman of Revelation 12, pregnant with Jesus and ready to give birth, clothed with the sun, with the moon at her feet. Scholars regard the Woman as a figure of the Church, and especially of Mary, as the holiest and most representative member and symbol of the Church.[1] I felt at one with Mary in her experience of being full of grace, while realizing that I had a long way to go in responding to grace. I felt a desire to imitate Mary in her full and free surrender to grace, in her total self-giving to Jesus, who had given himself to her and to the whole human race in the Incarnation. It enthralled me that Mary, in receiving her beloved Lord, was in fact the complete fulfillment of the magnificent bride of the Song of Songs. Since, as Saint Augustine says, Mary is the perfect disciple of Jesus

1. See Chapter 13 for more details on the identity of the woman.

Christ, how could we not see her as embodying the role of the bride in a preeminent way? No human being ever received God's love and grace as fully as did Mary, to the point of God becoming man in her. She conceived Christ in her heart and then in her womb. Mary, as spouse of the Holy Spirit, shows us our capacity to receive God and be entirely possessed by him. In receiving Christ, she was also empowered to completely give herself to him, spirit, soul, and body, in love as his mother. She became his partner in the work of salvation and was exalted to reign with him as Queen of heaven and earth. I prayed to imitate Mary the bride who experiences the fullness of God's life of grace and the eternal fulfillment of her being.

The Song of Songs (also called the Canticle of Canticles) is a book about love, our deepest desire and eternal destiny. Since God is love, the Song is first of all about the love that God has in himself as a holy Trinity of persons in a mutual exchange of love. The Song is also about the love that God has for each of us, both individually and collectively as the body of Christ, the Church. God created us to be a communion of love to reflect the love that he has in himself, and to participate in his love. He created us male and female in his image to mirror the perfect exchange of love among the distinct persons of the Trinity. The love of man and woman in the Song reflects the Trinity's love and serves as the best analogy of the love God has for us. The book is a metaphor for the love, light, and life that God gives us through intimate relationship. We are awakened to love the Lord in return with fervor, knowledge, and commitment. The Song offers a poetic description of God's intimacy with us, enabling us to name and express our relationship with the Lord. Ellen Davis says:

> the cultivation of real intimacy—with God, with other humans, with the creatures—is the greatest social and spiritual challenge of our time. Precisely because it addresses us in

> the language of yearning, not satisfaction, the Song can help us grow to meet that challenge. Unhealthy yearning—greed, lust—may destroy us and even the planet, as we are now beginning to recognize. But there is immense healing power in yearning for the *shalom* (health, wholeness, peace) for which we were created. The Song can guide us because it expresses our deepest desire and seeks to direct it toward healing in all these areas.[2]

The love poetry in the Song of Songs is laden with symbols. The Temple signifies the Bridegroom, and the land and people of Israel are the primary images connected with the bride. The Song is also rife with allusions to the Lord's presence and activity in the salvation history of his chosen people. Solidly based in this literal understanding, the Spirit leads us to greater spiritual understanding of the inexhaustible truths of his Word in these Scriptures. According to this spiritual understanding, Church Fathers and Mothers fathom the Song as the love of God for Israel, of Christ for his Church, and of Christ for the individual Christian. Christ is truly the Bridegroom of our souls, a union realized most fully in the life of the Blessed Virgin Mary as the Mother of God and perfect disciple of Jesus. Scripture scholar D. Bertotto declares that in light of current biblical exegesis and the commentaries of the Fathers of the Church and Scholastic masters, the bride of the Song of Songs symbolizes both the Daughter of Zion and the Israelites in their faithful bond of love with their Bridegroom Yahweh. The figure of the bride also symbolizes the Catholic Church, and each faithful member, as the new Israel. The bride is typified in a preeminent way by the

2. Ellen F. Davis, *Getting Involved with God, Rediscovering the Old Testament* (Lanham, MD: Cowley Publications, 2001), 81.

Church's most holy member and representative, Mary. She is most notably a fulfillment of the "garden locked, the sealed fountain" (Song 4:12) which describes her virginity; and the "you are all fair . . . there is no flaw in you" (Song 4:7), describing her immaculate nature.

Medieval commentators regarded Mary as the fulfillment of the figure of the bride throughout the entire Song of Songs. The Song of Songs became a complete interpretive key to understanding the mysteries of the relationship of Mary to the Most Holy Trinity. According to Ann Astell, "Mary's historical relationship to Christ establishes a narrative context in which the Song of Songs becomes literally true."[3] Rupert of Deutz (d. 1129), Honorius of Auton (d. 1156), and Alain de Lille (d. 1202) all wrote expositions of the Song that recognize Mary as the fulfillment of the bride. Although Bernard of Clairvaux did not attribute everything spoken of the bride to Mary, he interpreted certain passages of the Canticle as pertaining to Mary. He popularized the Marian interpretation.[4] Alain de Lille writes: "It must be known that everything in this Canticle which is said about the blessed Mary refers to her corporal or spiritual acts."[5] In his introduction he states, "And so, although the song of love, Solomon's wedding song, refers particularly and according to its spiritual sense to the Church, in its most particular and spiritual reference it signifies the most glorious Virgin."[6]

---

3. Ann W. Astell, *The Song of Songs in the Middle Ages* (Ithaca, NY: Cornell University Press, 1990), 44.

4. Ibid., 44.

5. Alain de Lille, *Elucidatio in Cantica Canticorum*, PL 210, C58, in Astell, 44–45.

6. Alain de Lille, in Denys Turner, *Eros and Allegory, Medieval Exegesis of the Song of Songs* (Kalamazoo, MI: Cistercian Publications, 1995), 294.

The Bridegroom of the Song refers to the Lord, and the bride refers to both the Church and the individual Christian. Mary, as the greatest disciple of Christ, is the preeminent Christian. She exemplifies the bride in an exceptional way.[7] Mary is the New Testament fulfillment of the Old Testament bride, Israel's desire for covenantal marriage with her Lord in the coming of the Messiah. According to Hans Urs von Balthasar, Mary is the only historical figure who could embody the perfections of the bride of the Canticle: "The Song of Songs stands alone in the Old Testament: an ideal which nowhere is realized in the history of salvation and which must wait for the New Testament before it can become the inner kernel of all thought about the history of salvation: when for once in all historical seriousness there would be found a sinless bride to correspond to the idyllic Shulamite."[8] Mary sums up Israel's call to be completely faithful to God in stainless virginity, to be humble servant and spouse of the Lord in his covenant. According to the Marian interpretation, the Song of Songs fathoms the depths of Mary's passionate love for the Lord by framing it within the context of the divine romance. Mary, whose life remained so hidden, and whose interior life defies description, is cast in a whole new light of mystical union with the Holy Trinity. If the bridal mystics such as John of the Cross could find in the Song a language to express their intense longings, how much more so would the Virgin full of grace experience the intensity of these Scriptures.

---

7. For an excellent contemporary commentary see Paul Griffiths, *Song of Songs* (Grand Rapids, MI: Brazos Press, 2011). The author applies the verses pertaining to the bride to both Mary and the Church.

8. Hans Urs von Balthasar, *Elucidations*, trans. John Riches (San Francisco: Ignatius Press, 1998), 101. (The bride is called "Shulamite" in Song 6:13) www.ignatius.com. Used with permission.

Two objections may arise. First, if Mary is without sin, how can she be the bride who has not kept her own vineyard (Song 1:6)? Without being sinful herself, Mary represents Israel, the sinful bride. According to Stefano Manelli, "by her original purity—in contrast to the adulterous infidelity of Israel—she recapitulates, reflects and sublimates in herself the 'new Israel,' i.e., the Church, and every soul, bride of the Lord."[9] Second, the carnal images seem inappropriate to attribute to Mary who is the purely chaste ever-virgin. But remember that the primary interpretation of the Song of Songs is of the Bridegroom representing the Lord and the bride representing Israel (whom Mary epitomizes). God's love for his people is passionately oriented toward union. The marital imagery is the best metaphor we have as human beings for symbolizing God's love for us. This imagery suggests a fundamentally spiritual meaning of God's union with the Christian.

When reading the Song of Songs, women might easily place themselves in the role of the bride alongside the divine Bridegroom, while men may find that more difficult. But for all of us, Christ is the Bridegroom of our souls. Saint John Paul II notes that "in the context of the 'great mystery' of Christ and of the Church, all are called to respond—as a bride—with the gift of their lives to the inexpressible gift of the love of Christ, who alone, as the Redeemer of the world, is the Church's Bridegroom."[10] It is crucial that men, in imitation of Saint John, take Mary into the home of their hearts in order to learn a spousal knowledge of the Bridegroom. The male person understands

9. Stefano Manelli, *All Generations Shall Call Me Blessed, Biblical Mariology*, trans. Fr. Peter Damian Fehlner, F.I. (New Bedford, MA: Academy of the Immaculate, 2005), 93.

10. Saint John Paul II, *Mulieris Dignitatem*, no. 27.

the mystery of bridal love for the son through filial love of the mother. Some virtues (such as hospitality, receptivity, compassion, sensitivity, and nurturing care) that might seem more feminine are common to us all, male and female alike. Both men and women must cultivate these virtues to be receptive to God's grace. All Christians are called to imitate Mary in her receptivity and responsiveness to God. As I stated in my previous book, "while men excel at giving themselves in a way that is receiving of the other, women excel at receiving the other in a way that is giving to the other."[11] Before God we are all called to first excel at receiving in a giving way. We see this in the account of Martha and Mary, where Mary chose "the better part" (see Lk 10:42). She received Jesus in hospitality by sitting at his feet and listening intently to his words. As the Lord gave himself to Mary, she simply received him, and in doing so, she also gave him love. God desires to give himself totally to each one of us. By receiving God, we are giving ourselves in return to him. God is pleased to give himself to us and delighted when we receive his gift of self in prayer.

Overview of the Parallels between Mary and the Song of Songs

Mary, like the bride, is "Daughter Zion" (Zeph 3:14), representing Israel in her intense longing and waiting for the coming of the Messiah. Her virginity is oriented solely toward her Lord, the Bridegroom of Israel, whose presence is realized in his divine kiss. Grace has prepared her to receive her Lord wholeheartedly.

---

11. Gregory Cleveland, OMV, *Awakening Love: An Ignatian Retreat with the Song of Songs* (Boston: Pauline Books & Media, 2017), 4.

Mary is the purified Daughter Zion, conceived sinless in view of her role as Mother of God. She is the bride who is dark and lovely, beautiful in grace, yet bearing the sins of her people. In her immaculate conception, Mary was kept free from original sin from the first moment of her existence. This grace does not separate her from us, but draws her closer to us, since grace unites us with one another, whereas sin divides. We share in the experience of receiving grace at baptism, which washes away our sins. Mary who is full of grace teaches us how to live by grace in the joys and sorrows of life in the most fully human way.

The first work of grace is to bring us into the union of contemplative prayer, symbolized by the King and his bride on their couch of rest. Mary enters contemplative prayer, "pondering" the events of life with her son and "keeping" them in her heart. The Bridegroom and bride gaze upon one another and admire one another's beauty. This is a perfect image of contemplative prayer. The incarnation of the Son of God made possible this loving gaze of Mary and Jesus, which we can all imitate. In prayer, Mary finds strength in her weakness, like the bride, who swoons in love for her Bridegroom and begs for nourishment. In the presence of her King, the bride is convinced of her commonness and humility as a mere lily of the valley. Mary, in her humility as the humble servant of the Lord, is chosen to be mother of the Son of the Most High.

The next work of grace is to invite us to generous self-giving to others. The Bridegroom draws close to his beloved and calls her to "arise and come." As Jesus draws close to Mary in the Incarnation, he calls her to arise and go to visit Elizabeth. Mary is prompt and generous in her response, compassionately bearing Christ's presence to her cousin. Most of Mary's self-giving to her son was offered during her hidden life with him for thirty years. She is the dove in the clefts of the rock (see Song 2:14), with Nazareth being the place of hiddenness where she receives her son's love, where he hears her sweet voice and beholds her lovely face. Mary experiences the pain of losing her son and searches for him with tribulation, finding him in the Temple. The bride similarly goes in anxious search of her lover who has disappeared, finding him and holding on to him. Mary's self-giving to Jesus and her sacrifice to the Father reach their zenith as she stands faithfully by him during his crucifixion. Her sacrifice in union with her son bears fruit in our salvation.

At the wedding feast at Cana Mary demonstrates her role as intercessor before Jesus on our behalf. Mary is a powerful intercessor because she always asks in Jesus' name according to his will, and Jesus will not refuse her. The Bridegroom's heart is likewise ravished by the beauty and power of his beloved. He describes her appearance in formidable terms as a protective warrior woman. Mary, who grew in her capacity for grace, receives a greater outpouring of the Holy Spirit at Pentecost and, in union with the Holy Spirit, becomes our advocate. She teaches the nascent Church to pray and to await the Spirit's coming. She continues to prayerfully sustain the Church by her deep union with God. The bride in the Song calls on the wind, a symbol of the Holy Spirit, to blow upon her garden, stirring its fragrance and wafting it about. She willingly endures pain as she shares in the sufferings of her Bridegroom. As the woman of Revelation, Mary becomes our mother, having borne the labor pains of giving birth to the Church at the foot of the Cross. She sustains us in difficult circumstances by her comforting presence. Mary shows us the essential motherhood of the Church and teaches us how to be mothers to Christ, hearing his word and keeping it.

Mary is assumed into heaven body and soul to be with her son. Her body is glorified after the pattern of Christ's resurrection. Her destiny is ours as we are all called to share in Jesus' risen life. The Bridegroom extols the bodily glory of his bride, who now resembles him in liveliness, power, and radiance. Her dance captivates and reconciles peoples, just as Mary's dance of joy in the presence of the Holy Trinity brings about peace among us all. Mary is also crowned as queen of heaven and earth, sharing in her Jesus' kingly rule. As queen she is not only exalted by God, but also draws closer to us, and by her power helps us in our need. The bride is likewise described as a queenly maiden, with power that instills fear in her enemies and can conquer even the most hardened hearts. As the woman, the new Eve, the mother of all the living in Christ, Mary is also the woman of Revelation 12, clothed with the sun, revealing God to us. By her spousal union with the Holy Spirit she becomes, like the bride in the love of her Bridegroom, the flame of the Lord himself (see Song 8:6).

How to Use This Book

This book can be used in various ways:

As a way to pray through the Song of Songs with Mary: As you read this book, you will discover the passionate depths of Mary's love for her Lord growing throughout her earthly life and ultimately fulfilled in heaven. Mary's experience of the Spirit is not foreign or beyond our reach. Instead it is a paradigm we can imitate, one which engenders our own union with God. Put yourself in Mary's place as the spiritually mature bride of the Song of Songs, with whom the Lord desires the deepest union through the joyful, luminous, sorrowful, and glorious experiences of your own life.

As spiritual reading to nourish your soul: Go beyond mere reading to prayerful consideration of the questions at the end of each chapter. Apply the stories and quotes to your own life.

As a personal retreat in daily life: Ideally, you could read one chapter per week while lingering over the prayer exercises. Let the Holy Spirit guide you to deeper meanings of the Scriptures in contemplation. Imagine yourself to be like Mary in her mysteries of union with the Holy Trinity, and the bride in her intense marriage with her beloved. Return to any moments of greater feeling, inspiration, or insight in your prayer experiences and deepen your understanding of what God is revealing.

Chapter 1

Virgin Daughter Zion

[B] Let him kiss me with the kisses of his mouth!
For your love is better than wine,
    your anointing oils are fragrant,
your name is perfume poured out;
    therefore the maidens love you.
Draw me after you, let us make haste.
    The king has brought me into his chambers.
[D] We will exult and rejoice in you;
    we will extol your love more than wine;
    rightly do they love you (Song 1:1–4).[1]

In the sixth month the angel Gabriel was sent by God to a town in Galilee called Nazareth, to a virgin engaged to a man whose name was Joseph, of the house of David. The virgin's name was Mary. And he came to her and said,

1. In the quotes from the Song of Songs, the bride is indicated as B; the bridegroom as G; and the daughters of Jerusalem as D. —Editor.

"Greetings, favored one! The Lord is with you." But she was much perplexed by his words and pondered what sort of greeting this might be. The angel said to her, "Do not be afraid, Mary, for you have found favor with God. And now, you will conceive in your womb and bear a son, and you will name him Jesus. He will be great, and will be called the Son of the Most High, and the Lord God will give to him the throne of his ancestor David. He will reign over the house of Jacob forever, and of his kingdom there will be no end." Mary said to the angel, "How can this be, since I am a virgin?" The angel said to her, "The Holy Spirit will come upon you, and the power of the Most High will overshadow you; therefore the child to be born will be holy; he will be called Son of God. And now, your relative Elizabeth in her old age has also conceived a son; and this is the sixth month for her who was said to be barren. For nothing will be impossible with God." Then Mary said, "Here am I, the servant of the Lord; let it be with me according to your word." Then the angel departed from her. (Lk 1:26–38)

Mary's gift of her whole being to the Lord inspired my own consecration in religious life. In 1993 I was ready to make my final vows of poverty, chastity, and obedience to the Lord with the Oblates of the Virgin Mary. I had spent seven years of formation in prayer, study, ministry, and community life, and now I was prepared. Our ceremony was held on a Friday evening at Saint Clement Eucharistic Shrine in Boston, where my seminary training had begun. I went to pick up my family members in the midst of a severe nor'easter rainstorm that had lasted all day. All the flights were delayed, and I spent the day in the airport. As I drove back from the airport with my family, we stalled in the Sumner Tunnel due to a car fire on the expressway. We had already missed dinner, and I was not amused as my brother joked about missing the ceremony. Finally, we arrived at 6:45 for a 7:00 P.M. ceremony. My provincial superior greeted me with the news that my friend and classmate of seven years had decided to postpone his vows. Stunned, I tried to take it all in. My provincial saw the disappointment on my face and told me I could postpone if I needed to. I had no doubts, but I was terribly disheartened. I told my sister about my classmate and she asked alarmingly, "You're not thinking of backing out, are you?" "No," I answered, "but it sure feels lousy," hoping for some compassion that I didn't receive. I told the news to my spiritual director, who was sitting in the back of the church. He just shook his head, indicating that I'd come too far to be swayed by the desolation of the moment. Even though I had had a good experience of seminary formation over seven years, I was now tempted to dwell on all the moments of hardship, pain, and disappointment of that period and let them sabotage my decision.

I hearkened back to my retreat of the previous June, when I had been inspired by our Lady's yes to God. I had felt swept up by God's grace as I contemplated her *fiat*. I knew that my life's decision was founded on solid ground, and I would not waver. My years of preparation and waiting culminated with a joyful yes that was tinged with pain as I uttered the words: "I, Gregory Cleveland, into your hands, O Lord, vow for all my life, chastity, poverty, and obedience. . . . I pledge myself to the proper apostolic services of the Congregation which will be assigned to me. My God, you have inspired this consecration in me; fully aware of my weakness I pray to you: confirm within me this holy resolve. Mary, I place myself in your hands so that you may bring me to God." By divine grace and inspired by Mary, my consecration to the Lord was the culmination of many trying years of preparation.

I first experienced the kiss of the divine Bridegroom during the Marian Year proclaimed by Saint John Paul II in 1987. It was the final day of the novena to the Divine Mercy in April. I went to holy Mass with my friends Cindy and Tony, and, when I received Holy Communion, I felt flooded with the love of God. I looked up and saw the priest purifying the vessels, and the thought came to me that God might be calling me to the priesthood. Later that day, I was going to a pro-life banquet with my friend Rosie, and we passed Saint Nicholas Albanian Orthodox Church. I had heard that there was a weeping icon of our Lady there. I had always wanted to see it, so we stopped and went in. I was captivated by the beauty of the icon and noticed that she had begun weeping on my birthday, December 6, which is also the feast day of Saint Nicholas. Her tears were for the suffering Christians in Albania, but I felt as if they were a kind of confirmation of my calling. Later that summer, I applied to the Oblates of the Virgin Mary and joined the seminary.

Throughout my formation process, I came to discover that the Lord loved me with a passionate desire, which made me come alive as never before. My studies became an intense pursuit of knowledge of him whom my soul loved. During my novitiate I discovered that the Lord didn't just want my obedience and service; he wanted my heart. While praying with the Song of Songs, I felt the Lord calling me beautiful in his grace. And I knew that he was captivated by me. He was keenly interested in everything about me and wanted me to share my heart with him. While I always knew that my heart was marked by a God-shaped hole that only he could fill, I came to realize that God's heart had a place that only I could fill. That was why he loved me into being and died out of love for me. I had been reluctant to share myself with him or others, hiding my heart, putting up defenses, not feeling like I had much to offer. Becoming more aware of his love for me, I was able to surrender my heart to him in all my weakness and goodness, even to the point of consecrating myself to him as a religious.

Our Yearning for God

While the Lord's way of truth was stimulating my intellect in my theological studies, his way of beauty in the Song of Songs was captivating my heart in prayer. I desired his grace to transform me into a mirror of his beauty in holiness of life. In the Song, the bride's desire for the presence and kiss of her beloved in marital union is symbolic of the soul's longing for an intimate relationship with God. This yearning for union is fulfilled in the angel's address to Mary, "Greetings, favored one, the Lord is with you" (Lk 1:28). While we commonly render the angel's greeting as "Hail, full of grace," the meaning of *grace* is a relationship of friendship and deep intimacy with God. Ratzinger elucidates:

> "Full of grace" means that Mary is a wholly open human being, one who has opened herself entirely, one who has placed herself in God's hands boldly, limitlessly, and without fear for her own fate. It means she lives wholly by and in relation to God. She is a listener and a pray-er, whose mind and soul are alive to the manifold ways in which the living God quietly calls to her. She is one who prays and stretches forth wholly to meet God; she is therefore a lover, who has the breadth and magnanimity of true love, but who has also

> its unerring powers of discernment and its readiness to suffer.[2]

Mary experiences grace as an openness and receptivity to receive the Lord's gift of self and to give herself in return. God, as the Bridegroom of his people, is the supreme lover who gives himself totally. Mary, representing the bride, receives his love completely and reciprocates it with her gift of love. Her experience of complete surrender to her loving Lord is meant for us all.

The bride's desire for her bridegroom is exceeded only by the Bridegroom's yearning for union. As Saint Augustine says, our thirst for God is a pale reflection of his thirst for us.[3] Having created Mary to be the beautiful spouse of the Holy Spirit, God desired to enter into that beauty. In the Incarnation, God himself experienced beauty. He experienced that ecstasy by which he came out of himself and became flesh in Mary. The great apostle of Marian consecration, Saint Louis de Montfort, says that in Mary, God experienced beauty, first in creating her, and then in admiring her virtues: "The angels and even God himself were filled with rapturous admiration for her. Her humility, deep as an abyss, delighted him. Her purity so otherworldly drew him down to her. He found her lively faith and her ceaseless entreaties of love so irresistible that he was lovingly conquered by her appeals of love."[4] Montfort sings to our Lady: "You have enraptured God. . . . Attracted by your beauty, he took human nature.

2. Joseph Ratzinger, *Mary, The Church at the Source,* trans. Adrian Walker (San Francisco: Ignatius, 2005), 68.

3. See *Commentary on Gospel of John,* 15, 11.

4. Saint Louis Marie de Montfort, *Love of Eternal Wisdom,* 105, 107, in *Jesus Living in Mary, Handbook of the Spirituality of Saint Louis Marie de Montfort* (Bayshore, NY: Montfort Publications, 1995), 75.

He could not help himself."[5] God has conferred beauty on each one of us and is drawn by that beauty to enter our hearts. Like the bride we invite God's presence to unite with us: "Let him kiss me with the kisses of his mouth" (Song 1:2).

The sole desire of the bride's heart is the arrival and the kiss of her bridegroom. The bride exclaims "your name is perfume poured out" (Song 1:3), referring to the Messiah, "the one anointed" with the Holy Spirit. She immediately adds, "your love is better than wine." The Messiah would also be the bridegroom of Israel whose role was to supply the wine for the wedding feast of the covenant. It was foretold that when the Messiah came, there would be an abundance of wine. The restoration of the kingdom meant the mountains would drip sweet wine of joy and all the hills would flow with it (see Amos 9:13; Joel 3:18). Jesus is the Messiah, the one anointed with the Holy Spirit, who is also the Bridegroom. At Cana he provided an abundance of wine for the wedding feast (see Jn 2:1–11). Mary is the bride who symbolizes Israel in her longing for the kiss of the Bridegroom and for his love, which is better than wine. The Incarnation brought these gifts. We know that Mary had the hopes and dreams of her people in mind when in her Magnificat she exclaims that the Lord has "helped his servant Israel, in remembrance of his mercy" (Lk 1:54). Mary also refers to herself as the "handmaid of the Lord," just as Israel was called to be the servant of the Lord. In doing God's will, Mary anticipates Jesus' own mission to do the will of the Father.

Throughout the Scriptures, the Lord had called his people "daughter Zion," whom he had raised and would marry as his

---

5. De Montfort, *Hymns* 63:5; cf. H. 81:3, in *Jesus Living in Mary*, 75.

bride so that she would bear fruit (see Hos 2:19–20). In a unique way Mary embodies Israel's relationship to the Lord as daughter Zion. A comparison between the prophets and Luke shows these parallels:

1. The Messiah will bring joy

The prophet Zechariah prophesies the coming of the Messiah to Israel: "Rejoice greatly, O daughter of Zion! Shout aloud, O daughter Jerusalem! Lo, your king comes to you" (Zech 9:9). When the Angel Gabriel appears to Mary he hearkens back to Zechariah in greeting her with the same word "rejoice"[6] addressed to daughter Zion (Lk 1:28).

2. The presence of the Lord

Just as the prophet Zephaniah had proclaimed to Israel, "The king of Israel, the Lord, is in your midst" (Zeph 3:14), so now Gabriel proclaims to Mary that "the Lord is with you" (Lk 1:28).

3. No more fear

Zephaniah charges Israel to "fear disaster no more" (Zeph 3:15), while Gabriel says "do not be afraid, Mary, for you have found favor with God" (Lk 1:30).

What is foretold to daughter Zion is now directed to Mary: "She is identified with daughter Zion, she is daughter Zion in

---

6. Rendered "Hail" or "Greetings" in some translations, but most accurately "Rejoice." See Edward Sri, *Rethinking Mary in the New Testament* (San Francisco: Ignatius Press, 2018), 13–22.

person . . . the bridal people of God."[7] Mary carries in herself the fulfillment of the saving plan of God and herself becomes the very personification of the new Israel, the truest abode of Yahweh, through the incarnation of the Son of God, who restores the kingdom of Israel with an unending rule.[8] Mary is the true Israel in whom the Old and New Covenants, Israel and Church, are indivisibly one. She is the "people of God" bearing fruit through God's gracious power.

The Jews intensely longed for the coming of the Messiah. In his book *The Day Christ Died,* the American Catholic journalist Jim Bishop describes this longing, which speaks to us of the bride's longing for her Bridegroom: "The coming of the Messiah was a sweet national obsession. It was a joy beyond imagining, happiness beyond belief. It was comfort for the weary farmer's bones as he lay in bed at night with his family waiting for sleep. It was the dream of every gray-haired person. It was the thing a small child looked to a mountain of white clouds to see. It was the hope of Judea in chains. The Messiah was always the promise of tomorrow morning."[9] We can imagine how intense was this desire for the coming of the Messiah during the age of the prophets, especially while Israel was in exile, waiting to return to their homeland and the Temple. We can imagine that hope waning 400 years later, the length of time since the last prophet had spoken. Some faithful Jews, like Simeon and Anna, still felt in their bones that they might live to see the Messiah's coming. We can imagine the peoples' anticipation rising to fever pitch when John the Baptist appeared. He was a new prophet in the desert who

---

7. Joseph Ratzinger, *Mary, The Church at the Source,* 65–66.

8. See Manelli, *All Generations Will Call Me Blessed,* 95–104.

9. Jim Bishop, *The Day Christ Died* (New York: HarperOne, 1957), 76.

exhorted Israel to prepare the way for the Messiah's arrival. Any expectant Jewish woman might wonder if her developing child was a son and whether he might be the Messiah.

The Meaning of Mary's Virginity

As a representative of her people and to anticipate the Messiah's coming, Mary experienced a call to virginity.[10] According to Isaiah's prophecy, the Messiah was to be conceived and born of a virgin and be called Immanuel (Is 7:14–16). The only way such a prophecy could be considered as a miraculous sign from God would be for the young woman to conceive virginally. The Hebrew term for young woman and virgin were used interchangeably, and young women were expected to be virgins. As a sign of fidelity, a young woman prepares for marriage with her husband by remaining a virgin. She will belong

---

10. Mary's question to the angel "How can this be since I am a virgin?" makes no sense unless she felt called to remain a virgin. With her impending marriage to Joseph, conceiving a child would be entirely natural, and she would have no need to question how it would come about. Many scholars assert that Mary likely took a vow of virginity in accord with Numbers 30:6–8, 13–16. See Brant Pitre, *Jesus and the Jewish Roots of Mary* (New York: Image Books, 2018), 100–115. De la Potterie states that even if Mary did not make a vow of virginity, her question to the angel suggests her desire to remain a virgin. Cf. Ignace de la Potterie, SJ., *Mary in the Mystery of the Covenant*, trans. by Bertrand Buby, SM (Staten Island, NY: Alba House, 1992), 22–29. Saint John Paul II asserts: "We can wonder why she would accept betrothal, since she had the intention of remaining a virgin forever. . . . It may be presumed that at the time of their betrothal there was an understanding between Joseph and Mary about the plan to live as a virgin. Moreover, the Holy Spirit, who had inspired Mary to choose virginity in view of the mystery of the Incarnation and who wanted the latter to come about in a family setting suited to the Child's growth, was quite able to instill in Joseph the ideal of virginity as well." *General Audience, August 21, 1996*, http://www.vatican.va/content/john-paul-ii/es/audiences/1996/documents/hf_jp-ii_aud_19960821.html.

exclusively to him, and he to her, and so she preserves herself for him exclusively. Christ conceived and born of a virgin signifies something new that God is doing that is beyond human imagining, as Isaiah prophesies: "I am about to do a new thing; now it springs forth, do you not perceive it?" (Is 43:19). Previously God had prophesied the birth of a child in the face of old age, barrenness, or other seemingly impossible situations. But God had never bypassed a human father in creating a child. This new creation is not of man's making, but something totally from God. Mary as a virgin shows that God alone can bring about the conception of one so holy as the Son of God and that this is clearly a work of God. Jesus' very existence as the Son of God made man points to and glorifies the heavenly Father. Mary's virginity necessarily guarantees the Incarnation as God's work.

Whereas previous births were merely announced to the women of the past, God asks for Mary's consent to his plan. God draws people to himself only by his love, never by force. By his grace, he conditions our free will to orient us toward choosing the good, and we experience greater freedom in God to choose the good. In her *fiat,* Mary shows a more daring confidence than her ancestors. She completely trusts the Lord and his promise to accomplish this new and incomprehensible work. Like the bride in the Song of Songs, she lives for her Bridegroom completely and he is her sole concern. Grace has so prepared Mary that she is available to live for the Lord alone in total service and confidence. Her yes is a marital consent of bride to Bridegroom, just as God had said: "And I will take you for my wife forever; I will take you for my wife in righteousness and in justice, in steadfast love, and in mercy. I will take you for my wife in faithfulness" (Hos 2:19–20). Scripture scholar Ignace de la Potterie explains that this marital bond between God and the Daughter of Zion is the foundational scriptural image to express the relationship of the covenant between God and his people: "For Mary, the desire of virginity, her desire to live fully for God, to live in entire fidelity to the Covenant is basically the desire to live this spousal relationship with God."[11] Theologian Jean Galot suggests that the more profound significance of virginity isn't that a woman goes into a self-preservation mode but that she surrenders herself more immediately and fully to the Lord. It is a quest for the nearest conceivable contact with God. We affirm the reality of intimate spousal love of the Lord. We should perceive its constructive worth, which is a spousal association with God, who loves us with a personal love.[12] Paradoxically, Mary's virginity is completely oriented toward a nuptial relationship with the Holy Spirit and serving her Lord. No wonder that Saint Paul, in encouraging virginity as a state in life, emphasizes that the virgin is concerned exclusively with the things of her Lord (see 1 Cor 7:32–35).

We don't have to embrace physical virginity in order to love God wholeheartedly. Many people who are married, or those who experience the struggle against lust, might have difficulty relating to Mary as a virgin. Some think that only virgin nuns and celibate priests can imitate Mary. What is more important than virginity of the flesh is Mary's virginity of the heart, that is, the integrity and purity of her faith. Mary's physical virginity was a sign of a virginity that was more interior and spiritual, based on her fidelity to the covenant. Mary had already been purified and sanctified by grace in preparation for the Incarnation,

---

11. Ignace de la Potterie, SJ., *Mary in the Mystery of the Covenant*, trans. by Bertrand Buby, SM (Staten Island, NY: Alba House, 1992), 147.

12. See Jean Galot, "Maria, la donna," 139 in Rosa Lombardi, *Mary, Reflections of the Trinity and First-fruits of Creation*, trans. Matthew J. O'Connell (Hyde Park, NY: New City Press, 2008), 59.

living her fidelity to the Lord in virginity of heart. It is not the virginity of the *flesh,* but virginity of the *heart* which is proposed to all believers. In faithfulness to all God asks, all Christian women and men ought to be virgins of heart like Mary. Saint Augustine asserts that Christ was born physically of a virgin in order to make us understand that the members of his Body should be reborn according to the Spirit, of the Virgin Church.[13] Saint Maximus the Confessor writes: "Christ always anew and on his own initiative is born in a mystical manner in the soul. He becomes flesh in those who receive salvation, and the flesh in which he is born, he transforms into a virgin mother."[14] The Incarnation is repeated in the life of each Christian who is spiritually called to be, like Mary, virgin and mother.[15] We are made children of God by virginal faith, born "not of blood or of the will of the flesh or of the will of man, but of God" (Jn 1:13).

Grace Transforms Us

While virginal motherhood in the flesh is an experience unique to Mary, it does not separate her from us, but rather unites her more closely with us. Before she conceived Jesus in the flesh, she first conceived him in her heart. Since we can all experience Christ in our hearts, we are one with Mary in participating in the grace of God. The divine favor of God's

---

13. See Saint Augustine, Sermons 72A, 8 Miscellanea Agostiana, I, p. 164 in Raniero Cantalamessa, *Mary, Mirror of the Church,* trans. Frances Lonergan Villa (Collegeville, MN: Liturgical Press, 1992), 69.

14. Saint Maximus the Confessor, *Commentary on the Our Father, PG* 90, 889, in Cantalamessa, 69.

15. See De la Potterie, 140.

presence does not remain extrinsic to us, but transforms us interiorly for a life of personal holiness in union with the Lord. Thomas Merton once had an epiphany on a street corner of the shopping district in Louisville. He suddenly felt totally connected with all the strangers who were present, realizing he loved them as Christ loved them. That graced encounter led him to ponder the secret beauty of the human heart at the core of each person. Merton reflected on the concept of the "virgin point" of the human soul:

> At the center of our being is a point of nothingness which is untouched by sin and by illusion, a point of pure truth, a point or spark which belongs entirely to God, which is never at our disposal, from which God disposes of our lives, which is inaccessible to the fantasies of our own mind or the brutalities of our own will. This little point of nothingness and of absolute poverty is the pure glory of God in us. It is so to speak His name written in us, as our poverty, as our indigence, as our dependence, as our sonship. It is like a pure diamond, blazing with the invisible light of heaven.[16]

At the virginal point of his soul where God was most present and vibrant, Merton also felt most connected with other human beings. Mary, united to the Spirit in her virginal heart, is also most united with us.

Mary experienced that virginal point of her human soul as a place of emptiness and utter dependence on God. Spiritual author Caryll Houselander describes Mary's emptiness as not just a meaningless void, but a cavern shaped by God's purpose. Her emptiness is like the hollow contour of a flute, that receives

---

16. Thomas Merton, *Conjectures of a Guilty Bystander* (New York: Image Books, 1968), 158.

the musician's breath of air and plays God's melody of eternal love. Mary was filled with the breath of the Spirit in her virginal heart to sing the divine melody.[17] Mary is attuned to God's Word, allowing it to flourish in her heart, allowing it in all its capacity to possess her completely. She makes a wholehearted self-gift, with no resistance or reservation in her mind and will. Her being is completely ordered to her free surrender to the Lord's possession of her. Mary gave herself to God in complete self-abandonment: "Let it be done to me according to your will." Mary's answer represents the height of religious devotion to God. Her willingness to be open to God's action was joined to her readiness to cooperate with God through her obedience.[18] The virgin point was the place of union of her human spirit with the Spirit of God. Like the bride, she experienced the kiss of her beloved in this innermost place of union in her heart.

Each of us who received baptism was consecrated completely to God, dedicated to his worship and service. It remains for us to live out this consecration of our hearts daily and in renewed acts of fidelity to the Lord's covenant with each one of us. Our first orientation as Christians should be to present ourselves to God, the source of our being, surrendering ourselves into his hands with childlike trust. We promise the Lord our faithfulness and trust that we will receive all we need from him. We allow the Lord to draw near to us in prayer with the loving kiss of the Holy Spirit. The Spirit in turn empowers us to utter our joyful yes to all God proposes to us and to respond wholeheartedly to his promptings. Like Mary we can respond in

---

17. See Caryll Houselander, *The Reed of God* (Notre Dame, IN: Ave Maria Press, 2006), 21–22.

18. See H. Shurmann, *Das Lukasevangelium*, Freiburg in Br., 1982, ad. loc., in Cantalamessa, 39.

freedom and allow the Lord to do as he wills in us. In the virginal point of our hearts we can allow the Lord to take complete possession of our souls and radiate the invisible light of the divine.

Saint Teresa of Calcutta was known to radiate the divine presence. She gave herself totally to God in response to the Lord's complete self-gift. She knew that if God had given himself wholly to her, she could not reciprocate by only giving a fraction of herself. In giving herself completely to God, she was receiving him completely and allowing him to possess her soul. She knew that she would lose nothing in giving herself completely to her Lord. When Teresa began her street ministry, many ridiculed her as foolish or prideful, but she did not worry about her reputation. She trusted in the Lord's promises and wanted to please him alone. The only wise choice for us is to completely abandon ourselves to the God who made us, redeemed us, and continually sanctifies us. We surrender ourselves totally into his hands, willing to serve him, confident of his promise to remain with us. The bride of the Song has made her initial surrender to her Lover, who takes her to the secret depths of his heart, his "chambers" or "wine cellar" (Song 1:4). There the Lover and beloved are united and share hidden depths of intimacy and union. In surrendering all of herself, she receives his complete gift of Love.

As we observe the complete self-abandonment of great saints like the Blessed Virgin Mary or Saint Teresa of Calcutta, we might be tempted to discouragement. In some degree we have all neglected to love the Lord as we should. But that need not hinder us from beginning again and renewing our consecration to the Lord. I have fallen far short of serving God in my own religious life and priesthood. In countless ways I have often settled for mediocrity. I frequently refuse to remain in a state of poverty of spirit and to base my identity on my relationship with

God as a son. It is difficult to persist in that place of nothingness and remain totally dependent on God when it feels more secure to build up my own ego. I feel safer resting on my own accomplishments, relying on my own capabilities and possessions. Acknowledging these shortcomings and failures, I must surrender my entire being, good and bad, to the Lord's mercy. God wants all of us, not only our goodness, powers, gifts, and nobility of soul, but also our brokenness and sinfulness. When we refuse to surrender our dark side to him, when we hide behind masks of fear and defensiveness, we put up obstacles to experiencing the Lord's mercy in the depths of our hearts. We are to love God as we are with our poor hearts and know his power to transform us into his likeness.

Our consecration and fidelity to God will be tested in ways we can't imagine. In marriage one promises to be true to one's spouse in good times and in bad, in sickness and in health, for richer or for poorer, and for better or for worse. Truly in challenging moments spouses experience unconditional love for one another in the way God loves us. According to this ideal, one gives and receives love no matter what the circumstances, even on one's worst day. In these times of trial we experience our own weakness and dependence on the Lord to sustain us in faithfulness to him and one another. A priest tells an inspiring story of patience and reliance on God in fidelity. On a visit to China in the 1980s he met an elderly couple who were both doctors. They had studied together at medical school, fallen in love and married. She was a Catholic, he was not. She wanted to convince him that he should join the Church, but he did not wish to be baptized. A short time later she had a child. During one of China's political upheavals, the husband, along with several other intellectuals, was arrested and sent to a labor camp. The separation was very difficult for the wife, who had to work long hours at the hospital during the day and care for her son at night. In addition to her loneliness, she was under pressure from the government to divorce her husband and to renounce her religion, so that she could gain political advantages. But she refused. Every night after she returned home, she and her son knelt down to pray and ask strength from God to endure the difficulties. At the end of the 1970s, she heard that her husband and other intellectuals were to be allowed to come home. When the day arrived, she and her son went to the railway station, where they were the only family members on the platform to welcome the men. Unable to endure the long separation, caving under pressure from the government, all the other women had divorced and remarried. Deeply moved, her husband took instruction in the faith and was later baptized.[19]

This wife showed extraordinary patience in longsuffering while keeping her heart fixed in faithfulness, waiting for her husband's return. Her power to remain faithful came from her relationship of utter dependence on God in prayer. God did not abandon her, but sustained her in fidelity to his covenant in baptism and marriage, as he will do for us. We feel emboldened to imitate Mary's availability to God and his divine plan for our lives in our own consecration to the Lord. We remain hopeful in his presence, especially in difficult moments, trusting that he will sustain us in our fidelity to him. United with Mary the bride, we rejoice constantly in the kiss of the divine presence of the Bridegroom in our hearts.

---

19. See Flor McCarthy, *New Sunday and Holy Day Liturgies, Year B*, Advent Week 3 (Dublin: Dominican Publications, 1999), 22–23.

Questions for Reflection and Discussion

1. How has your longing for God been satisfied or frustrated? Have you grown in faith, hope, and love through this longing, or have you wavered in these virtues? Do you feel as though God has fulfilled his promises to you?
2. Since your baptism, have you renewed your consecration to God through Mary? If not, do you feel a desire to do so? If you have made a Marian consecration, how has it affected your Christian life?
3. How do you relate to Mary under the aspect of both her physical and spiritual virginity? Does it make you feel closer to her or more separate from her? How does the reality of spiritual virginity speak to you?
4. What have been the challenges to a more complete self-giving to God in your life? What obstacles keep you from greater surrender? How does Mary's presence and example inspire you?

Prayer Exercises

1. Consider Israel's longing for the Messiah (p. 21) along with the bride's desire for the kiss of the Bridegroom. Pray with Song 1:1–4 and ask for the grace to realize the Lord's presence within.
2. Reflect on the concept of spiritual virginity (p. 26). Pray with Luke 1:26–38 and ask for the desire and grace to live totally for God.
3. Ponder the Thomas Merton quote on the "virgin point" of the soul (p. 26). Pray with John 15:1–11 and ask for the grace to live in Christ and depend on him.

4. Consider the story of the Chinese woman (p. 29). Pray with Matthew 11:1–19 and ask for the grace to be faithful to Christ in time of trial.
5. Reflect on the meaning of your baptismal consecration and how you might deepen that consecration in union with Mary. Pray with Matthew 3:11–17 and ask for the grace of a deeper self-abandonment to Christ.

Chapter 2

Robed in Salvation

[B] I am black and beautiful,
O daughters of Jerusalem,
like the tents of Kedar,
like the curtains of Solomon.
Do not gaze at me because I am dark,
because the sun has gazed on me.
My mother's sons were angry with me;
they made me keeper of the vineyards,
but my own vineyard I have not kept!
Tell me, you whom my soul loves,
where you pasture your flock,
where you make it lie down at noon;
for why should I be like one who is veiled
beside the flocks of your companions?
[G] If you do not know,
O fairest among women,
follow the tracks of the flock,
and pasture your kids
beside the shepherds' tents.
I compare you, my love,

to a mare among Pharaoh's chariots.
Your cheeks are comely with ornaments,
your neck with strings of jewels.
We will make you ornaments of gold,
studded with silver (Song 1:5–11).
You are altogether beautiful, my love;
there is no flaw in you (Song 4:7).

In the sixth month the angel Gabriel was sent by God to a town in Galilee called Nazareth, to a virgin engaged to a man whose name was Joseph, of the house of David. The virgin's name was Mary. And he came to her and said, "Greetings, favored one! The Lord is with you." (Lk 1:26–27)

Original Sin and Mary's Immaculate Conception

Original sin is something we all inherit generationally from our first parents, passed down through our own parents. We are born into a sinful state, as David says: "Indeed, I was born guilty, a sinner when my mother conceived me" (Ps 51:5). This results in disorder in our souls and an inclination to sin. By grace we are saved through baptism, and original sin is washed away, but its effects remain. Still, we are created in the image of God and given the grace to overcome sin and live godly lives. But we also experience the damaging effects of the sins of others, especially within our own families. As relational beings, our sins affect one another for the worse. We are born into an injured network of human relationships in a world broken by sin. A retreat master once received a note from a girl at the end of a retreat he was giving. He put the note in his pocket and forgot about it. Later he found it, opened it up and read:

> For the past eight months I have been in psychotherapy, a fact known to only a few people. As a child I experienced overwhelming fear because of hatred and abuse. A major focus of my life right now is to overcome and transform that fear. The details are unnecessary, but much of my fear is centered on my mother. . . . I had become so turned off to the concept of mothers that I consciously rejected the love of Mary, the mother of Jesus. After your talk, I walked outside—feeling terribly alone. I prayed for the grace to break through the wall that was keeping me from trusting. . . . I wanted to cry, but haven't in months. You may have noticed a small, round building near the cemetery. Curiosity is one of my strongest traits—I walked to it and opened the door. When I looked inside, I was filled with fear. There stood a large statue of Mary. My first impulse was to run away in anger. But something drew me closer to the kneeler at her feet. Then, I fell to my knees, weeping in the folds of her robes. When it was over, I felt cleansed and new. I felt willing to be a trusting child. . . . Even more important, I felt that a mother's love had touched me—leaving in me a true desire to forgive my natural mother."[1]

We see the destructive effects of sin in the life of this girl, as well as the healing effects of God's grace working through Mary. The girl's experience points to the importance of Jesus being born to a sinless mother. As Jesus grew to full stature in wholesome and virtuous character, he could not be psychologically disfigured by sin.

---

1. Mark Link, *Illustrated Sunday Homilies, Years A, B, C/Series I*, January 1, Mother of God, Year C (Saint Louis: Tabor, 1989), 15.

Like Mary, Christ, the New Adam, is at once sinless while identifying with and emerging from sinful Israel. He is the innocent Lamb who will take upon himself the sins of his people in order to deliver them from sin. "For our sake he made him to be sin who knew no sin, so that in him we might become the righteousness of God" (2 Cor 5:21). As Daughter of Zion, Mary similarly identifies with her people Israel, who are sinners in need of purification. She represents Israel purified and ready to receive her Lord. God had promised to purify Israel his unfaithful wife and transform her into a sinless bride (see Hos 2:14–23). "By her original purity, contrasted with the adulterous infidelity of Israel, Mary recapitulates, reflects and sublimates in herself the 'new Israel,' namely, the Church, and every soul as bride of the Lord."[2] Here in the Song of Songs, the bride refers to herself as swarthy. The bride represents Israel in her sin and exile, having been burnt and disfigured by her hard labor, suffering in a foreign land. She continues to suffer under foreign oppression, first by the Greeks and now by the Romans. She suffers the consequences of her own infidelity. Mary keenly feels the effects of her nation's sin and suffering, yet is aware of her own innocence and interior purity. "Mary is well aware of her people's infidelity, and she wants personally to be a Bride who is faithful to her most beloved divine Spouse."[3] As the bride is dark and lovely, so Mary represents the best of her people in her beauty, while bearing her people's ills. She is Israel rejoicing, transformed into a lovely bride:

> I will greatly rejoice in the LORD,
>   my whole being shall exult in my God;
> for he has clothed me with the garments of salvation,
>   he has covered me with the robe of righteousness,

---

2. Manelli, *All Generations Shall Call Me Blessed*, 93.
3. Saint John Paul II, General Audience, December 4, 1991.

as a bridegroom decks himself with a garland,
and as a bride adorns herself with her jewels (Is 61:10).

Already at the annunciation, Mary is called "full of grace," (in Greek *kecharitomene*). This word means that she always has been and remains filled with the divine favor of God's presence. God has bestowed his abundant favor upon her in anticipation of Christ's conception. Amazingly, Mary is already free of original sin and filled with God's grace. How could she be full of grace before Christ was conceived? How could she be redeemed from sin before Christ died on the cross to save us? If Mary is "full of grace" beforehand, the Lord must have delivered her from sin beforehand. By a special grace of anticipation, the Lord applied the merits of his death and resurrection to preserve her from the stain of original sin from the moment of her conception.

An illustration from the history of the Church will help us understand how Mary could be preserved sinless from the moment of her conception. In the Middle Ages many Christians were held captive by foreign armies and bartered as slaves to non-Christian nations. These subjugated Christians bore children, who, as children of slaves were destined to become slaves themselves. Eventually, Christians ransomed the children who were born of slave parents, giving the children freedom. Sometimes the ransom was arranged before a child was born, or even conceived. Even though the child was conceived and born of slave parents, it was already free. The child's independence had been bought beforehand. This analogy may help us understand how Mary was conceived without sin. Though Mary is born of parents enslaved by sin, she is conceived and born in freedom.[4] Christ's death is a ransom from sin, in this case applied

4. See Mark Link, *Illustrated Sunday Homilies*, Years A, B,C/Series 1, 6.

before Mary's conception and birth in view of the merits of Christ. Many theologians consider it fitting that Christ's death and resurrection have, at least in one singular instance, the effect of not only saving people from sin after having sinned, but completely preserving one from sin beforehand. God's grace is so efficacious that it can even preserve one from sinning at all, as happens with Mary. God gave her this grace because of her unique mission to become the Mother of God.

Mary is not only the Mother of God, but she also represents the Church, the fulfillment of the people of Israel. Like the bride in the Song, the Church is at once both swarthy and beautiful. Saint Bernard exclaims: "O humility! O sublimity! Both tabernacle of cedar and sanctuary of God; earthly dwelling and celestial palace; house of clay and royal hall; body of death and temple of light; and at last both object of scorn to the proud and bride of Christ! She is black but beautiful, O daughters of Jerusalem, for even if the labor and pain of her long exile may have discolored her, yet heaven's beauty has adorned her."[5] What God has given to Mary, her brightness and glory, he intends and has in fact given to his Church. What he has given collectively to his Church in her essence, he will give to each of her members. While the Church is certainly composed of sinful members, in her essence she is pure and without stain, because of her union with Christ who has cleansed her. She is Christ's body. Saint Paul teaches "Christ loved the church and gave himself up for her, in order to make her holy by cleansing her with the washing of water by the word, so as to present the church to himself in splendor, without a spot or wrinkle or anything of the

5. Saint Bernard of Clairvaux, *On the Song of Songs,* Sermon 21, in *Catechism of the Catholic Church,* no.771.

kind—yes, so that she may be holy and without blemish" (Eph 5:25–27). Paradoxically, the Church is at once holy, yet always needs purification. Many people find it easy to look on the dark side of the Church, the sins and scandals of her members, but fail to see the glory of her essential holiness. As baptized Christians each of us participates in Christ's holiness, while we are being cleansed of our sins. It is only in the person of Mary that the Church has already realized her nature as the spotless bride (see Song 4:7).

As immaculate and all holy, Mary transcends our sinful condition but she is not so unlike us in her reception of God's grace. Indeed, she is a paradigm for us in how to receive grace and live by it. Karl Rahner, whose exposition on grace influenced Vatican Council II, explains: "Mary does not differ from us because she possessed these gifts. It is her possession of them from the beginning, and incomparably, that is the sole difference between her and us. As for the content of this gift, its nature and intrinsic meaning, the eternal Father could not intend anything for the mother of His incarnate Son, without intending it for us too, and giving it to us in the sacrament of justification."[6] From all eternity God has desired his saving grace for us. We need to realize that salvation is not from us, but purely a gift from God. From the moment of our conception, God has been at work, not only creating us to be the unique individuals we are, but also preparing us to receive his indwelling presence. At the moment of our baptism, the Lord stands ready to enter into the inmost center of our hearts, cleansing us from all sin, both original sin inherited from our ancestors and any actual sin committed in

6. Karl Rahner, *Mary, Mother of the Lord* (New York: Herder and Herder, 1963), 49.

our will. The Lord has set his seal upon our hearts (see Song 8:6) in our redemption, making us the temple of the indwelling God. We are chosen in order to be sent by him to carry his light to the darkness of this world and to dwell in his eternal radiance for eternity. All that Mary has received as pure gift from God, in her immaculate conception and in the incarnation of Jesus Christ, is intended for us. Even now in some way we participate in the same divine favor she has received, though she in a unique and preeminent way.

Benedict XVI clarifies that the grace of the Immaculate Conception is not given to Mary as a merely personal grace for her alone, but rather as a grace for the entire people of God:

> In Mary, the Church can already contemplate what she is called to become. Every believer can contemplate, here and now, the perfect fulfillment of his or her own vocation. May each of you always remain full of thanksgiving for what the Lord has chosen to reveal of his plan of salvation through the mystery of Mary: a mystery in which we are involved most intimately since, from the height of the cross which we celebrate and exalt today, it is revealed to us through the words of Jesus himself that his Mother is our Mother. Inasmuch as we are sons and daughters of Mary, we can profit from all the graces given to her; the incomparable dignity that came to her through her Immaculate Conception shines brightly over us, her children.[7]

Benedict explains that Mary is not separate from us in her unique experience of being redeemed beforehand from sin.

7. Benedict XVI, Angelus Address, Lourdes, France, September 14, 2008, Vatican website: http://w2.vatican.va/content/benedict-xvi/en/angelus/2008/documents/hf_ben-xvi_ang_20080914_lourdes.html.

Rather, it is because she is without sin that she is more united with us. Sin divides and grace unites. Removed from the torrent of sin, she becomes more fully a member of the human race and more closely united with us. Since Mary is supremely filled with grace, she is one with us. Everything in the gift she has received from God is oriented toward us, so that in some way she may share her gifts with us. The fullness of grace leads to a fullness of love and therefore to a generous response that has never been marred by sin.

Mary's purity makes her infinitely close to our hearts. She is attentive to each of us and desires our true good. More fully human because of her freedom from sin, she can be more compassionate toward us. Christians understand her love. One can easily observe this in the throngs of people who flock to Marian shrines and confide their inmost thoughts, needs, and desires to her Immaculate Heart.[8]

How We Can Experience Grace in Our Lives

We need to appreciate Mary as all holy in her true and full humanity. The author George Maloney maintains that she opened herself to the beauty of God's loving presence in her love toward each person to whom she related. She came alive and discovered God inside each human encounter. Her faith allowed Mary to find God's loving presence everywhere. Her trust allowed her to give herself to each human situation without fear or nervousness. God's Spirit of love allowed her to be delicately open and sensitive to the needs of others. As she gave herself to

8. Ibid.

God in each person, her knowledge, understanding, and wisdom of herself and of others grew. Her growth in humanness and holiness was shaped by her freedom to be opened totally to God's presence in each human encounter.[9]

The Seven Longings of the Human Heart

Mary is all holy because her God-given desires are not corrupted to something evil or less than good. Being without sin, she is able to experience the fullness of life and love. We fallen sinners experience a fundamental distortion of our God-given desires. We pursue intentions and actions that we think will bring fulfillment to our lives, but leave us feeling empty and corrupt. We can see how Mary remained true to her deepest desires and practiced the virtues that lead to life and freedom. Catholic counselor Gregory Popcak explains how our struggle to overcome the seven capital sins is really a recovery of seven longings of the human heart. "When we stop fighting against our brokenness and instead simply seek to heal that brokenness by fulfilling the God-given longings hidden behind our sins, we stop working against ourselves and start working toward both our present fulfillment and our ultimate destiny to become gods through God's grace."[10] When we satisfy our divine longings, we no longer feel much inclined toward sin. We can observe how Mary always remained faithful to those God-given longings, and herself never experienced a tendency to sin. She serves as a model of virtue for us to imitate.

---

9. See George Maloney, *Mary: The Womb of God* (Denville, NJ: Dimension Books, 1976), 120.

10. Gregory Popcak, *Broken Gods, Hope, Healing, and the Seven Longings of the Human Heart* (New York: Image Books, 2015), 28.

Pride twists the God-given yearning for plenitude, for living a life full of meaning, intimacy, and virtue.[11] Jesus came in order that we might have life, and have it to the full (see Jn 10:10). Pride misshapes this desire for bounty by leading us to think that only we know best how to live a fulfilling life. Pride makes us egotistical and condescending, separate from others. In opposition to pride, the virtue of humility empowers us to acknowledge that we should relate to God and others in order to experience fullness of life. Humility enables us to offer ourselves and our gifts for the benefit of others. It helps strengthen our bonds with others and empowers us to cooperate with them in order to become fully human and fully alive. Mary always remained the humble maidservant of the Lord. She let things be done to her according to God's will, not her own (See Lk 1:38). In her humility, she experienced the fullness of life by conceiving and bearing Christ for the sake of us all.

Envy disfigures the heavenly yearning for dignity, the longing to have our value as human beings recognized and affirmed.[12] God wants to confer on us as his children a worth greater than anything we could envision. Envy suggests that we have no importance unless we have the same gifts as everyone else, and unless we can achieve everything that they do. We contend with others in order to be the best. In opposition to envy, the virtue of kindness empowers us to realize our true worth by enabling us to help others experience their own value. Our kind presence can foster the prosperity of others. Mary knew that her human dignity came from the Almighty who had done great things for her, and that all generations would recognize this and call her blessed.

11. Ibid., 28–29.

12. Ibid., 29–30.

She bestowed kindness on Elizabeth and made her aware of her own dignity.

Anger warps the heavenly yearning for justice and order that prevents injury to ourselves and others.[13] Justice helps us transcend ourselves and show charity toward others. Wrath twists justice by convincing us to look for selfish remedies to injustices that end up harming others as much as they have injured us. Anger exacerbates wrongs by persuading us that retribution is the most effective way to correct injustices. We fulfill our yearning for justice only when we practice the heavenly virtue of patience. Patience directs our endeavors to overcome wrongs as opposed to imposing hurried, ill-conceived remedies that harm others or compound the situation. Mary rejoiced in God's justice in her *Magnificat,* exclaiming: "He has scattered the proud in the thoughts of their hearts. He has brought down the powerful from their thrones, and lifted up the lowly; he has filled the hungry with good things, and sent the rich away empty" (Lk 1:51b–53). Mary showed great patience in awaiting the coming of the Messiah who would bring about justice for the oppressed. She patiently accompanied Jesus' development into manhood. She patiently longed for her crucified son to be vindicated by God's justice in his resurrection.

Sloth falsifies the heavenly yearning for peace and an amicable life, in accordance with the divine plan.[14] Sloth distorts our yearning for harmony, leading us to think that the easy and effective way to promote harmony is to ignore issues. Sloth causes us to evade necessary confrontations in laboring for right order and the common good. We can only fulfill the heavenly

13. Ibid., 30.

14. Ibid., 30–31.

yearning for peace by exercising the virtue of diligence, laboring for right order regardless of the cost or length of time. Mary experienced inner peace by doing God's will, not her own, and diligently working to bring about God's reign of peace in the life of her son. She was faithful in performing all the religious practices of Israel according to the Law (see Lk 2:22–24). Mary continued to work to bring peace in the Church after her son's ascension until her own assumption into heaven.

Avarice distorts the heavenly yearning for trust.[15] By avarice we seek to feel sure that both we and what we have are enough to meet life's difficulties. Avarice allows fear to overcome us and suggests that we rely on our hoard of possessions as our main security. Ravenous greed compels us to heap up more goods and achievements. Our longing for trust is only fulfilled by the virtue of generosity, sharing our possessions in order to show trust in God and his Providence. Jesus reminds us not to worry about our lives and that he will provide for all our needs (see Mt 6:25–34). Mary trusted God for all that she was and had. She exclaimed that God who is mighty had done good things for her, and that he had filled the hungry with good things. Jesus was all that she needed. In her hour of greatest need, when she became pregnant with Jesus, Mary gave of herself to Elizabeth. She continued to give herself wholeheartedly to Jesus even to his death on the cross. Mary gave Jesus to us for our salvation.

Gluttony warps our heavenly yearning for prosperity, that is, our longing for mental, physical, and spiritual wholeness.[16] Gluttony suggests that gorging ourselves with food and drink is

15. Ibid., 31–32.

16. Ibid., 32–33.

better than leading a healthy and wholesome life. Comforting ourselves with food, and seeking excessive pleasure with drinks, drugs, or other stimulants is often a way to numb ourselves against the turmoil and disorder in various aspects of our lives. Ravenous gluttony also compels us to seek integration by fixating on the type of food we eat or being fussy about how our food is prepared. While we need good nutrition, it nevertheless cannot save us. The virtue of temperance enables us to seek and utilize every beneficial thing, not only food, in a balanced way that promotes the health and equilibrium we all need. Mary was a fully-alive woman, whose soul glorified the Lord (see Lk 1:46). She knew the favor of the Lord's grace (see Lk 1:48), which made her whole and complete as a human being. Mary knew the value of celebration in prompting her son to change the water into wine at Cana.

Lust falsifies our heavenly yearning for communion, our longing for personal relationship, our desire to understand and to be understood by others and God.[17] Lust promotes the falsehood that genuine fellowship and intimacy is pointless, that all one needs is an imagined or superficial association with another. The virtue of chastity enables us to love each person we know appropriately, never seeking the other as a means to our selfish purposes. Mary in her virginity experienced the incarnation of Jesus, realizing the most profound union possible with her Lord. Mary chastely loved Joseph as her husband and loved all the people in her life as well as possible. She loved and nurtured the Church as a mother in the Upper Room and throughout her last days on earth.

17. Ibid., 33–34.

Mary all-holy remained focused on all her divine longings and found them completely satisfied in her son Jesus and in relationship with the Holy Trinity. We are all like Mary in that we have the same human yearnings for the divine that she experienced. Although in us these yearnings have been distorted by sin, we can, by grace and imitation of Jesus and Mary, reorient our desires toward their proper end. Whenever we experience disordered desires and sinful tendencies, we need to recognize what we are honestly looking for. Then, relying on grace, we can seek to live the virtues that will lead us to the fulfillment of our true and deepest desires.

Various Ways We Experience Grace

Mary's experience of being full of grace parallels our experience of receiving God's grace. Grace is a participation in the life of God that affects and transforms human freedom and loving. His love is accepting and forgiving, raising a person to a new kind of existence. While God in his grace saves us by washing away original and actual sin in us, God saved Mary by preserving her from sin from the moment of her conception. Because she was not affected by the consequences of sin, she posed no obstacle to the working of God's grace in her life. Just as pure gold is a perfect conductor of electricity, so Mary in her purity and sinlessness is a perfect conductor of God's power working through her. It is because of Mary's cooperation with God's grace that we are saved by grace, though we still pose obstacles to God's grace due to our history of sin.

Saint Andrew of Crete asserts that with the birth of Mary, humanity receives anew the gift of its original creation at the hands of God, restored to its ancient loveliness: "Today the reshaping of our nature begins and a world grown old is divinely transformed and receives the first fruits of a second creation."[18] With Mary, humanity is restored to the freshness of the original graced creation. In Mary's consent to God, and because of it, grace is at work transforming our own history and that of the world. We experience God's grace especially in significant moments of self-transcendence, when we experience the fullness and richness of God beyond ourselves. According to Denis Edwards, some of these moments would be experiences of interpersonal love, childbirth, creativity, forgiveness, and the beauty of nature.[19] In these graced moments we can see Mary's fully graced humanity and her experience that parallels our own. We will look at each of these in turn.

In the encounter of interpersonal love, two persons transcend themselves in the giving and receiving of the other.[20] Married couples share in this graced experience of self-giving and receiving as a gift from God. For Mary, this happened in the mutual exchange of selves that occurred in her virginal marriage to Joseph. She discovered God's love in Joseph's pure love and self-sacrifice for her and Jesus. In our graced experiences of love of family and friends, God's love is mediated to us. Mary experienced the joy of familiarity and friendship in her exchange of interpersonal love with her cousin Elizabeth. John the Baptist leapt with joy in his mother's womb on hearing Mary's voice and at the presence of the Savior. Elizabeth perceived who Mary was in her interior essence as the one who trusted that God's promise would be fulfilled (see Lk 1:45).

---

18. Andrew of Crete, Sermon 1: (PG 97-912), in Lombardi, *Mary, Reflections of the Trinity*, 249.

19. See Denis Edwards, *The Human Experience of God* (Ramsey, NJ: Paulist Press, 1983), 29.

20. Ibid., 29–30.

Grace is also manifest in the conception, development, and birth of a child.[21] Parents experience the privilege of being co-creators with God as they provide not only the genetic material, but also to some degree the form of a child's personality. Parents often come to a greater understanding of God's love and responsibility through the awareness of how much they love and care for their child. They continue to wonder in awe as the child matures. We can imagine Mary's magnanimous love and tender self-giving to her child. God chose to depend upon her to give his Son human flesh. We might picture how Jesus resembles his mother in his looks and personality, and presume her impact, together with that of Joseph, on his psychology and character.

Human creativity can be a channel of God's grace.[22] Musicians and poets often attribute their compositions and talents to something greater than themselves. Filled with the Holy Spirit, Mary composed the most beautiful Magnificat to the praise and glory of God. Her song spoke of God's faithfulness in fulfilling his promises and prophesied great things to come. As a devout Hebrew woman, Mary would have been skilled and industrious in ordinary creative works, such as growing a vineyard, providing food, making tapestry and garments, and selling her wares (see Prov 31:10–31). God's grace works in us as we use our gifts and talents in being co-creative with him.

The favor of God often takes the form of mercy in our relations with others.[23] We are called to imitate our Father, who "makes his sun rise on the evil and on the good, and sends rain on the righteous and on the unrighteous" (Mt 5:45). We have

21. Ibid., 30–31.

22. Ibid., 31–32.

23. Ibid., 32.

many opportunities to offer forgiveness "seventy times seven" to those we love, as well as to those we might consider enemies. We experience something of God's unconditional love toward us when we love others despite their faults and the ways they have hurt us. As we consider our own sinfulness and how the Lord has forgiven us so much, we find ourselves in solidarity with our neighbors who are sinners. Since Mary was without sin, she must have been extra sensitive to sin in others and to the hurt it caused. Yet she must have also been more compassionate in her response to sinners. As full of grace, she no doubt allowed God's forgiveness to flow upon others, even the many who must have judged her for being pregnant before she lived with Joseph. Mary refused to go down the path of judging others in return, most likely returning a blessing instead (see 1 Pet 3:9).

Creation is filled with God's blessings and becomes an occasion for us to be filled with grace.[24] We can imagine Mary as a devout Hebrew always giving thanks in psalms and canticles to God for the gifts of his creation. Creation was a reminder of God's presence in and through the sun, the moon, the wind and rain, the fish in the sea, the birds of the air, and the animals that roamed the earth. We can be overwhelmed with thanks and praise at the beauty of nature, from the tiny marvel of a flower to the multitude of stars in the sky. Mary would have experienced a special oneness with nature as the fulfillment of the bride of the Song of Songs. The land of Israel provides not merely the scenery for the love encounter in the Song of Songs, it is also identified with the beautiful features of the bride's body.[25]

24. Ibid., 33.

25. See Ellen F. Davis, *Proverbs, Ecclesiastes, and the Song of Songs* (Louisville: Westminster John Knox Press, 2000), 233.

Grace in Times of Sorrow

We discover God's grace not only in the joyful experiences of life. God is also to be found in seemingly negative situations, such as moments of vulnerability, death, failure, alienation, and loneliness.[26] Mary did not return to the Garden of Eden due to her privilege of being sinless. Her grace is not a grace of original justice (which Adam and Eve had at first); it is really a Christian grace—a greater grace of redemption.[27] This grace implies deeper and more exclusive divine demands and involves a body capable of undergoing suffering and a soul susceptible to sorrow, capable of bearing the pains due to sin. Mary had many such experiences of sorrow and loss in which she found God present. Mary found herself pregnant and certainly vulnerable as a young woman who was legally married but living in the time before the marriage would have been consummated. (Jewish weddings took place in two stages: a time of betrothal when the spouses lived apart, and a time when the wedding feast was celebrated and they would begin to live together. In both stages the man and woman were legally, fully married).[28]At the time of the annunciation, Mary was betrothed to Joseph, but they had not lived together. She must have wondered if Joseph would divorce her. At the presentation of Jesus, Mary faced the future with a

26. See Edwards, 34.

27. "*Mary* means, in a sense, a going beyond the limit spoken of in the Book of Genesis (3:16) and a return to that 'beginning' in which one finds the 'woman' as she was intended to be in *creation*, and therefore in the eternal mind of God: in the bosom of the Most Holy Trinity. Mary is the new beginning of the *dignity and vocation of women*, of each and every woman." Saint John Paul II, *Mulieris Dignitatem*, 11.

28. See Brant Pitre, *Jesus and the Jewish Roots of Mary* (New York: Image Books, 2018), 103ff.

certain sense of dread in knowing that her heart would be pierced with a sword of sorrow because of the rejection of her son. Witnessing her son's crucifixion, she would have experienced a horrifying feeling of obliteration and a sense of having been abandoned by God. We sinners tend to distract ourselves or put up defenses that cover our vulnerability to life. Instead, we should allow ourselves to experience our own fragility and dependence on God for our identity and importance. Like the bride who has suffered in exile and yet is lovely, we can experience grace in our own suffering.

In moments of failure we learn to face the limitations of our human condition.[29] We have to surrender our egocentric selves to God, whose ways are not our ways. Mary and Joseph likely experienced a keen sense of regret in having to welcome Jesus into the world in a lowly cave. They probably felt they had failed God when they lost Jesus in the Temple at Jerusalem. Jesus' own death on a cross was a major failure by human standards, and Mary would have been devastated as she witnessed it, yet it resulted in the exceeding fruitfulness of our salvation. As we face failures in our own lives, we learn to surrender ourselves to God who can make all things work together for the good.

Experiences of loneliness and alienation can leave us reeling and feeling empty inside.[30] We can feel alienated from God, our neighbor, and even our very selves. Mary likely felt alienated from her family and friends who judged her at her pregnancy, but she found connection with her understanding cousin Elizabeth. When her kinsfolk thought Jesus to be mad, and when her fellow townspeople rejected him as altogether

---

29. See Edwards, 36.

30. Ibid., 36–38.

too much for them, she experienced hostility and separation. She had to learn to live alone as a widow after Joseph died, when Jesus departed from her side to begin his public ministry.

Death is the final constraint on our being and the ultimate experience of the poverty of our existence.[31] The grief we feel at the loss of a loved one can be unbearably painful and dark, yet it also opens us to the reality of the mystery of life beyond death. Mary lost Joseph her spouse and eventually watched as her son was cruelly put to death, standing faithfully beneath his cross. Though she always believed in his resurrection, her grief and darkness were immense. In the Western Christian tradition, it is believed that Mary died, experiencing the loss of her dear ones on this earth. Like Mary we can face the anguish of death with hope and fortitude. We can experience the Lord's compassion because he is close to the brokenhearted.

We see that in all the joys and sorrows of Mary's life, she is the one who is full of grace and who teaches us how to live by grace. Because she is pure and sinless, she is more fully human in experiencing all that is truly human in our existence. She savors the joy of human life and drinks its sorrows to the dregs. She is not shielded from the effects of sin in others and, in union with Jesus, she bears with the sins of her people. Like the bride who is scorched yet lovely, burnt by the sufferings of human life, Mary radiates beauty as the most fully graced human creature the world has ever known.

31. Ibid., 35.

Questions for Reflection and Discussion

1. Is there any parallel in your life with the way Mary and Jesus innocently bore the sinfulness of their people in order to redeem them?
2. Which of the seven capital sins do you struggle with the most? How does awareness of the true divine longing associated with that sin help you to strive for what you honestly want and need? How can you better practice the opposite virtue?
3. In what way have you seen Mary as someone separate and so different from yourself that you cannot identify with her or relate to her?
4. How do you see Mary as more human and like yourself in many ways? Do you ever experience her compassion? In what ways could you see yourself imitating Mary?
5. In what manner do you see your life as full of grace? What in you is an obstacle to God's grace, and what in you is more receptive to his grace?

Prayer Exercises

1. Which of the seven divine longings (p. 42) do you tend to distort with one of the seven deadly sins? Pray with Song 1:5–11 and ask for the grace of repentance and the ability to live in the fullness of Christ's life.
2. Reflect on the ransomed slaves of the Middle Ages (p. 37). Pray with Revelation 5:6–14, or 1 Peter 1:13–25 and ask for gratitude to realize that you have been bought for the price of Christ's blood.

3. Ponder Mary's fullness of humanity in the purity of her Immaculate Conception (p. 34). Pray with Song 4:4 and Luke 1:26–38 and ask for the grace to relate to Mary on a very human level.
4. Consider the positive experiences of life that are graced (p. 47). Pray with Isaiah 61:9–62:5 and ask for the ability to savor God's grace in your own transcendent moments.
5. Consider the limiting and more negative experiences of life that are graced (p. 51). Pray with Matthew 2:13–23 and ask for the ability to know God's presence in difficulties and sufferings.

Chapter 3

Enraptured Gaze

[B] While the king was on his couch,
    my nard gave forth its fragrance.
My beloved is to me a bag of myrrh
    that lies between my breasts.
My beloved is to me a cluster of henna blossoms
    in the vineyards of En-gedi.
[G] Ah, you are beautiful, my love;
    ah, you are beautiful;
    your eyes are doves.
Ah, you are beautiful, my beloved,
    truly lovely.
Our couch is green;
    the beams of our house are cedar,
    our rafters are pine (Song 1:12–17).

While they were there, the time came for her to deliver her child. And she gave birth to her firstborn son and wrapped him in bands of cloth, and laid him in a manger, because there was no place for them in the inn. . . . But Mary treasured all these words and pondered them in her heart. (Lk 2:6–7; 19)

A woman once noticed that her teenage son seemed to be walking on air. Since she knew he was dating a nice girl she asked him, "What does Nancy like about you?"

He happily responded, "She thinks I'm handsome, talented, clever, and a good dancer."

"Oh, that's wonderful," his mother replied, "and what do you like about Nancy?"

"She thinks I'm handsome, talented, clever, and a good dancer."

Once we get past the humor of his romantic infatuation, we realize this vignette points to a sublime truth. We love God because he has loved us first, awakening our desire for him in return. Our love for God is a pale reflection of his infinite love for us. Here in the Song of Songs the bride is aware of the Bridegroom's captivated interest in her. He lies on his couch within the enclosure, symbolizing the Temple in Jerusalem encircled and protected by the surrounding hills. The worship of God is the moment of rest for Israel, who enters into God's repose. God's rest can be traced back to the seventh day of creation, when God rested from all he had done (see Gen 2:3). The Hebrew word *menuha*, or "rest" means much more than the English translation suggests. For the Jews, "rest" is better understood as "purposeful contemplation," wherein one becomes tranquil in order to ponder life deeply. *Menuha* is living well in both exterior and interior peace in quiet reflection.[1] The Lord

1. Abraham Joshua Heschel, *The Sabbath* (New York, NY: Farrar, Straus, and Giroux, 1978), 22–24.

leads his people beside restful waters and makes them lie down in green pastures (see Ps 23:2). God is the one who first contemplates the goodness of his creation, loving it and seeing it as good. The Lord invites us into his loving contemplation of us as we are invited to enter his rest. Mary knew herself as the Lord's chosen, his loved one from the beginning. "The Father blessed Mary more than any other created person 'in Christ with every spiritual blessing in the heavenly places' and chose her 'in Christ before the foundation of the world, to be holy and blameless before him in love.'"[2] He imagined Mary from all eternity and created her with a rich endowment of gifts in view of her role as Mother of the Redeemer.

The Pondering Heart

Mary is the fulfillment of the bride who has captivated the Bridegroom, God, and holds him closely in her heart. The bride compares her lover to the nard of finest fragrance at her heart, the place of her deep, cherished love. In Scripture, the heart symbolizes the inmost center of the person wherein a person chooses fundamentally for or against God. God's word penetrates most deeply to the heart of the human person and is to be contemplated and appropriated in prayer. Mary *kept* all the events of her life with Jesus, the Word incarnate, reflecting on their meaning in light of God's word. Scripture scholar Edward Sri notes that the Old Testament patriarch Jacob *kept in mind* the dreams of his son Joseph about his brothers reverencing him (see Gen 37:9–11). King Nebuchadnezzar *kept* Daniel's interpretation of his dream in his heart, as Daniel *kept* in his own heart the meaning of the vision in his dream (see Dan 7:28). In each case, the

2. *Catechism of the Catholic Church*, no. 492.

biblical figure is concerned to understand God's message in the right way so that he or she can live according to his revelation. The psalmist *keeps* God's word in his heart so that he will not sin (see Ps 119:11). The father instructs his son to let his heart keep his commandments (see Prov 3:1). Finally, Sirach explains that the wise man carefully *keeps* the stories and prophecies given to him, penetrating their subtleties and seeking to understand their obscurities (see Sir 39:1–3).[3]

Luke tells us that Mary "pondered" in her heart the events of the birth of her son, that she held and cherished them deeply at the center of her being. The Greek word for "ponder," *symballein,* means to throw together, to compare, to consider from all possible angles until one arrives at understanding. Mary pondered her life experiences in light of God's revelation of his Word and in the person of his son. In her pondering she is the perfect image for us of a Christian at prayer. In our praying we first pay attention to what God is saying to us in the ordinary events of our daily lives, trying to accept our lives as they are and to find meaning. Ambiguous and seemingly contradictory messages in our lives often confound our understanding. Instead of always expecting answers, we learn in prayer to be comfortable with the sometimes-unresolved situations in our lives, entrusting our lives to God until he brings clarity.

It can be a challenge to notice what God is saying to us when things seem to go wrong. We often have an ideal of how our lives should be, while we miss the meaning of the way they really are. There was once a twelve-year-old boy named Willie who resented not getting the role of Joseph in the parish nativity play. Instead

---

3. See Edward Sri, *Walking with Mary: A Biblical Journey from Nazareth to the Cross* (New York: Image, 2017), 87.

he received the bit part of inn keeper. As the weeks of rehearsal progressed, Willie plotted how he would take revenge on his younger brother Tommy who was chosen to play Joseph. The night of the play arrived. Tommy, as Joseph, and their sister Nancy, as Mary, arrived at the inn in Bethlehem. Tommy knocked at the door and braced himself for the expected rejection. Having plotted all these weeks, Willie the inn keeper was ready for them with a surprise. He opened the door slightly, peering at them with suspicion. Then he flung the door wide open and exclaimed, "Come in, come in! You shall have the finest room in the inn!" Tommy was shocked, but with great presence of mind he responded, "Just a minute Mary, I'll look inside." He walked in, looked around, shook his head and replied, "Look at this filthy place! We're not staying in a dump like this. Come on Mary, I'd rather sleep in a stable!" With that, he was back on track. Such a humorous event reminds us how rarely things turn out the way we expect, but that God has a plan to fulfill his will. God's plan might seem beyond our comprehension, yet we are called to ponder, understand, and accept it, adapting our lives to it.

Mary could have pondered her own vision of how the Son of God and King of Israel should have been born—in a palace, receiving royal treatment. Instead he was subject to a Roman census. Mary had difficulty traveling while pregnant, giving birth to Jesus in a cave for animals. In accepting the reality of the lowly circumstances of Christ's birth, Mary perceived God's wisdom. God used the census to ensure that Christ fulfilled the prophecies that the Messiah would come from Bethlehem. Knowing that Herod was an evil king seeking to destroy the child, Mary realized God's wisdom in having Jesus born in poverty and obscurity, "behind enemy lines" so to speak. In Jesus' rejection at the inn, Mary encountered the first sign of his rejection by his own, which would culminate with the cross.

Mary would have pondered the irony of the angels' revelation to the shepherds. Shepherds were dirty and despised citizens of Israel. They were scorned as incapable of keeping the Law, since they were preoccupied with caring for their sheep, working even on the Sabbath. God should have revealed the Savior's birth to anyone *but* shepherds. Yet some of Israel's greatest heroes, such as Moses and David, were shepherds who reflected the care and providence of God, the true shepherd of Israel. Jesus would eventually refer to himself as the Good Shepherd who tends his sheep and seeks out the lost, the poor, and the lowly. It was fitting that the angels would announce Jesus' birth to outcasts like these shepherds.

Finally, Mary pondered the visit of the Magi, the wise men of Persia, the king's consultants who were often offered key governorships. But the religious leaders of Israel disrespected and even shunned the Magi. They were considered dangerous and misleading with their enticing illusions. They summed up all that was considered repulsive in Gentile aliens and idolaters.[4] Yet the best of these men had core beliefs rooted in wisdom, which they studied and taught. The influence of the prophet Daniel, who was once persecuted by these same Magi in Persia (see Dan 2:6), brought some interaction with the truth and the prophecies of the God of Israel, making the Magi well-disposed to seek more of the truth. Mary must have been awestruck at their unexpected visitation and their account of following the star. She would have recognized that somehow the prophecies of Isaiah (see Isa 60:11) and the Psalms (see 72:10) proclaiming that kings of the earth would bring gifts in procession to Israel, were being fulfilled in her child. She could have recognized that

---

4. See Scott Hahn, *Joy to the World* (New York: Image, 2014), 108–109.

the gold, frankincense, and myrrh were all used in temple worship. The Magi were now using them to honor her son as the great high priest of Israel. Mary pondered all these experiences in light of God's revelation in order to discover meaning and purpose for her life with Jesus.

Mary holds Jesus and the mysteries of his birth, life, and death close to her heart, just as the bride holds her Bridegroom close to her heart. "My beloved is to me a bag of myrrh, that lies between my breasts" (Song 1:13). Myrrh is a natural gum or resin secreted from a small thorny tree. Its perfume is so captivating and penetrating that it can make one faint, and so it epitomizes well the magnetism of the Bridegroom. The Psalmist suggests of the Bridegroom of Israel that his "robes are all fragrant with myrrh and aloes" (Ps 45:8). Isaiah has spoken of the perfume boxes hidden in the garments of the women of Israel (see Is 3:20). The bride now states that the Bridegroom is the very sachet of myrrh that lies between her breasts, "Constantly breathed in, rising up from her breast, mixed with her own breath, he is the secret radiance of her whom he loves."[5] Her continual awareness of his fragrant presence serves as a perfect image of unceasing prayer (see 1 Thess 5:17). Mary exercised this unceasing prayer as she pondered all the mysteries of Jesus' life, death, and resurrection, permeated by the fragrance of myrrh. The Magi offered myrrh as one of their gifts to the newborn King. Even then in his infancy, the somewhat bitter scent of the myrrh was exuded in his poverty and sufferings. At Jesus' birth, Mary wrapped him in swaddling clothes and laid him in the manger (see Lk 2:7), which foreshadowed how Jesus would

5. Blaise Arminjon, *The Cantata of Love* (San Francisco: Ignatius Press, 1988), 120. www.ignatius.com. Used with permission.

be wrapped in burial bands and laid in a tomb (see Lk 23:53).[6] During the crucifixion, Jesus was offered wine mixed with myrrh (see Mk 15:23) to deaden the pain, but he refused it so as not to mitigate his own sufferings. Myrrh must be bruised and crushed, as Jesus was during his passion, to release its scent. Jesus' body is anointed at burial with myrrh in anticipation of his resurrection (see Jn 19:39). Throughout her life, Mary was constantly aware of the fragrance of Christ (see 2 Cor 2:15), the one she held close within her heart. She carried him about physically as a child throughout the day and night; later, she continued to carry him in her heart. Through Mary the heavenly fragrance of Jesus was being released in a way that others could perceive. They would then be drawn to her because she radiated Christ.[7]

When Mary gave birth to the Lord, her love for him increased as she beheld him face to face. All the pain of her trials must have melted away in the peaceful radiance of Jesus' countenance. Their physical presence to one another, once visible, made possible a loving gaze and loving actions as Mary began to care for Jesus. In that moment, Mary and Jesus relived the scene in which the bride and Bridegroom behold each other face to face and declare each other's beauty in the Song of Songs. The Bridegroom first says of the bride, "How beautiful you are, my love . . . your eyes are doves" (Song 4:1). God has so regarded beauty in the Virgin Mary, that enraptured, he has been drawn out of himself to take on flesh through her. Having created her full of grace, he delighted in her virtues and could not resist taking his human nature from her. "You have ravished my heart

6. Luke uses the same words, "wrapped" and "laid" in both passages.

7. See George Maloney, *Singers of the New Song* (Notre Dame, IN: Ave Maria Press, 1985), 40.

with a glance of your eyes" (Song 4:9). When Mary found favor with God, he found her beautiful. Her beauty is the work of grace in her, her response to and cooperation with the divine enterprise. God himself has been charmed and conquered by the beauty of his most perfect bride. In the person of the Bridegroom, he can only exclaim ecstatically, "Behold, you are beautiful, my love!"

And the bride says in return, "Behold, you are beautiful, my beloved!" Mary, now seeing the face of the Infant Jesus, is spellbound by his serenity and charm. Jesus delights and deeply touches all those who look at him, from the lowly shepherds to the exalted Magi. The great orator Bishop Fulton Sheen once remarked that Mary would have pondered the paradox and spiritual beauty of the Incarnation in her heart. She would have been in awe that the little baby who was lying on straw in the manger was the same God who created the universe. Though he was born in time, he existed before time began.[8] Mary found endless food in her contemplation of the Word made flesh in the Incarnation as she laid her son in the manger. God's loveliness was made visible and led her to contemplate the infinite beauty of God, who is not limited by appearance and defies human understanding.

This mutual gaze and admiration of the Bridegroom and bride exemplifies our experience of contemplative prayer. In this prayer the Lord gazes on us with love and calls us beautiful. We contemplate Christ and his mysteries, finding beauty in his radiant face and in all his actions. In his nativity, Jesus depended completely on his mother. He expected everything from her, which

8. See Fulton Sheen, *The Eternal Galilean* (New York: Alba House, 1997), 11.

she willingly gave. We can imagine the tenderness of every action she performed on his behalf. Her whole life was reordered to care for her child. She wrapped him in swaddling clothes, nursed him, and remained sensitive to his cries in the night. She would hold Jesus to her breast to warm him with tender care for his fragility. Mary performed all these gestures with great reverence for her son's divinized humanity. She could more easily ponder his beautiful physical presence as she held Jesus in her arms.

As Mary pondered in prayer, she interpreted the events of her life with Jesus in light of God's revelation.[9] While the circumstances of Jesus' birth were filled with hardship and were not what she had expected, Mary received the grace to accept and even cherish them. Once she beheld her child, her life began to make sense. We too have the choice to pay attention to our life experience and its meaning in light of God's revelation. If we neglect to ponder the Word of God, our lives may seem like a string of random, meaningless events. Our hearts will become hardened and closed to God's grace. Often, we have our own narrowly focused agenda for our lives and miss out on God's gift of self to us in the real events that happen. We become preoccupied with life's problems and our failings. The more we try to solve our problems without God, the more deeply we dig our own pit. Instead, we need to learn to surrender our lives completely to the Lord and his Providence. "Cast all your anxiety on him, because he cares for you" (1 Pet 5:7). When we contemplate

---

9. All Mary's words echo Old Testament passages, suggesting a keen awareness of revelation and ability to interpret her own life in light of Sacred Scripture. For instance, her *fiat* echoes 1 Sam 1:11 and Ex 19:8. Her *Magnificat* harkens back to 1 Kings 2:1–10; Hab 3:3–19; Ps 33, 56, 102, 112, 146; Isa 61:10; and Jdt 16:6–7, among other references.

the Lord's face in prayer and ponder the meaning of his mysteries for our lives, our lives begin to make sense.

This is shown in the example of a woman named Dorothy who purchased a potted gardenia. She faithfully watered the plant, which produced rich green leaves and a good number of buds. Sadly, each of the buds died, one after the other. Disheartened, she removed the potted plant from inside her home and relegated it to the outside patio, feeling she had wasted her money on it. Meanwhile, Dorothy suffered a series of setbacks in her life. She had financial difficulties, a misunderstanding with a friend, and an illness in her family. The more she tried to work on her problems, the worse they got. Everything seemed to go wrong for Dorothy, who fell into self-pity. Her depression worsened. One day she collected her dirty clothes to do the one thing she could still do—laundry. As she walked through the patio on her way to the basement laundry room, she was overcome by a pungent aroma. She turned around to find a large and beautiful gardenia flower. As Dorothy admired the gardenia and breathed in its scent, she realized that it had flowered because she had put it in the sun. All her diligent watering and fertilizing were important, but not enough to make it bloom. Then she realized that the same was true of her life. Everything she was doing to address her problems was important, but not enough. She still lacked something. If her life were to flower and bear fruit, she needed to put herself and her problems before the light of Christ. Dorothy needed to open her heart to the Lord in prayer. Once she did, her life and her attitude improved.[10]

---

10. See Mark Link, *Illustrated Sunday Homilies, Sundays Year A, B, C/Series II* (Saint Louis: Tabor, 1990), 63.

As we ponder our lives, memories from our past often come up, memories of events that God has used to make us who we are. We can interpret our entire lives, including our past, in light of the Gospel of Jesus Christ. Mary must have marveled at how her life had brought her to the point of giving birth to the Savior. She could look back at all the events from her childhood and teenage years that had prepared her for this moment—her desire for virginity,[11] her betrothal to Joseph, the angel's appearance and message, her time with Elizabeth, and even the census and journey to Bethlehem. She could perceive a pattern of the Lord's favor to her in her growing relationship with her son who was now visible before her. Imagine Mary's gratitude for all God had done for her over the years, her sense of fulfillment in the present moment. Many saints have used their memories in prayer to recognize how present God has been to them throughout their lives. Saint Augustine wrote his *Confessions* as a remembrance of his life, interpreting all that happened to him in the light of God's grace. As he reflected on his life before his conversion, he became aware that God was within, while he was without. God called, shouted, and broke through his deafness. God flashed, shone, and dispelled his blindness. The Lord was present and seeking to communicate himself to Augustine, who was not paying attention. Eventually Augustine experienced conversion while pondering God's word. He then reviewed his life through the prism of his newfound awareness of how God had always been present to him, despite Augustine's failure to recognize him. Saint Thérèse of Lisieux also used her memory to review her life in conversation with the Lord, unearthing many profound experiences of his grace. In her autobiography she reveals

11. See footnote 10 in chapter 1.

how she discovered God's power at work in her most painful experiences, such as overcoming the need to be pampered with gifts from her father on Christmas Eve.

We can use our own memory to consider our whole lives, period by period, in the context of God's favor. First, offer a prayer for enlightenment. Then consider our earliest memories with a sense of how God was blessing us with so many gifts, whether we were aware of his presence or not. Besides the gifts, there may have been moments of pain or trials. But in them we discover how God has sustained us and enabled us to overcome difficulties. We may discover incidents in which we hurt others or were hurt by them, pointing to our need for healing and forgiveness. Such memories can help us converse with the Lord in order to find a new awareness of his presence throughout our lives. We may also discover patterns of God's grace—the way he often deals with us, so that we can be more sensitive to his approaches to us in the present. Many life events will remain a mystery, but we will have a greater sense that God makes all things work for the good for those who love him (see Rom 8:28).

In John English's book *Choosing Life,* a woman named Jane describes praying through her life history, having suffered through the sadness and pain of growing up in a poor family. Jane relates the following prayer experience:

> After asking for the grace to appropriate my history in faith, I felt constrained to stay with the Lord. He seemed to indicate that he wanted me to stay in his presence, rather than have me call up events in my life. The feeling of being drawn to him intensified. There was no dialogue, no exchange, simply a sense of deep presence, intense peacefulness and joy at being together. At one point, however, he intimated that he is the beginning and the end of my history, that he lovingly designed generations of ancestors to bring me into life, that all comes

> from him and flows back to him. This period of loving presence continued for perhaps an hour or more. No recollections, no reminiscences of any kind occurred.
>
> Suddenly, from nowhere, a childhood scene flicked on. As a child on the family farm I was standing in the middle of a waving field of golden wheat. The wind blew the wheat like an ocean of gentle tides, ebbing and flowing, under a blue sky with puffy, white clouds. This scene lasted but moments. There was no message, only the scene. The sense of gentle presence continued.
>
> A second childhood scene turned on sometime later. I was in the school cafeteria, eating homemade bread that had been spread with a mixture of cream and corn syrup. Again, the scene lasted only seconds, followed again by silence for a few minutes. Then came the softly spoken words, "I have fed you with milk and honey." Strong sentiments of love and gratitude welled up in me for his tender care. A period of silence followed.
>
> Suddenly, a third childhood scene flashed into my memory. As I was coming up the gravel road toward home, I could smell the baking bread. As I entered the kitchen, I saw again the many loaves of plump, golden bread. For a few minutes there was silence again. Then came the Lord's voice once more, "I have filled you with the best of wheat." Waves of gratitude and love flooded over me. He seemed to enrobe me with himself.[12]

Jane realized the meaning of her life in God's loving design and gained a sense of acceptance of her life history. Such prayer over one's personal history is life-giving, producing peaceful contemplation and profound attentiveness to God.

12. John English, *Choosing Life* (New York: Paulist Press, 1978), 133.

As I reflected like this, using memories from my novitiate, I discovered that my prayer not only focused on thoughts in my head, but also opened more deeply to feelings rushing in at the heart level. I experienced Christ as a companion who encompassed my whole past. Such prayer resulted in my greater self-acceptance as a loved sinner, affirmed in my dignity as a child of God. I no longer needed to obsess about past failures in the futile hope of doing away with them. I could laugh at my own idiosyncrasies, life's nuisances, and annoying people. Past resentments and anxieties faded so that I came to better appreciate God in my daily routine. I became more aware of and responsive to the needs of others. I found renewed meaning in ordinary events as memory revealed their origins and the providential hand of God. Greater peace in acting flowed from the abundance of my contemplation and union with Christ and his values. Finally, as I felt more lovable and more loving toward others, I expressed greater confidence in God and hope for myself and my community. I discovered that the Lord can draw good not only from our virtue, but even from our past failings and present weakness.

Mary is aware of her son's loving gaze upon her. He has long contemplated her from all eternity, fashioned her existence and now delights in his perfect creature. He desires to take up his dwelling in her inmost essence, in her heart in which he delights. She is aware of the beauty of her whole life, past, present, and future, in his eyes and of his eternal, loving embrace. She keeps and ponders him in her memory, in the deep recesses of her being, finding meaning in all the graced moments of her life. She finds purpose in all that she does as life-giving surrender in doing his will and serving him. Keeping these things and pondering them in her heart, Mary is fruitful in producing an awareness and responsiveness to the full outpouring of God's favor. Aware of her own beauty in his eyes, she views her beloved with "dove eyes," with the same contemplative awareness of his beauty. She is moved to respond as the bride, "Ah, you are beautiful, my beloved!" (Song 1:16)

Questions for Reflection and Discussion

1. How has the notion of the "Sabbath rest" of purposeful leisure and contemplation influenced your life? Do you value contemplation of the divine and make enough room for God?
2. How does God's presence cause an upheaval in the mystery of his birth? How would you feel if you were Mary and Joseph and experienced all that happened to them?
3. As you look back at your life, how have your own expectations been met or dashed? How well have you responded in faith to both successes and setbacks? How have setbacks been graced moments? How has the Lord made all things in your life work together for the good?
4. How do you experience the loving gaze of contemplation? What does it mean for you to seek the face of the Lord with your whole being and especially with your imagination?
5. In what ways do you perceive Mary and Jesus as beautiful? Can you imagine Jesus calling you beautiful?
6. What difference does it make for you to ponder the events of your life and interpret them in the light of Scripture?

Prayer Exercises

1. Ponder the image of the king on his couch in restful contemplation (p. 58). Pray with Song 1:12–17 and ask for the grace to enter into the Lord's rest.
2. Consider the meaning of the Greek word *symballein* (p. 60). Pray with Luke 2:1–22 and ask for the grace to ponder your life in light of the mystery of the Incarnation.
3. Reflect on Mary's experience of the census, the shepherds, and the Magi (pp. 61–63). Pray with Luke 2:1–22 and ask for the grace to find God's purpose in seemingly negative events.
4. Ponder the image of myrrh in the life of Jesus (p. 63) Pray with Song 1:12–17 and ask for the grace to live recollected in the presence and fragrance of the Lord.
5. Consider the beauty of Mary and Jesus (pp. 64–65). Pray with Psalm 45 and ask for the grace to perceive both the natural and supernatural beauty of Jesus and Mary, and your own graced beauty.
6. Reflect on Jane's story (pp. 69–70). Pray with Isaiah 49:1–18 and ask for the grace to know how God has always been present to you throughout your own salvation history.

Chapter 4

Love's Vanquishing

[B] I am a rose of Sharon,
    a lily of the valleys.
[G] As a lily among brambles,
    so is my love among maidens.
[B] As an apple tree among the trees of the wood,
    so is my beloved among young men.
With great delight I sat in his shadow,
    and his fruit was sweet to my taste.
He brought me to the banqueting house,
    and his intention toward me was love.
Sustain me with raisins,
    refresh me with apples;
    for I am faint with love.
O that his left hand were under my head,
    and that his right hand embraced me!
I adjure you, O daughters of Jerusalem,
    by the gazelles or the wild does:
do not stir up or awaken love
    until it is ready! (Song 2:1–7)

> In the sixth month the angel Gabriel was sent by God to a town in Galilee called Nazareth, to a virgin engaged to a man whose name was Joseph, of the house of David. The virgin's name was Mary. And he came to her and said, "Greetings, favored one! The Lord is with you." But she was much perplexed by his words and pondered what sort of greeting this might be. The angel said to her, "Do not be afraid, Mary, for you have found favor with God. And now, you will conceive in your womb and bear a son, and you will name him Jesus. He will be great, and will be called the Son of the Most High, and the Lord God will give to him the throne of his ancestor David. He will reign over the house of Jacob forever, and of his kingdom there will be no end." Mary said to the angel, "How can this be, since I am a virgin?" The angel said to her, "The Holy Spirit will come upon you, and the power of the Most High will overshadow you; therefore the child to be born will be holy; he will be called Son of God. And now, your relative Elizabeth in her old age has also conceived a son; and this is the sixth month for her who was said to be barren. For nothing will be impossible with God." Then Mary said, "Here am I, the servant of the Lord; let it be with me according to your word." Then the angel departed from her. (Lk 1:26–38)

T. S. Eliot once remarked that human beings cannot bear much reality, especially the reality of God. The Jews were convinced that no one could see God and live, except for Moses, who was given the grace to meet with God face to face in the meeting tent. The experience of God's presence is an awesome and daunting thing. There was once a young sister named Gianna preparing to make her final vows to the Lord. She was inspired by the example of sisters in her religious community who had recently made their lifelong commitments. As she spoke with one of her classmates who was also preparing for the same choice, her friend asked her if she had prayed to God about making final vows. Gianna admitted that she had not prayed enough, resolving to do so now in her room. As she prayed, she asked God whether he desired her to make her final commitment. Her room was immediately flooded with a supernatural light and her heart was filled with God's love. Gianna was so overwhelmed by the suddenness and force of the Lord's presence that she ran out of her room. Walking back and forth in the hallway, she met her friend, who wondered if she had been praying. Gianna replied that she had prayed and that God was in her room at that very moment. Her friend wondered why she was out in the hallway and not back in her room. Gianna answered that she had received plenty in reply from God for the moment.[1]

The Humility of Mary

Gianna's encounter offers us a glimpse into Mary's experience of both love and fear in the annunciation of the Angel Gabriel. Angels are awesome in appearance. In the Old Testament, human beings such as Lot, Balaam, and Daniel fell to the ground before angels. Mary was certainly in awe of Gabriel's appearing to her, troubled at his greeting. She might also have been surprised and taken aback when he addressed her as "full of grace" (sometimes rendered "favored one"). "Full of grace" is

1. See Janet Ruffing, *Spiritual Direction Beyond the Beginnings* (New York/ Mahwah, NJ: Paulist Press, 2000), 37.

Mary's true name, which expresses a special calling. In her nation's past, great figures like Abraham had received new names that expressed their callings. Furthermore, Gabriel tells her "The Lord is with you" (Lk 1:28), the same message given to great figures of Israel chosen by God for heroic missions. The Lord told leaders such as Jacob, Moses, and Jeremiah that he would be with them in their all-important and dangerous assignments. Not only would the undertaking be challenging, but the entire future of Israel would depend on it. No wonder that Mary was greatly troubled by the angel's saying. She knew God would be asking her to dedicate her whole being in generous self-sacrifice to fulfill his will. In her humility Mary also knew that her task did not depend on her own ability, but on God and his power at work through her.

Like Mary, the bride in the Song humbly thinks of herself as common as the rose of Sharon and the lily of the valley (see 2:1). The latter small wildflowers grew in abundance in the countryside and lower valleys of Palestine in the springtime. The bride is aware of her small stature in comparison with the great cedar and cypress beams of the temple (see 1:17). Immediately drawn to the bride's humility, the Bridegroom exclaims that she is a lily among thorns (see 2:2). This suggests her singular and superior beauty. Just as the angel called Mary "full of grace," fashioned by God as his loved one from the beginning, so the Bridegroom expresses his singular and exclusive choice of her to be his own. In reply the bride exclaims that her Bridegroom is an apple tree among other trees of the wood (2:3), far transcending her little-flower nature. Just as the apple tree bears fruit, Mary knows that her fruitfulness in accomplishing the Lord's mission does not depend on her, but on God.

In her humility and dependence on God, Mary knows that her role is to remain in God's presence and rely on his help.

Similarly, the bride is taken to the banquet house where she delights in remaining in the shadow of the Bridegroom's presence, eating his fruit. She is overcome with her own weakness, crying out for her lover to sustain her with fruit as she swoons with love (see 2:6). Like other great heroes chosen by God, Mary protests her own inability. She asks how she can accomplish God's plan because she does not know man. Gabriel reassures her that the conception of the Savior will happen by the power of the Holy Spirit. The power of the Most High will overshadow her, just as Israel was overshadowed by the divine presence throughout her journey through the desert to the Promised Land. Mary is to turn her attention totally to the divine presence to remain in God's strength and accomplish his will. Aware of her limits and powerlessness to do what only grace can achieve, Mary is still able to offer her whole being in consent to the Lord. Like Mary, we too are called to remain in God's presence, which overshadows us from our baptism onward. The Benedictine monk Laurence Freeman suggests:

> We become most freely present to ourselves when we turn from ourselves (our egoism). Our greatest good is found beyond (and within) ourselves in being present to God. The free alignment of our attention is the work of faith and expresses love as the basic energy of all human growth. The presence of Christ in us through his gift of the Spirit (Jn 14:16) is what empowers this free gift of ourselves to be with God. The Spirit is in a special sense the presence (or self-knowledge) of God, being the love that flows between Father and Son (Jn 15:26).[2]

---

2. Laurence Freeman, OSB, "Presence: Presence of God," in *The New Dictionary of Catholic Spirituality* (Collegeville, MN: Liturgical Press, 1993), 781.

In prayer we constantly remain in this divine presence and are caught up in God's love. In the sacraments, especially the Holy Eucharist, we abide in Christ and are nourished by his love, as the bride in the banqueting hall is sustained by her lover's fruit.

The Gift of Grace

In the mid-nineteenth century a family from a Croatian village was about to emigrate to the United States. The villagers threw a party for them and bought them parting gifts. Among the very practical gifts were large loaves of bread and big discs of cheese that would help sustain the family on their long sea journey. The family boarded the ship on a cold winter day. Since no one else on the ship spoke their language, they quickly descended to their third-class cabin below the deck. They remained below for the entire three-week journey until the last day, when the weather became pleasant and the teenage son asked if he could explore the ship's deck. The father reluctantly consented, but insisted his son be back within an hour. The hour came and went, and when his son didn't return, the exasperated father went to look for him. After a long search, he finally found his son in the galley, devouring a large plate of meat, potatoes, and vegetables, with dessert on the side. Since the father had no way to pay for the meal, he imagined spending his first days in America in jail. As he looked at his son dumbfoundedly, his son said: "Don't worry dad, while we've been fasting on bread and cheese, everyone else has been feasting every day on meals like this. They're included in the ticket price!"[3] Grace is like those free

---

3. Mark Link, *Illustrated Sunday Homilies*, Series II, Years ABC, 93.

delicious and nourishing meals in the banquet hall. God's presence, his very gift of self, is gratuitously given to us to enjoy and to make us strong and fruitful in our faith. Our life of faith can be a feast or a starvation diet. We feast when we pray with God's word and receive the sacraments, especially the Holy Eucharist. Our lives become full of meaning and purpose. If we fail to live by God's grace, we are like the family living below the deck.

Grace will make demands upon us, even the surrender of our whole lives. Love makes this possible. Saint Teresa of Avila was called to a great mission by the Lord and the superior of the Carmelite order. It was to establish new convents according to the original, more rigorous rule of life of the order. She faced enormous religious and civil opposition, which caused her great suffering. She hesitated to move forward. One day while praying after Holy Communion, she begged the Lord to enlighten her so that she might conform to his will in everything. While aware of her tepidity, she would not allow it to subtract one bit from her desire to do his will. The Lord challenged her: "What do you fear? When have I failed you? I am the same now as I was before. Do not neglect to make these two foundations." She exclaimed in her heart, "O great God! How different are your words from those of men!"[4] Teresa was then filled with such determination and courage that she felt the whole world could not oppose her. At once she began to make arrangements for the foundations, and the Lord provided her with the means. Teresa experienced some human fear based on her own weakness and doubt. Deep down she experienced a holy fear of the Lord, desiring only to do his will. Like Mary and like the bride, Teresa did not let her

---

4. Saint Teresa of Avila, *Life, The Book of Her Foundations*, in *The Collected Works of Saint Teresa of Avila*, trans. Kieran Kavanaugh, OCD, and Otilio Rodriguez, OCD (Washington, D.C.: ICS, 2012), par. 6, 278.

inadequacy stop her. She wholeheartedly abandoned herself to the Lord and his designs.

Power in Weakness

It is good to be aware of one's inadequacy as a pre-condition for achieving God's will. We do not rely on our own strength, but on the Lord's help. In a homily to newly ordained Jesuit priests, Michael Buckley, S. J., asked them a counter-intuitive question, "are you weak enough to become a priest?"[5] Usually persons qualify for various professions by their talents and capabilities. One person might have the type of great analytical mind needed to be a physicist, or another the physical talent to be an athlete. But in following Christ, and especially in order to be his representative, one must break out of the mindset that catalogues our talents and focus instead on Christ. He was beset by weakness and suffering, and was tempted in every way that we are (see Heb 5:1–10). For the priest, weakness means "the experience of a peculiar liability to suffering. A profound sense of inability, both to do and protect even after great effort, to author, perform, effect what we have wanted or with the success we would have wanted, an inability to secure one's own future, to protect oneself, to live with clarity and assurance or to ward off shame and suffering."[6] This weakness not only places us in solidarity with humanity that needs a Savior, but also becomes the opportunity for God to manifest his power. Saint Paul glories in his own weakness as he experiences the power of Christ resting upon

5. Michael Buckley, "Letter to the Ordinands," http://www.servant-leader associates.com/Servant-Leader_Associates/Faith_Perspectives_files/The%20Wisdom%20of%20Rev%20Michael%20J%20Buckley.pdf.

6. Ibid.

him. He is content with weakness, mistreatment, hardship, persecution and calamities, aware that when he is weak he is strong in grace (see 2 Cor 12:10).

Why does God allow us to suffer our human weakness and sense of nothingness? Because it is a way to prepare us for greater union with him and greater fruitfulness in our ministry. Jesus calls himself the true vine, and his Father is the vinedresser. Jesus says that the Father "removes every branch in me that bears no fruit. Every branch that bears fruit he prunes to make it bear more fruit" (Jn 15:2). This experience of being pruned will be painful, especially when we are confronted with our nothingness. God removes our sense of security, strength, and importance to lead us to greater humility, dependence, and trust in him. In 2014 I assumed leadership of *The Lanteri Center for Ignatian Spirituality*, which is dedicated to offering one- on-one spiritual direction, retreats, and training for spiritual directors. Our founder and previous director had been transferred to Boston, leaving us pruned back to one priest instead of two and three lay staff members. I felt not only the daunting task of taking over responsibility from the founder and director, but also the challenge of maintaining and extending the mission. I felt like the Israelites being commanded to make more bricks without any straw (see Ex 5:7ff.). Experiencing my own inadequacy as a leader, I prayed my usual holy hour each morning, asking for the strength and grace to do whatever God might be asking. Ask he did, and I found myself inspired to begin a new program to bring Ignatian spirituality to the parish level. I felt the desire to offer parish retreats on prayer and discernment in a mission format, making the Ignatian experience accessible to a much wider audience. As I pondered this inspiration, I felt trepidation. I wondered how I would find the time and energy to do this while keeping up with all our other programs and my new administrative tasks.

I brought the inspiration to the staff and my spiritual director. Everyone was supportive, though concerned I might be overextending myself. We had a great initial response to our offerings, with requests for five missions within the first two months. Powerful experiences of prayer and discernment in the Spirit began to happen on a popular level, continuing to this day. At the very moment I felt most inadequate and overwhelmed, the Lord chose to accomplish his plan.

Trust in God

Our weakness should not make us shy away from God's will but embolden us to trust more in his power and Providence. Mary hears God's intention to bring about a Savior for Israel and an everlasting kingdom. She knows this will not be her work, but totally God's work, and she will be a willing cooperator. The angel tells Mary that her cousin Elizabeth, advanced in age, has conceived a son and that "for God nothing will be impossible" (Lk 1:37). Mary knows that God's word is productive:

> so shall my word be that goes out from my mouth;
> it shall not return to me empty,
> but it shall accomplish that which I purpose,
> and succeed in the thing for which I sent it. (Is 55:11)

By the grace of God, Mary believes in God's word and cooperates with his plan. Mary responds to God's proposal with words of complete surrender, never before spoken in the Scriptures by any great figure addressed by God. She responds, "Here am I, the servant of the Lord; let it be with me according to your word" (Lk 1:38). Her reply shows her total abandonment to the will of God and the generous gift of herself. Mary is willing to be a handmaid or servant of the Lord. She is willing to give up her own plans and preferences to be totally available to God's plan. Mary anticipates Jesus' absolute commitment "not to do my own will, but the will of him who sent me" (Jn 6:38).

According to De la Potterie, the Greek grammatical form of "let it be to me" indicates "the '*fiat*' of Mary is not just a simple acceptance or even less, a resignation. It is rather a joyous desire to collaborate with what God foresees for her. It is the joy of total abandonment to the good will of God. Thus, the joy of this ending corresponds to the invitation to joy at the beginning."[7] Mary's *fiat* is not mere compliance or acquiescence, but a joyful embrace of God's will for her life and for her people. While we often experience the Lord's will as a burdensome cross, it is ultimately meant to be delightful.

Some might object that offering to be a servant restricts freedom and human growth. Freedom is not a license to do whatever we want, which ironically leads to enslavement to our desires. Rather, freedom is given us to do good and to love, especially as God loves. The closer we get to God, who is infinitely free, the freer we become as we share in God's very freedom. Jesus never did his own will, but only the will of his heavenly Father. In this he was supremely free to choose according to his divine nature. Liberty is the power to choose the transcendent good. Liberty stems from an inner delight in the good, which is a gift of the Holy Spirit, and the effect of grace. God conditions our will to choose what is good, overcoming our own selfishness and inclination to evil. Our freedom is expanded to desire and choose what is ultimately important and permanently valuable. Mary staked her whole existence on God's promise to her and pledged to serve him

7. Potterie, *Mary in the Mystery of the Covenant*, 35.

alone. Grace conditioned her to make her full response to God's proposal in unbridled freedom.

We are inspired by Mary's example to listen to God and respond in freedom, even when external circumstances would restrict that freedom. Karol Wojtyla grew up in Poland in the face of adversity from foreign occupying powers. Even while losing family members he was able to freely respond to God's call to the priesthood. When young Karol was in third grade, his mother Emilia died of kidney failure and congenital heart disease. His older brother Edmund, a young doctor to whom he drew closer in his early high school days, died after contracting scarlet fever from one of his patients. This tragedy hit Karol even harder. Then, in his late teens, Karol came home from working in the quarries one day and found his father dead. He spent the entire night on his knees praying beside his father's body, and later recalled that he had never felt so alone. During the Nazi conquest and occupation of Poland there were police round-ups, deportation to camps and forced labor in Germany or elsewhere, beatings by secret servicemen, and fatal shootings in the streets. Shots were frequently heard at night after curfew hours, when police arrested people who were caught walking the streets without passes and fired at any who did not stop when challenged. Karol and his townspeople were continuously hungry for five years, surviving on potatoes. Each winter they were desperately cold in the brutal subzero temperatures.

Amid pain and loss, Karol surrounded himself with books, immersed himself in studies of the arts, sciences, and languages, and read Polish philosophers and the Bible. He belonged to a theater troupe, which performed powerful underground dramas aimed at preserving the culture, history, and truth of Poland, and the dignity of the human person in the face of Nazi persecution. As he worked as a stone-cutter in a quarry, he discovered the spiritual dimension of human work. After working the night shift, Karol would stop to pray or attend early morning Mass. Karol joined the Living Rosary, founded by a devout layman named Jan Tyranowski. Young people would gather in these groups to receive spiritual instruction on how to improve their daily lives by living in the presence of God. Karol's conviction about the truths of his faith was deepening. He was introduced to contemplative prayer as he studied John of the Cross. With this growing interior illumination, Karol discovered a call to the priesthood, which proved to be an even more effective way to resist the degradation of human dignity and freedom by brutal Nazi ideology. Pursuing the priesthood was also fraught with danger. Seminarians were rounded up, and some of his classmates were taken. Karol studied secretly, meeting teachers clandestinely. After the war the Soviet Union moved in and ousted the Nazis. Matters didn't improve under Communism. Karol was ordained in a secret ceremony in the bishop's chapel in Krakow. As a young priest, as bishop of Krakow, and finally as Pope John Paul II, he would be a tireless advocate for the freedom of the Polish people. Karol taught us by his life the humble, fervent, and complete dedication to God that characterizes true freedom. Abandoning oneself to be led in God's direction as one confronts and reaches one's destiny is the highest expression of freedom.

Christ's sacrifice in his death and resurrection is the source of our living in freedom. Hans Urs von Balthasar offers a beautiful reflection on the free self-giving of Christ that is mirrored in the self-offering of Mary in her *fiat*:

> Understand what it means to give oneself away. To strip oneself of one's freedom out of freedom; and out of love, no longer to be free or to be lord over oneself; no longer to be able to determine where the journey will take you; to surrender

> oneself, to deliver oneself over to the series of consequences that carry us off in a direction we did not want — where to? You leap down from a high cliff. The leap is freely made, and yet, the moment you leap, gravity leaps upon you, and you tumble exactly like a dead stone to the very bottom of the gorge. This is how I decided to give myself. To give myself right out of my hand. . . . I wanted to be the one given away par excellence. The corpse over which the vultures gather. The Consumed, the Eaten, the Drunk, the Spilled, the Poured Out. The Plaything. The Worn Out. The one squeezed to the very dregs. The one trod upon to infinity. The one run over. The one thinned to air. The one liquified into an ocean. The Dissolved. This was the plan; this was the will of the Father. By fulfilling it through obedience (the fulfillment itself was obedience), I have filled the world from heaven down to hell, and every knee must bend before me, and all tongues must confess me. Now I am all in all, and this is why the death which poured me out is my victory. My descent, my vertiginous collapse, my going under (under myself) into everything that was foreign and contrary to God — down into the underworld: this was the ascent of this world into me, into God. My victory.[8]

There is nothing Christ would not do to show his love for us, and nothing Mary would not do for God in return, giving her whole self in exchange for his self-gift. Such radical self-giving in humility, freedom, and abandonment to the will of God is possible only in God's grace. Mary is overshadowed by the Holy Spirit and surrenders to the power of the Most High God. In her heart she willingly abandons herself to the life of her son

8. Han Urs von Balthasar, *Heart of the World* (San Francisco: Ignatius Press, 1979), 180–181. www.ignatius.com. Used with permission.

who will become incarnate in her womb. Mary is the bride overshadowed by the presence of her Lover, overcome by his ardent proposal.

The bride of the Song is pierced by the dart of love aimed at her heart and is made lovesick in the banqueting hall. The phrase "his intention toward me was love" (Song 2:4) is more literally translated "his army against me is love." To win her heart, the Bridegroom shows the bride the intensity of his passion for her. She is made ecstatic in her faculties as she eats and drinks of his love, so that nothing of the world matters except in relation to him. In her swooning weakness she cries out to be sustained with raisins and apples so that she can remain alive in his love. As painful as the wound of love is, she only desires to experience greater union. The Bridegroom immediately comes to her aid, embracing and consoling her, cradling her head. She releases herself in complete surrender and trust. She is now so conquered by love that she will consent completely to his will. He awaits her awakening to say yes to all he desires. Mary is the bride so overcome with love that nothing else in the world matters except her Lord. In her selfless ardor and consent to all that God wishes to do in her, she is strengthened by grace to receive an even greater outpouring of his love.

The Bridegroom commands, "do not stir up or awaken love until it is ready!" (Song 2:7). God does not force Mary's will, except by the weapon of his love. Now he patiently awaits her response to also be awakened only by his love. Saint Bernard of Clairvaux captures the anticipation and intrigue of the whole universe waiting for Mary's awakening in loving consent to the divine Word's proposal to become flesh in her:

> Adam, with all his race, Adam a weeping exile from Paradise, implores it of you. Abraham entreats you, David beseeches you. This is the object of the burning desires of the holy

> fathers, of your fathers, who are still dwelling in the region of the shades of death. Behold the entire human race prostrate at your feet in expectation. And rightly, for on your word depend the consolation of the wretched, the redemption of the captive, the freedom of the condemned, the salvation of your entire race, of all the children of Adam. Hasten, then, O Lady, to give your answer; hasten to speak.[9]

God from all eternity, the people of Israel through centuries, indeed all of creation from the time of the fall—all patiently await the Virgin's reply.

Questions for Reflection and Discussion

1. Have you ever had a powerful encounter with God in prayer? How would you describe your experience? What was God saying to you?
2. When have you felt God asking something of you? Were you disposed to obey and cooperate with his desire? Were you afraid or unwilling? Did you feel graced to say yes and to follow through?
3. How aware are you of your weakness in the presence of God? In what ways does your weakness hinder you from stepping forth to serve God? In what ways does your weakness embolden you to rely more on God in serving him? How have you felt God's strength in the very midst of your weakness?

---

9. Saint Bernard of Clairvaux, *In Praise of the Virgin Mother,* Hom. 4, 8–9: https://archive.org/stream/sermonsofstberna00bernuoft/sermonsofstberna00bernuoft_djvu.txt.

4. How has the Lord's love conquered you? How does the Lord's love for you cast out all fear? Do you feel like you would be willing to do anything out of love for the Lord? In what areas might you be tempted to hold back?

Prayer Exercises

1. Consider Sister Gianna's prayer experience (p. 77). Pray with Luke 1:26–28 and ask for the grace not to fear the Lord's presence.
2. Ponder the bride's and Mary's humility (p. 78). Pray with Song 2:1–7 and ask for the grace of humility before God's greatness.
3. Reflect on the story of the Croatian family (p. 80). Pray with Song 2:1–7 and ask for the grace to be nourished and strengthened by the Lord in your weakness.
4. Consider the story of Saint John Paul II's losses of family members (p. 86). Pray with 1 Kings 19:1–18 and ask for the grace to be strengthened by the Lord to continue to grow in your service to him.
5. Ponder Balthasar's quote about Jesus' complete self-giving (pp. 87–88). Pray with 2 Timothy 4:1–18 and ask for the grace to pour yourself out in love for the Lord and others.

CHAPTER 5

Daring Generosity

In those days Mary set out and went with haste to a Judean town in the hill country, where she entered the house of Zechariah and greeted Elizabeth. When Elizabeth heard Mary's greeting, the child leaped in her womb. And Elizabeth was filled with the Holy Spirit and exclaimed with a loud cry, "Blessed are you among women, and blessed is the fruit of your womb. And why has this happened to me, that the mother of my Lord comes to me? For as soon as I heard the sound of your greeting, the child in my womb leaped for joy. And blessed is she who believed that there would be a fulfillment of what was spoken to her by the Lord."

And Mary said,

"My soul magnifies the Lord,
    and my spirit rejoices in God my Savior,
for he has looked with favor on the lowliness of his servant.
    Surely, from now on all generations will call me blessed;
for the Mighty One has done great things for me,
    and holy is his name.
His mercy is for those who fear him

from generation to generation.
He has shown strength with his arm;
he has scattered the proud in the thoughts of their hearts.
He has brought down the powerful from their thrones,
and lifted up the lowly;
he has filled the hungry with good things,
and sent the rich away empty.
He has helped his servant Israel,
in remembrance of his mercy,
according to the promise he made to our ancestors,
to Abraham and to his descendants forever."

And Mary remained with her about three months and then returned to her home (Luke 1:39–56).

[B] The voice of my beloved!
Look, he comes,
leaping upon the mountains,
bounding over the hills.
My beloved is like a gazelle
or a young stag.
Look, there he stands
behind our wall,
gazing in at the windows,
looking through the lattice.
My beloved speaks and says to me:
[G] "Arise, my love, my fair one,
and come away;
for now the winter is past,
the rain is over and gone.
The flowers appear on the earth;
the time of singing has come,
and the voice of the turtledove
is heard in our land.
The fig tree puts forth its figs,

and the vines are in blossom;
they give forth fragrance.
Arise, my love, my fair one,
and come away.
O my dove, in the clefts of the rock,
in the covert of the cliff,
let me see your face,
let me hear your voice;
for your voice is sweet,
and your face is lovely (Song 2:8–14).

Jim Croce was a famous folk singer in the early 1970s. Married and deeply in love with his wife, he worked hard to support her before he became well known. One day his wife told him she was pregnant. Jim was stunned at first, then ecstatic at the news. He was so overwhelmed with enthusiasm and creative inspiration that he wrote one hundred songs over the next two weeks. Among them were classic hits such as *Operator; Bad, Bad Leroy Brown;* and *Don't Mess Around with Jim*. One of the most beautiful ballads Croce wrote was *Time in a Bottle*. Although most people assumed he wrote it about his wife, he actually wrote it for his unborn child. In it he sang of his desire to capture time in a bottle, saving every day so that he could spend them all with his son. In the song, Jim also expressed frustration that he never had enough time to do the things he desired, but that he still wanted to journey through time with his son. Croce beautifully captured the sense of time and eternity in the birth of his child. Then came the tragic irony. The very songs Jim Croce wrote under the inspiration of being a new father made him an overnight sensation. His career skyrocketed. He signed a big record contract, requiring him to go on countless tours. Jim was never home to see his child for two years. His wife was starved for attention, and the demands of Jim's career strained their marriage. Weary of the exhausting tour schedule, Croce grew disillusioned with his fame. He reconciled with his wife, and they agreed he would give up touring at the end of his current circuit. Then it happened—the plane crash that ended his rise to stardom—just as he was planning to make time for his family.[1]

The beautiful aspirations in Croce's song, his desire to spend every day with his son, tell us something of God's desire for us. God so loves us that he desires to spend every moment of every day of our lives with us. When God created Adam and Eve, he walked and talked with them throughout the day. Even though we lost God's friendship, he continued to be present to us. God revealed himself to Moses in the burning bush as the one who is present for us. As he led Israel out of slavery from Egypt, he continued to be present to them in the desert, guiding them as a pillar of fire by night and as a cloud by day. Later God told Moses to build the Ark of the Covenant as a divine dwelling place (see Ex 25:10ff.). All these modes of God's presence to humanity were meant to prepare for God's ultimate coming to us in the Incarnation, by which God came to share our very humanity, dwelling among us. Jesus wanted to relate to us in the most intimate way possible, being present in the womb of the Virgin Mary, and after his birth, living with us as our brother and Lord.

The Song of Songs also brings out this theme of presence. The Bridegroom represents God in his transcendence, bounding

1. See *Behind the Music: Jim Croce,* Documentary produced by Daniel Bowen, 1997.

across the mountains and leaping over the hills. The Bridegroom traverses a great distance to draw close to his bride. This is an excellent symbol of God's immanence, or closeness, in the Incarnation. Although he is God and is with the Father, Christ empties himself. He did not cling to his divinity so that he could share in our humanity, arriving gently and secretly in love (see Phil 2:6ff). Christ's self-emptying to take on a human nature is his self-revelation to us. The almighty power of his divinity is expressed in his assuming our weak humanity. God chooses to become dependent on a humble maiden to give him flesh and to nurture his humanity.

Mary is that humble maiden, the bride of God who consents to allow him to take on our human flesh by the power of the Holy Spirit. Conception of a child brings about a unique biological bond between mother and child. When a woman is pregnant, fetal cells from the child proliferate within her body and remain with her throughout her lifetime. Jesus would have been nurtured through Mary's bloodstream. Since he took his human nature from her, his genetic makeup was hers, and his blood was her blood. The saints often reflected on this. For example, Saint Elizabeth Ann Seton meditated on the truth that the blood of Christ, which would redeem the world, came first from the blood of his mother through her milk. As human beings we not only possess bodies, but more accurately we are our bodies, in addition to being soul and spirit. Our bodies are a real expression of who we are as human beings. The biological unity between Mary and Jesus shows how related and interdependent they are, how she continues to support and donate herself to him.

In the Incarnation, Christ even became dependent upon Mary for the initial proclamation of the Gospel. Mary was inspired by the Holy Spirit to go and visit her cousin Elizabeth who was six months pregnant. Elizabeth lived in the hill country of Ain Karem. Like the Bridegroom of the Song, Christ went bounding over the hills to draw close to his people. Sharing Christ's life, Mary shared his longing to be with his people in need. She desired to be with her cousin Elizabeth in her pregnancy and share the good news of what God had revealed to her. At the sound of Mary's greeting, Elizabeth immediately sensed God's presence and exclaimed, "And why has this happened to me, that the mother of my Lord comes to me?" (Lk 1:43). The presence of God had come to Elizabeth through the presence of Mary just as the presence of the Lord came to David in and through the Ark of the Covenant (see 2 Sam 6:1–19).[2] Just as David danced before the Ark in procession, John the Baptist leapt for joy in his mother's womb. The presence of the Incarnate Christ brings about joy and the proclamation of God's mighty deeds. Mary proclaims her own dependence on God for all the good he has done for her and glorifies him. "For the Mighty One has done great things for me, and holy is his name" (Lk 1:49). The Christ life within us should make us dance for joy and proclaim the greatness of the Lord, as the following story illustrates.

A young husband and father named William relates his experience in praying with the mystery of the Visitation. As he meditated on the words "Mary set out and went with haste," he was filled with interior joy. He felt permeated with the life of Christ and energized to fulfill the demands of his daily life. William rose from prayer filled with love and zeal for the seemingly minor tasks of the day, like helping to see his children off to school. He felt inspired by the servant mentality of Jesus and

---

2. For more on Mary as the Ark of the Covenant see Brant Pitre, *Jesus and the Jewish Roots of Mary* (New York: Image Books, 2018), 41–70.

Mary, and, interacting with his clients at work, he regarded their needs as his own. William took great satisfaction as he assisted clients and colleagues alike in solving problems. As he paused for a coffee break in his busy day, he reflected on how God's life within him seemed to be overflowing to others. He felt very fulfilled in his experience of serving others. Giving to others was feeding him spiritually. William expressed quiet gratitude to the Father and offered a short prayer to remain united to Jesus and that he might glorify the Lord by his life. As the days progressed, William didn't always feel the same enthusiasm and love. But he persevered in ardent service to his family and in his workplace with the same sense of purpose and fulfillment. Like the bride in the Song of Songs, William experienced the divine Bridegroom drawing close to him in prayer and calling him to arise and come away. He experienced union with the Lord not only in prayer, but in service to others.

This example shows us how the grace of the Incarnation elevates our focus first toward God and then toward others. From the annunciation onward, Mary's whole universe shifted toward presence and availability to the Son of God, just as the bride became totally available to her Lover as he arrived. The miracle of pregnancy suggests that it will take a reconfiguration of our entire being to nurture the Christ life within us. Many of these bodily changes are painful and require great sacrifice of the woman on behalf of her child. It suggests to us that while the new life of Christ within us is joyful, it also results in some pain and suffering on our part. It would have been easy and even justifiable for Mary to rest comfortably with the burden of pregnancy in view of her new role as Mother of God. But Mary is humbly self-effacing, thinking not of herself, but of others. Sensitive to her cousin's need and to the Holy Spirit's promptings, she rises in haste and goes immediately.

Similarly, in our love for Christ are we willing to bear the inevitable suffering of life in union with him as we adjust our lives to his? One woman who had experienced a great deal of growth in following Christ reported feeling upset about letting go of some of her attachments and familiar ways of doing things:

> It seems I don't really know what I'm doing anymore. I used to have a nice solid sense of who I was and where I was heading in life. I used to be able to decide what I wanted for myself and plan for it, and go out and get it. Now, because it seems more important to wait for God's call and to give myself to God's purpose, I'm at a loss as to what to do with all my drive and ability to figure things out for myself. It seems now that so much of my knowledge is contrived and not really on target. I trust in God, but it's still frightening. And there's something sad about it, not to be able to rely so much on my own resources.[3]

We may experience some distressing upheaval of familiar attitudes and behaviors along with the joy of our new life in Christ. We need to remain rooted in our contemplative life and our relationship with Jesus. We can follow the example of Mary, who was constantly aware that she carried his divine presence within her, communicated with him, and followed his promptings.

The incarnate Christ in his fetal development had not only a unique human nature with a unique personal identity, but he also profoundly depended on the conditions provided by his mother. Each human fetus draws nourishment from its mother to grow according to its genetic pattern. The mother provides

---

3. Gerald May, M.D., *Care of Mind, Care of Spirit* (San Francisco: Harper Collins, 1992), 99.

the specific and complete environment which the child appropriates in order to live. A kind of symbiosis develops between a mother and her child in the womb. What she experiences, the child in some way experiences, and vice-versa. Jesus appropriated the ups and downs, the peace and anxiety, the joys and sorrows that affected Mary's spirit throughout his life in her womb. Jesus experienced Mary's anguish at any misunderstanding and judgment of her family and neighbors at Nazareth. He felt her enthusiasm for charitable service during the visit to Elizabeth. During the journey to Bethlehem he experienced her feelings of frustration at the inconvenience of the census, as well as the hardships of the birth in the cave. Even on a human level, Jesus was already developing a compassionate awareness and sensitivity to his mother's reactions.

Mary shows us how to be compassionate, as she made Elizabeth's needs her own. Paul Miller tells the story of his son John who was a chaotic, insolent, and despondent teenager. He and his wife had tried everything in terms of positive and negative reinforcement of his behavior, to no avail. As Paul and his wife grew more distressed, Paul decided to put himself in John's shoes. John was a good student who didn't like conventional sports, which put him outside the popular social circle. He didn't feel like he was good at much and needed something to build his confidence. Paul pondered John's strengths—being quick and tough—and wondered if he would like wrestling. John was intrigued, and the school athletic director agreed to let Paul start a team if he could come up with funding for equipment and a coach. No coach was available, so Paul, with no experience, decided to become one. He checked books out of the library to learn about the philosophy and techniques of the sport. Paul would sit on the floor with a book in one hand trying to practice wrestling moves, and then teach them to John. His son went on to become a two-time MVP and was soon able to easily pin his dad. John wore his school coat that sported his varsity letter with newfound self-esteem. Paul learned that compassion is more than lending a supportive ear or saying affirming words; it must be considerate of and conformed to the other's needs.[4]

Jesus invites us to be the compassionate extension of his incarnation in the world today. Saint Augustine asks the question "What does love look like?" and replies: "It has the hands to help others. It has the feet to hasten to the poor and needy. It has eyes to see misery and want. It has the ears to hear the sighs and sorrows of men. That is what love looks like."[5]

While Jesus was in the womb, Mary became his feet to travel to Ain Karem to visit Elizabeth. Mary was his voice to greet her and utter his words of praise and consolation. Mary became his hands to tend to Elizabeth's needs. We are all called to be the extension of Christ to our brothers and sisters in need. The Grail Prayer makes an excellent response to Jesus' invitation to incarnate his love in service:

> Lord Jesus I give you my hands to do your work. I give you my feet to go your way. I give you my eyes to see as you do. I give you my tongue to speak your words. I give you my mind that you may think in me. I give you my spirit that you may pray in me. Above all, I give you my heart that you may love in me your Father and all mankind. I give you my whole self that you may grow in me, that it is you, Lord Jesus, who live and work and pray in me.[6]

---

4. See Paul Miller, *Love Walked Among Us* (Colorado Springs, CO: NavPress, 2001), 72.

5. Attributed to Saint Augustine, source uncertain.

6. The Grail Prayer, Catholic Social Teaching UK Website, http://www.catholicsocialteaching.org.uk/themes/solidarity/reflection/grail-prayer/.

Venerable Bruno Lanteri, founder of the Oblates of the Virgin Mary, sums up the meaning of the Grail Prayer: "The life of the Christian properly speaking is none other than the expression and the continuation of the life of Christ, which in a certain sense is not yet completed, but is being completed daily in the life of the saints who follow his example, and will be completed at the end of the world."[7]

The life of Christ becomes noticeable in our life and actions. Once when I was rector of the seminary in Boston, a woman in need came to our door. We sat down in the front room and I listened to her describe her problems. I sensed her burden lifting as we spoke. All she needed was a place to store her luggage, which I was able to provide for a short time while she searched for a place to live. When she came a few days later to pick up her things, she handed me a thank you card. She had composed the loveliest note I have ever received:

> "I know that he lives, for I saw him today in a hand that was offered to me on my way, in the warmth of a smile that was offered to cheer me, in the welcome of a friend who took time just to hear me. I heard his voice in the words of support whispered to me when my hope had run short. Yes, I know that he lives for I see how he sends his love every day in the caring of friends. You touched a moment of my day, my life, with your beautiful spirit in a way that only you could do. What a blessing it is knowing you. In a world where people are so consumed with themselves, it's harder to find kind people who take away a little of the pain, because that's what you did. I truly appreciate it from the bottom of my heart and am very thankful. Jesus in you came through."

7. Venerable Pio Bruno Lanteri, *The Spiritual Writings of Venerable Pio Bruno Lanteri, A Selection*, ed. David N. Beauregard, OMV (Boston: Oblates of the Virgin Mary, 2001), 76.

Rarely have I received such gratitude, and for such a small act. I realized then how even the slightest act of kindness could be the occasion of God's grace. Saint John Henry Newman once wrote: "Dear Jesus, help me to spread your fragrance everywhere I go. Flood my soul with your spirit and life. Penetrate and possess my whole being so utterly that my life may only be a radiance of yours. Shine through me, and be so in me, that every soul I come in contact with may feel your presence in my soul. Let them look up and see no longer me, but only Jesus!"[8]

Mary was the perfect radiance and fragrance of the life of Jesus. The Spirit moved her to utter the words, "My soul magnifies the Lord, and my spirit rejoices in God my Savior" (Lk 1:46). Christ so shines through her that her very being manifests and amplifies the presence of Jesus. No wonder Christians turn to Mary to encounter Jesus. Mary's humility turns our attention not to herself, but to Christ. She exclaims that the Lord "has looked with favor on the lowliness of his servant," and "the Mighty One has done great things for me" (Lk 1:48–49). Mary seeks only to glorify God for all that he has done, and takes no credit herself. Mary truly demonstrates the virtue of magnanimity, which literally means "great-souled." Magnanimity is a courageous stretching forth of the soul to honorable and noble deeds. Saint Thomas Aquinas notes that magnanimity is about striving to do the honorable thing without thinking much of the honor conferred on oneself by others.[9] Mary is aware of the honor that will be bestowed upon her as the Mother of the Savior, stating that all generations will call her blessed (Lk 1:48),

---

8. John Henry Newman, "Fragrance Prayer," World Prayers Website, http://www.worldprayers.org/archive/prayers/invocations/dear_jesus_help_me_to.html.

9. See Saint Thomas Aquinas, *Summa Theologiae*, IIa–IIae, q. 129, art. 1, ad 3.

while she continues to give God the glory. She has the humility to know what she is capable of by God's grace and the confidence in God to do it. Unlike arrogant, vainglorious souls, Mary has no interest in how others perceive her from a worldly standpoint.

Saint Teresa of Calcutta was criticized for not doing enough to eradicate poverty on a grand scale. She responded by stressing the importance of loving one person at a time. Her heart was truly magnanimous in embarking on a worldwide mission of loving those most abandoned in society, without sacrificing personal care for these poor. One day in Melbourne, Australia, she visited a poor man whom nobody knew existed. The room where he was living was in a terrible state of disorder and neglect. There was no light in the room. The man hardly ever opened the blinds. He hadn't a friend in the world. Mother Teresa started to clean and tidy the room. At first he protested, saying, "Leave it alone, it's all right as it is." But she went ahead anyway. Under a pile of rubbish she found a beautiful oil lamp covered with dust. She cleaned and polished it. Then she asked him, "How come you never light the lamp?"

"Why should I light it?" he replied. "No one ever comes to see me. I never see anyone."

"Will you promise to light it if one of my sisters comes to see you?"

"Yes," he replied, "if I hear a human voice, I'll light the lamp."

Two of Mother Teresa's nuns began to visit him regularly. Things gradually improved for him. Then one day he said to the nuns, "Sisters, I'll be able to manage on my own from now on. But do me a favor. Tell that first sister who came to see me that the light she lit in my life is still burning."[10] The small spark lit

10. See Flor McCarthy, *Homilies for Sundays and Feast Days*, Year A, 3rd Sunday in Ordinary Time (Dublin: Dominican Publications, 1998), 171.

by Mother Teresa's personal acts of love ignited a great blaze of love in the Missionaries of Charity.

Living in God's grace, drawing close to Christ, we are inspired with magnanimity in desiring great things for Christ and in the hearts of his faithful. Whatever God wills for our lives may be considered great, although not necessarily by worldly standards. Cardinal Mindszenty once wrote that "the most important person on earth is a mother. She cannot claim the honor of having built Notre Dame Cathedral. She need not. She has built something more magnificent than any cathedral—a dwelling for an immortal soul, the tiny perfection of her baby's body. . . . Mothers are closer to God the Creator than any other creature; God joins forces with mothers in performing this act of creation."[11] Mary generously cooperated with the Holy Spirit's work of giving the King of the Universe his human nature. As awesome as this work was, she did not neglect to bring him to others in comparatively small gestures like visiting Elizabeth. It is equally important to do God's will with great love in little works and in minor details, however he prompts us.

Mary's magnanimity extends far beyond her own relationship with her son. She proclaims what Jesus will mean for her people Israel, and ultimately, for all nations. Her hand that rocks his cradle will also rock the world! The Lord will cast down the mighty from their thrones and lift up the lowly. He will fill the hungry with good things while the rich will be sent away empty. Jesus will be opposed by religious and civil leaders, but he will bring about staggering upheavals to society and culture. Filled with the Holy Spirit Elizabeth exclaims to Mary, "Blessed are you

11. Joseph Cardinal Mindszenty, *The Mother* (St Louis: Cardinal Mindszenty Foundation) http://www.mindszenty.org/mother.htm.

among women." She is hearkening to the Old Testament heroines Jael and Judith who both vanquished pagan oppressors of the Jews by striking or cutting off their heads. Both are extolled as "blessed among women" (Judg 5:24; Jdt 13:18).[12] Mary is now the most blessed among women as she strikes the head of the ultimate enemy of Israel, the devil. She does this through conceiving Jesus, who will save all people from their sins. We are the living beneficiaries of the work of Jesus as we participate in the grace that Mary received, conceiving Christ in our hearts and bearing him to the world. There is no greater work than this, and we should perform it with eagerness and magnanimity.

We shouldn't let fear get in the way of doing great things for the Lord. A woman named Susan had been meditating regularly with a group for several months. One morning she shared the following:

> "I've gotten so much from this, but lately, I've begun to fear where Jesus might be leading me. Is he going to ask some great sacrifice from me?"
>
> An older woman who had been listening intently said, "Susan, don't be afraid! I once felt the same way you feel now. And Jesus was, indeed, leading me—just as he is clearly leading you also. As a result, now I'm doing things I never dreamed I'd do. But it's filled me with a joy and a peace that I never dreamed existed."[13]

We ought to trust that God is leading us and that he will accomplish his great plans in us, as he did in Mary. The bride has welcomed the Bridegroom who has drawn close and now invites her to "arise . . . and come away" (Song 2:10). Mary has arisen in

12. Sri, *Walking with Mary*, 70–72.

13. Mark Link, *Vision 2000* (Allen, TX: Tabor Publishing, 1994), 128.

haste with her lover and gone forth magnanimously and with divine purpose to share his presence with others. We too are filled with the presence of the Almighty who has done great things for us as we seek to do great things for him.

Questions for Reflection and Discussion

1. Do you experience the Lord as being very close to you? Do you feel that he is interested in everything about you and your life, even the small details? Do you feel as if God wants to spend every hour of every day with you?
2. How does Christ's life within you bring you joy and move you to zeal in his service? Do you ever feel a sense of urgency about bringing his life to others?
3. How is your acceptance of God's presence and his will for your life like the pregnant woman's body adjusting to a new person within? What are the challenges to letting go of your attachments and conforming to what God wants?
4. How do you experience Jesus' and Mary's compassion for you and become their compassion to others? What are the special ways in which you radiate Christ?
5. Do you have any awareness of a great work God has called you to do in his service, even if it seems small by worldly standards? Do you I aspire to the virtue of magnanimity, while also remaining humble?

Prayer Exercises

1. Ponder the story of Jim Croce's desire to be with his son (p. 95). Pray with Song 2:8–14 and ask for the grace to know the Lord's intense desire to be with you.

2. Consider William's prayer experience (pp. 98–99). Pray with Luke 1:39–45 and ask for the grace to be prompt and zealous to bring Christ to others.
3. Reflect on the experience of pregnancy and adjusting to a new life within (pp. 100–101), and the woman who struggles to accept God's will in her life (p. 100). Pray with Luke 1:39–45 and ask for the grace to let go of your own agenda in order to follow Christ more closely.
4. Ponder the quotes from Saint Augustine, the Grail Prayer as well the quotes from Venerable Bruno Lanteri, and Saint John Henry Newman (pp. 102–104). Pray with Luke 1:46–56 and ask for the grace to magnify the Lord in your relationships with and ministry to others.
5. Consider Mary's magnanimity (p. 104) and the story of Saint Teresa of Calcutta (p. 105). Pray with Luke 10:1–11; 16–20; 12:49 and ask for the grace to desire to do great things in the Lord's service.

Chapter 6

Precious and Hidden

[G] O my dove, in the clefts of the rock,
    in the covert of the cliff,
let me see your face,
    let me hear your voice;
for your voice is sweet,
    and your face is lovely.
[B] Catch us the foxes,
    the little foxes,
that ruin the vineyards—
    for our vineyards are in blossom."
My beloved is mine and I am his;
    he pastures his flock among the lilies.
Until the day breathes
    and the shadows flee,
turn, my beloved, be like a gazelle
    or a young stag on the cleft mountains. (Song 2:14–17)

Then he went down with them and came to Nazareth, and was obedient to them. His mother treasured all these things in her heart. And Jesus increased in wisdom and in years, and in divine and human favor. (Lk 2:51–52)

Beautiful treasures are often formed in secret over long periods of time. Exotic pearls are molded over years of darkness in oysters deep in the heart of the sea. Carbon material remains ninety miles deep in the earth's mantle for one to three billion years before it erupts as magma and cools into precious diamonds. "It is the glory of God to conceal things" (Prov 25:2). Our often hidden and precious lives are formed over many years through ordinary events. We should treasure these everyday moments and realize they can become occasions of grace. Eating and drinking, laughing, playing, working quietly, walking, sitting down to relax or read a book—these ordinary activities often take place in solitude or within the walls of our family home. In our digital society, people seem to have less appreciation for privacy, often exposing all aspects of life publicly. Our concealed lives keep us more focused on God and less dependent on the opinions or approval of others. Prayer is the best expression of our hiddenness as we discover our true identities in God and experience his providential care. We become aware that God is slowly and quietly creating something precious out of our lives, often in secret.

This is seen in the witness of a woman named Charlotte. She speaks about the quiet but effective vocation of motherhood, describing herself as being practically "invisible," even to her husband and children. She felt very undervalued by her family, who took her for granted. One evening Charlotte was having dinner with a group of friends, celebrating the return of one of them, Nancy, from England. Nancy gave Charlotte a beautifully wrapped package, a book on the great cathedrals of Europe. She wasn't sure why Nancy had given it to her until she read the inscription made out to her. Nancy expressed profound respect for the significance of what Charlotte was building in her family, though no one else seemed to notice her.

Shortly thereafter, Charlotte was consumed with the book. She came to understand her seemingly invisible life in light of some noteworthy truths. Charlotte discovered that a series of anonymous workers had constructed these tremendous monuments to the glory of God, not themselves. Generations of workers sacrificed their entire lives for a work most of them would never see completed. They gave without counting the cost and without reward, except for the privilege of sharing in such a magnificent project. The fact that God looked with pleasure upon their project fueled their enthusiasm to work. The book told an amazing story of a rich man who visited the half-constructed cathedral. When he saw a laborer etching a small bird within a hidden wood rafter, he asked the man why he would bother to meticulously carve an image that no one would ever see. The worker replied, "God is watching." Charlotte was pierced by the truth that nothing escapes God's notice. He sees and delights in the small details of her life—getting the children off to school, driving them to practice, making their lunches, making the costumes for their school plays—and her every other act of kindness. She sensed that she was a cooperator with God in developing the character of her children, and that she too was involved in a project as great as building a cathedral, though most people would never notice.[1]

---

1. See Nicole Johnson, *The Invisible Woman* (Nashville, TN: W Publishing Group, 2005).

Like Charlotte, the bride in the Song is hidden in the clefts of the rock, humble before the presence of God. The Lord, the Bridegroom of Israel, desires to see the lovely face of his bride and to hear her dulcet voice. A bride in ancient Israel was veiled and hidden from the bridegroom before the wedding and unveiled before him on their wedding day. Now as Christ weds himself to our human nature, taking on human flesh from the bride of Israel, he desires to see, hear, and know us, in and through our humanity. Jesus came to know the fullness of humanity in the long, patient process of growing up in a family. The first faces Jesus saw and the voices he heard were those of Mary and Joseph, who would exert the greatest formative influence on his truly human life. The strongest emotional bond in the Hebrew family was not between father and mother, nor between father and son, but between mother and eldest son. Nowadays we understand that through secure attachment to his mother, a boy will experience peace. He will develop the emotional intelligence that leads to compassion and effective self-expression. The boy will be less likely to engage in risky behavior and will be formed to make good decisions. We can imagine what an immense impact Mary had on the fully human development of Jesus throughout his infancy, youth, and young adulthood. Jesus, as the Son of God, would also have had a reciprocal impact on Mary over thirty years, forming her into his first and most perfect disciple.

The Hidden Life at Nazareth

What did Mary do as a wife and mother in her hidden and ordinary life at Nazareth? We can imagine Mary as the wife of noble character of Proverbs 31, who brings good and gain to her husband and family throughout her life. A boy would accompany his mother in all her activity during his early formative years until he reached adolescence, when he would then mostly accompany his father in learning manual labor. We can imagine Jesus helping Mary or playing alongside her as she ran the household. Mary would weave fabric at the spindle and make clothing out of wool and flax with eager hands. She would plant crops, perhaps even a vineyard on a small plot of land, harvesting, processing, and cooking the produce. We can imagine Mary grinding wheat on stone hand mills and baking flat bread on a hot stone or in an oven. She would go to the market to purchase or trade for food and other necessities, such as oil for lamps. Jesus as a small child would accompany Mary on her errands and in her labors. Most importantly, Mary would give Jesus wise lessons about life. She would faithfully teach the truth about God and his revelation to his people Israel. Jesus would later use his experiential knowledge to convey truths of the kingdom in parables about children playing in the streets, women baking bread, and farmers planting seeds and watching them grow.

In my own experience of hidden life, growing up in my family, my mother was the heart of our home. The most important thing was her loving presence in our home. She was always there for us. She mirrored God's presence, the "I AM WHO I AM" (Ex 3:14), which is also translated as "I am for you." Just as God was always present and acting on behalf of his people, so my mother was always present and acting on our behalf. Her presence was a welcoming, inviting presence that, in loving us, let us know she desired our love. In her receptive presence she allowed us to show our love for her. My earliest memories are of running to cling to my mother's leg as she worked in the kitchen. At age four, I spontaneously picked little clover flowers to present to her, which she received graciously. I most remember my mother always smiling at me, especially as we had fun together. That smile was affirming to me. It let me know that I was loved just as I was. To this day, when people tell me I have a great smile, it reminds me of my mother who taught me to smile. Mary taught Jesus this same love in his sacred humanity, so that his human nature would become the effective means of giving his love to us all. Spiritual author John Haughey writes that Mary made room for Jesus in her whole being, not only in her womb but also by reflecting him to others. Jesus learned from Mary how to develop the capacity of his human nature to be present to others. Jesus as man grew in his relationship with his heavenly Father. Mary was the instrument that the Holy Spirit used to teach Jesus from his boyhood.[2]

My own mother was a woman of strong faith, which she imparted to each of her children. Watching her pray we knew that prayer was something sacred and important. God came first and putting our faith in him would be our salvation. Along with her rock-solid faith, my mother exuded a sense of well-being about life. She let us know that everything would turn out well, even if there was suffering involved. She had a great sense of balance and knew when to rest and when to work, never letting the demands of raising eleven children overwhelm her. She made sure that time for her children was the priority. Her trust in God gave her an inner peace that she conveyed to us. People in my religious community tell me that I convey a sense of peace, a feeling of stability and well-being. I know where it comes from; it's the same peace in the Lord that my mother conveyed to me. Jesus must have found that peace, that place of rest, in his own mother's heart. Jesus, who was the very peace of God in his divinity, was formed by his mother's peace in his sacred

---

2. See John Haughey, *The Conspiracy of God: The Holy Spirit in Us* (New York: Image Books, 1976), 14.

humanity. Jesus brings us the peace the world cannot give: "Peace I leave with you; my peace I give to you" (Jn 14:27), and his mother is a loving vehicle of that peace.

The most important aspect of Jesus' human development was his understanding of his Jewish faith. Though he was divine, he advanced in learning on a human level in his mind and will. Mary and Joseph fulfilled the prescriptions of the Jewish Law (see Lk 2:39). They would have spoken to the child Jesus about the God of Israel and practiced their faith in the home and local synagogue. Jesus would have absorbed the religion of his parents through a kind of osmosis by observing their example. Joseph knew all the prayers and benedictions, especially those prayed at the family meals. Mary and Joseph most likely kept some scrolls of Sacred Scripture in their home. Joseph would have led Bible readings and Mary would have helped her son learn his Hebrew faith. Jesus would have also been enrolled in the synagogue school, learning the Hebrew language of the Bible as well as how to read its scrolls. Eventually, Jesus would have the opportunity to sit beside his father in the synagogue as Joseph took his turn leading the service. Jesus may have celebrated his *bar mitzvah*, demonstrating his knowledge of the Mosaic Law. However, Luke seems to imply that Jesus was wise enough not to need one, since at age twelve he was the one asking questions of the scholars in the Jerusalem Temple, to their own amazement (see Lk 2:46–47). Ultimately Jesus would be a respected man of the synagogue, teaching school and taking turns at leading the Sabbath worship.

Bringing Out the Best

A mother brings out what is best in her children, forming them in virtue. As welcoming and unconditionally affirming as my mother was, she was also conscientious about training us to have a good character. She made sure we formed good manners, avoided evil things of the world (especially bad television programs), and learned to make good choices. I remember her challenging me to overcome my fear of joining the baseball team. I cried the whole way to the practice field for tryouts. When it was all over and I made the advanced team, I ran back to her, beaming, and she shared my joy. My mom was not overly demanding, but encouraging. She gently brought out the best in each of us, teaching us to be our true selves, living from our hearts. Mom encouraged me with my business career, but I know she sensed I had a greater calling, which she did not try to impose on me. When I discerned the Lord's call to priesthood, she was not surprised. In fact she sensed that it had always been there. A mother often realizes a child's true nature and calls him or her forth to be that person. At Cana Mary knew who her son was, and even when he seemed reluctant, called on him to act in accord with his nature as he began his public ministry.

My mother taught me to love the poor, not just in giving them money or material things, but in having regard for their dignity as persons, and especially by spending time with them. Mary's love and preference for the poor is exhibited in her Magnificat, in which she exclaims that the Lord has "lifted up the lowly" and "filled the hungry with good things" (Lk 1:52–53). Saint John Paul II asserts, "Mary is deeply imbued with the spirit of the poor of Yahweh,"[3] who in the prayer of the Psalms awaited from God their salvation, placing all their trust in him (see Ps 25; 31; 35; 55). Mary, who was poor in spirit and in fact,

3. Pope John Paul II, Encyclical *Redemptoris Mater* (Boston: Pauline Books & Media, 1987), no. 37.

shared in the life of the poor. At the presentation of Jesus in the Temple, Mary and Joseph offered a pair of turtledoves, the offering of a poor family, as a sacrifice to the Lord (see Lk 2:24). The Holy Family did not live in abject poverty as beggars. They lived a frugal existence, making enough to survive while also giving to the destitute. It is often poor people who are most generous with their own kind. Like the virtuous woman of Proverbs, Mary would open her arms to the poor and extend her hands to the needy. Mary's love for the poor would help to form Jesus' own care and concern for the needy.

Such a concern for the poor is illustrated in a story about the wealthy businessman Ross Perot, who ran for president of the United States. He grew up during the Depression in Texarkana, Texas. His parents worked hard, barely making enough for the family to subsist. During those years, many vagrants rode in and out of Texarkana, hungry and looking for a meal. They came to Ross' family home at 29th and Olive. Ross' mother, Lulu May, always fed them, but could never figure out why so many showed up on her doorstep. One day a vagrant told her that a white mark was etched into the curb to indicate that food was given away at her house. Ross found out and asked his mother if he should remove the mark. His mother told him not to erase it, but to leave it there. Reflecting on the influence of his mother's attitude, Ross said that when he saw his mother helping the vagrants, he learned the greatest lesson in the world. His mother didn't have to give a speech about it, she just did it. And Ross learned from her example of generosity.[4] We could imagine Jesus watching

4. See David Remnick, Washington Post, April 12, 1987, https://www.washingtonpost.com/archive/lifestyle/magazine/1987/04/12/our-nation-turns-its-lonely-eyes-to-h-ross-perot/daaa9b6a-6767-4ece-9d4c-8ef75861a1dc/?utm_term=.202dd14fcbdf.

Mary quietly extending her hands in love to the needy, learning from her example.

Mary delighted to see the physical, mental, and spiritual progress of her child. Luke says of Jesus that "The child grew and became strong, filled with wisdom; and the favor of God was upon him" (Lk 2:40). We can imagine her joy at hearing Jesus' first words and seeing him take his first steps. She watched him develop his social skills and personality in conversations and games with his friends. Joseph was a craftsman, which probably meant that he could do woodworking as a carpenter and stonework for building. Jesus would have learned his father's trade as a craftsman. He probably eventually managed his father's business in Nazareth. We can imagine Jesus being fair, friendly, and patient in his interactions with clients. He also knew what it was to toil with his hands. He experienced the joy of creativity and accomplishment. Mary must have been proud of her son's work and shared in his joy.

Jesus spent thirty long years developing his human nature by living the hidden life in Nazareth. In his divinity he was savoring human life in its beauty and grandeur. "What are human beings that you are mindful of them, mortals that you care for them? Yet you have made them a little lower than God, and crowned them with glory and honor" (Ps 8:4–5). Jesus must have delighted in his human nature. Through his humanity Jesus was redeeming mankind: "In the days of his flesh, Jesus offered up prayers and supplications, with loud cries and tears, to the one who was able to save him from death, and he was heard because of his reverent submission" (Heb 5:7). Though Jesus knew his mission for at least eighteen years (from the time he was age twelve until his public ministry at age thirty), he did not rush his preparation. John Haughey explains that during these years, Jesus did not simply "hang around" waiting for his time to come. Instead he lived an intense life with the Holy Spirit. Through the Spirit, Jesus grew in wisdom and grace, deeply aware that he was the Son of the Father.[5] Why would Jesus take so long to prepare for his public ministry? Fulton Sheen puts it eloquently: "He waited until the human nature which he had assumed had grown in age to full perfection, that he might then offer the perfect sacrifice to his heavenly Father. The farmer waits until the wheat is ripe before cutting it and subjecting it to the mill. So he would wait until his human nature had reached its most perfect proportions and its peak of loveliness, before surrendering it to the hammer of the crucifier and the sickle of those who would cut down the Living Bread of heaven."[6] Jesus was led by the Spirit in submission to the Father's will to patiently wait for the right moment to begin his public ministry.

Often we are way ahead of the Father's slow and patient will for our lives. Candidates for priesthood undergo many years of seminary formation before they are ready to be ordained. After I spent seven years preparing for ordination, I was informed that our congregation would be adding an extra pastoral year to the process. Deep down I knew the year would be a beneficial experience, and I also knew I needed the summer to finish my master's thesis. But I had been expecting to be ordained soon and wanted to get on with my vocation. As I prayed about my situation, Christ gave me the grace to accept the decision as a share in his sacrifice. As a result, I was much better prepared for the priesthood. Completing my thesis bore fruit in the eventual specialization of my ministry to give spiritual exercises.

---

5. See Haughey, 15.

6. Fulton Sheen, *Life of Christ* (New York: Image/Doubleday, 1977), 54.

Later when training seminarians, I would teach them patience during their eight years of formation by referring to the lesson of the Chinese bamboo tree. When the Moso bamboo tree is planted, there is no sign of visible growth above ground for five years. Then it suddenly explodes to a height of ninety feet within six weeks. Botanists explain that during those five years all the hidden activity happens underground. The tree develops miles of an elaborate root system to draw nutrients and prepare for the huge growth spurt. Without the five years of laying down roots, the tree could not emerge and rapidly climb skyward. How true this was for my own preparation for priesthood. All my hidden prayer, study, and pastoral experience in the seminary came into play and readied me for the graced moment of my ordination and subsequent ministry. The same was true for Jesus in his full understanding and experiential knowledge of being human. The obedience he practiced at Nazareth prepared him for his complete submission to the Father's will throughout his public ministry and finally at Calvary.

As human beings we easily grow impatient with God's workings. We expect satisfaction on demand and immediate results in our labors. Consumerism and technology have trained us to expect instant rewards. Even in our spiritual lives we expect quick outcomes. We want to become saints overnight. Saint Paul teaches us a great deal about patience. When we think of Saint Paul, we may think of an instant transformation. He who was the most zealous persecutor of Christians is converted by Christ and immediately becomes the greatest apostle and promoter of the Christian faith. Nothing could be further from the truth. After Paul's conversion on the road to Damascus, he spent three years in the Arabian desert in prayer and silence, studying and assimilating his new faith in Jesus Christ (see Gal 1:17–18). Humbled from his great position as a self-righteous Pharisee, he had to recast everything he knew of the Jewish faith into a Christian context. He would implore God for the conversion of his people in prayer before setting out to preach to them in person. We can imagine his regimen of prayer and asceticism during those days, during which his sole intention was to order his life completely to Jesus and remain in his presence. Subsequently, he spent about five years in relative silence and solitude in his native Tarsus, where he continued to quietly practice tent-making and study the Scriptures. Paul spent long periods of time in deep contemplation of the mysteries of Christ. In 2 Corinthians, he describes his mystical experiences of prayer during which unutterable truths were revealed to him. Saint Paul's eight years of hidden life in silence and solitude gave him an intimate union with the Lord Jesus. He was filled with a missionary zeal that bore fruit in the rapid expansion of the Church to the Gentiles. In living this hidden life Saint Paul was following the example of Jesus.

Jesus' thirty years of obscurity forged his human identity, which, united with his divinity, is the instrument of our salvation. The witness of Mary and Joseph was a crucial influence upon Jesus. No wonder a woman cried out during Jesus' ministry, "Blessed is the womb that bore you and the breast that nursed you!" (Lk 11:27). Jesus and Mary shared a reciprocal influence. Just as Mary had quietly formed Jesus humanly in his mind, body, and spirit for his public ministry, so Jesus was slowly and quietly forming Mary into his perfect disciple. During Jesus' hidden life, he, as the divine Bridegroom, could say of his mother:

> O my dove, in the clefts of the rock,
>   in the covert of the cliff,
> let me see your face,
>   let me hear your voice;
> for your voice is sweet,
>   and your face is lovely. (Song 2:14)

During those thirty years, Mary as the bride of the Song dwelt in the deep cave of the presence of Christ, our rock (see 1 Cor 10:4). Saint John of the Cross calls each Christian to remain in these clefts: "We will go up to the high caves of rock that are deeply hidden. In these caves the soul wants to go deeper and deeper, to be absorbed, to get intoxicated, to be deeply transformed in the love that the knowledge of the mystery will give to it and to hide in the bosom of her beloved. The latter, indeed invites her in the Song of Songs to enter into the gaps of the stone, into the caves of the wall."[7]

Mary entered the heart of her son as he associated her with the mysteries of his hidden life. Mary is a willing cooperator in the works of Jesus and is forever united to him in living the mysteries of his life, death, and resurrection. Mary enters these mysteries not just in her biological relationship, but with her whole heart and strength. She reflects on the meaning of these events as she lives them and continues to ponder them in recollection. Jesus' words and actions were the substance of her contemplation by which he enlightened her soul. In return for the human life and formation he had received from her, Jesus sustained her with his very self as her divine source. Christ and his mother are thus intricately united in every mystery. In these mysteries Mary has united us all in her heart with her divine son. In the hidden life of contemplative prayer, we enter into the clefts of the rock of the heart of Jesus. Like Mary, we discover that we live in him as he lives in us, that he desires to hear our voice and see our face.

---

7. Saint John of the Cross, *Spiritual Canticle*, Stanza 36, *The Collected Works of Saint John of the Cross* (Washington, D.C.: ICS Publications, 1991), 615–616.

Questions for Reflection and Discussion

1. What was your own experience of the "hidden life" in your family as you grew up? What are the parallels with the joys and trials of the Holy Family, and with the way Jesus increased in wisdom and grace?
2. In what way does the Holy Family's hidden life and daily routine inspire you? How do you continue to live a hidden life of grace and virtue?
3. Do you ever become upset about not being noticed or appreciated? Do you have a sense that God appreciates everything you are and do?
4. When have you become impatient when it seems that God is not doing anything with your life? Have you trusted in hope and eventually discovered that God brought forth fruit?
5. How have you felt your life hidden in Christ and been able to discover your life in him? Have you ever felt the Lord calling you to be more "public" in serving him?

Prayer Exercises

1. Consider Charlotte's story of feeling invisible (pp. 112–113). Pray with Song 2:14–17 and ask for the grace to accept being hidden from notoriety in many ways.
2. Ponder the daily life of the Holy Family and Jesus' gradual learning of our humanity (pp. 115–117). Pray with Luke 2:51–52 and ask for the grace to be sanctified in the ordinary routine of your home life.
3. Reflect on your own experience growing up in your family. Pray with Hosea 11:1–12 and ask for the grace to

know how the Lord manifested his merciful love to you in your youth.

4. Consider the example of Ross Perot's mother (p. 119). Pray with Proverbs 31:10–31 and consider Mary as the virtuous wife and mother.
5. Ponder the slow, hidden growth of the Moso bamboo tree (p. 122) and Saint Paul's gradual assimilation of the Christian faith (pp. 122–123). Pray with Colossians 3:1–17 and ask for the grace to be patient and trusting in the Lord's slow process of transforming you.

Chapter 7

The Sword of Sorrow

Now every year his parents went to Jerusalem for the festival of the Passover. And when he was twelve years old, they went up as usual for the festival. When the festival was ended and they started to return, the boy Jesus stayed behind in Jerusalem, but his parents did not know it. Assuming that he was in the group of travelers, they went a day's journey. Then they started to look for him among their relatives and friends. When they did not find him, they returned to Jerusalem to search for him. After three days they found him in the temple, sitting among the teachers, listening to them and asking them questions. And all who heard him were amazed at his understanding and his answers. When his parents saw him they were astonished; and his mother said to him, "Child, why have you treated us like this? Look, your father and I have been searching for you in great anxiety." He said to them, "Why were you searching for me? Did you not know that I must be in my Father's house?" But they did not understand what he said to them. Then he went down with them and came to Nazareth, and was obedient to them. His mother treasured all these things in her heart.

And Jesus increased in wisdom and in years, and in divine and human favor. (Lk 2:41–52)

[B] Upon my bed at night
    I sought him whom my soul loves;
I sought him, but found him not;
    I called him, but he gave no answer.
"I will rise now and go about the city,
    in the streets and in the squares;
I will seek him whom my soul loves."
    I sought him, but found him not.
The sentinels found me,
    as they went about in the city.
"Have you seen him whom my soul loves?"
Scarcely had I passed them,
    when I found him whom my soul loves.
I held him, and would not let him go
    until I brought him into my mother's house,
    and into the chamber of her that conceived me.
I adjure you, O daughters of Jerusalem,
    by the gazelles or the wild does:
do not stir up or awaken love
    until it is ready! (Song 3:1–5)

One day, the phone rang, and a little boy answered. "May I speak to your parents?"

"They're busy."

"Oh. Is anybody else there?"

"The police."

"Can I speak to them?"

"They're busy."

"Oh. Is anybody else there?"

"The firemen."

"Can I speak to them?"

"They're busy."

"So let me get this straight—your parents, the police, and the firemen are there, but they're all busy? What are they doing?"

"Looking for me."

Many parents know the agony of losing a child and what it means to marshal all possible resources to find him or her. Often, parents are blamed for losing their children, even in the midst of huge crowds and with many children to mind. In Jesus' time, the men and women traveled in separate groups, while part of the same caravan. Often cousins and family friends were part of the same travelling group. It would be easy for Joseph and Mary to assume the child was with the other or with extended family or friends. They might have assumed Jesus had the maturity and responsibility to remain with the caravan from Nazareth. But Jesus had other ideas. He was so absorbed in his Father's house of worship and so engaged with the teachers of the Law that he remained behind in Jerusalem. Luke explains that the finest teachers of the Law in the Temple were amazed at Jesus' questions and answers. Usually a Jewish boy of Jesus' age receiving a bar mitzvah is questioned and only gives the answers. Here, Jesus is the one teaching with authority and asking penetrating questions of the scholars of the Law. They are astonished at his wisdom, likely perceiving the divine presence in the mere lad.

After the end of the first day of travel, when the caravan reassembled for the night, Mary and Joseph realized Jesus was missing. They were filled with tribulation and began an anxious search for him. Imagine the emotional distress of going back to

Jerusalem, inquiring among other caravans, worried Jesus could have been harmed by robbers. Jerusalem was overflowing with over a million people during Passover, so looking for Jesus among such crowds in the city must have seemed hopeless. After another full day of searching, they finally came upon Jesus in the Temple on the third day. Mary asked Jesus how he could have been so inconsiderate. She expressed the anguish in her heart that she and Joseph experienced in searching for him. Jesus' response seems as callous as it is mysterious. "Why were you searching for me? Did you not know I must be in my Father's house?" (Lk 2:49). Other translations use terms such as "my Father's business," or "my Father's affairs." Jesus will not be primarily concerned about following Joseph in his trade as a builder, but will instead be consumed with following the will of his heavenly Father. Luke states that Mary and Joseph did not understand what Jesus meant, and that Mary pondered these events in her heart. Mary and Joseph knew that Jesus was destined for greatness, but they still had to absorb the magnitude of his conduct and explanation. Jesus' new mission was a lot to grasp and must have taken some adjustment.

Losing the Beloved

Mary is the fulfillment of the bride of the Song of Songs, who loses her lover and searches for him through the streets of the city. The bride is prepared to open the door to her bridegroom only to find he has disappeared. Like Mary losing Jesus, the bride is greatly distressed and searches frantically for her lover. She calls out his name but receives no answer. She hunts for him on every square of the city, asking the watchmen if they have seen him. This loss of the Bridegroom parallels the loss of Jesus in his passion and death. Jesus had spoken of a time when he as the Bridegroom would be taken away and that only then would his disciples fast. Jesus was taken away from his disciples in his passion and death. Mary his mother, Mary Magdalene, and John the beloved disciple were bereft at losing him. It was only on the third day that they found Jesus risen from the dead in Jerusalem, just as Mary had found Jesus on the third day after losing him in Jerusalem. Mary's experience of losing Jesus in the Temple prefigures her eventual loss of him in his crucifixion and death. Already Mary is sharing in the anguish of the crucifixion and loss of her son, but she is always oriented toward regaining him in a new way. Here at the finding in the Temple he is restored to her in a way that gives her a new purpose and a deepened understanding and surrender to God's plan. At the resurrection, Mary then relates to him in his risen glory and with a new mission to be mother to the fledgling Church. She is the bride who loses her beloved, searches for him and encounters him anew.

We too have times when we feel like we are losing Jesus, only to find him in a greater way. When we can't pray in our familiar ways, the Lord may be leading us to a deeper experience of prayer. In my early years of religious life in the seminary, I discovered the new experience of praying contentedly with just a word or phrase of the Song of Songs or other Scriptures. At first this caused me some concern because I wasn't applying the same mental effort as I usually did in meditative prayer, reasoning over Scripture passages to come to greater understanding and conviction in my faith. I could no longer focus my imagination or senses on any particular thing. I wondered if I was growing slothful, bored, or losing my ability to pray. With the help of my spiritual director, I came to realize that the Lord was leading me beyond my own efforts in prayer to surrender more to his work in me in a more simplified form of prayer. I noticed that I had a greater desire to practice solitary affective prayer more often and for a longer time. If I had clung to my old ways of praying out of fear of change, I would have hindered the work of the Spirit within me. I was finding the Lord in a new way.

When we experience dryness or darkness in prayer, the Lord is often preparing us to encounter him in a new way, as Mary and the bride do in the Scriptures. A woman named Diane had a long experience of God's seeming absence, which opened her to more profound experiences of his presence:

> It has been emptiness, longing, darkness, and there have been times when we did come together, and it was like color in a black and white scene for me. What I notice the most is that I feel empty. And when we're together, it will be something small in the environment that suddenly becomes loaded. Music is always very important. The images come from the texts of songs. . . . The image and the Scripture accompanied by the emotion and the music will suddenly be riveting. And I could stay with one image for over six months. One was God as the hiding place. The text was, "He will hide me in the shelter of his tents all the days of my life." That image from the psalms of being camped about and besieged—I listened to relentlessly. What happened inside was quite hard to put into words. It was not an experience of God as the strength and safety and the stronghold and shield. It was more of a reaching out to that. It was not the affirmation of it. It was, please let this be so. I hope like anything this is so. It was a reaching out. Some comfort for me. Some lessening of tension inside. But a really deeply tearful longing. That's what I felt.[1]

Diane's experience of emptiness was preparing her for a more intense desire to be surrounded and permeated by God's loving presence. Like the bride of the Song, she did not experience God

1. Janet Ruffing, *Spiritual Direction: Beyond the Beginnings* (Mahwah, NJ: Paulist Press, 2000), 116–117.

within, in her usual way. She was disposed to discovering God in her environment, in music and songs, which would lead her back to his presence within her. She experienced the Lord in surprisingly new ways beyond the ordinary, yet in ways that sustained her and manifested God in small, often hidden details of her life.

God Comes to Us in Hidden Ways

Throughout the Song of Songs the Bridegroom often disappears just when it seems that he will always be physically and sensibly present to the bride. She then must seek him more fervently, and her desire for him increases. She learns to never take his presence for granted. This motif of loss and recovery suggests that God often seems to be hiding himself so that we might seek him all the more. Joseph Ratzinger describes God's disappearing act in which, ironically, he becomes less recognizable and yet more manifest to us in hidden ways. God chooses one of the most insignificant planets—earth, a speck among all the marvels of the cosmos—to be the place of his divine action. God then chooses Israel, a nobody among the nations, to be the place of his entrance into this world. After that comes Nazareth, a backwater village of Israel, of which Nathaniel would comment, "Can anything good come out of Nazareth?" (Jn 1:46). Next, there is the shameful cross, which was reserved for those cursed by God, where Jesus becomes "a worm, and not human; scorned by others" (Ps 22:6), with his form marred beyond human likeness (see Is 52:14). Christ chooses the Church as the locus of the revelation of his divine presence, which, sadly, often obscures it.[2] Christ humbles himself to give us his Body and Blood under the

2. See Joseph Cardinal Ratzinger, *Introduction to Christianity*, trans. J. R. Foster (San Francisco: Ignatius Press, 2004), 256–257.

appearances of a mere piece of bread and cup of wine in order to nourish us in the Holy Eucharist. He vanishes, as it were, in order to enter our hearts and make them burn (see Lk 24:31–32). Ratzinger concludes, "Thus what is small by a cosmic or even worldly scale represents the real sign of God wherein the entirely Other shows itself, which even in relation to our expectations is once again the completely unrecognizable."[3] In his physical appearance at the crucifixion, Mary barely recognized Jesus as the beautiful son she had raised and as the Messiah whom the angel had prophesied. Yet in her mind and spirit she knew the heart of Jesus; by faith she knew that his passion and death were necessary for him to enter into his glory.

Ironically, it is in the apparent loss of Jesus in the crucifixion, in his hidden divinity, and even in his unrecognizable humanity that we often discover him most profoundly. Saint Thérèse of Lisieux often held a crucifix in her hand because she felt closest to God in her suffering. Amazingly she felt a desire to suffer that was like a magnet which drew her to itself. She thirsted for suffering and only craved to suffer for Jesus always. Thérèse did not love suffering for its own sake, but because it brought her closer to God. This made her cautious about asking for sufferings because she reasoned they would then be from her own will and she could never bear them alone. Instead she remained focused on conformity to God's will, accepting whatever suffering that entailed. Thérèse experienced few consolations and a barren prayer life, enduring remarkable spiritual and physical pain before she died. She reached the point in which she could no longer suffer because all suffering had become sweet to her. She wrote: "God is admirable, but he is especially lovable; let us love

---

3. Ibid.

him, then . . . let us love him enough to suffer for him all that he wills, even spiritual pains, aridities, anxieties, apparent coldness. . . . Ah, here is great love, to love Jesus without feeling the sweetness of this love . . . this is martyrdom . . . unknown martyrdom, known to God alone, which the eye of the creature cannot discover, a martyrdom without honor, without triumph. . . . That is love pushed to the point of heroism."[4]

Mary at the Cross

Thérèse's hidden, honorless, and generous suffering reminds us of Mary's silent witness of suffering at the foot of the cross. In Jesus' day a son's success would redound to the glory of his mother. The mother of James and John had approached Jesus asking that they sit at Jesus' right and left side, in positions of nobility in God's presence. Now Mary's hopes for her son, by contrast, are reduced to nothing in his passion and death. She can only hope in the Father's mercy for her son and those he will save. Mary is stripped of the rights and dignity of motherhood as she watches her son die a shameful death. As Jesus' mother and faithful disciple, Mary would know his pain like no other. At the presentation Simeon prophesied that a sword would pierce her heart, even as Jesus' heart was pierced by a lance. Simeon suggested that a large rapier would be thrust through Mary's soul as she faithfully remained standing at the foot of the cross. Her pain would primarily be mental and emotional anguish at her son's rejection and intense agony. Only by the gift of divine

4. Saint Thérèse of Lisieux, *The Letters of Saint Thérèse of Lisieux and Those Who Knew Her: General Correspondence*, Vol. I, trans. from the critical edition by John Clarke, OCD (Washington, D.C.: ICS Publications), 578.

fortitude could she remain faithful and compassionate toward her son in this tragic injustice. Mary had once prayed, "My soul magnifies the Lord." At the moment her soul is pierced with the sword her soul most magnifies the Lord by her participation in her son's passion and death.[5] We are all called to share in the Lord's passion and death as he invites each of us to take up our cross and follow him. We are never so Christ-like as when we share in his cross and resurrection. Like Mary, we can magnify the Lord in our sufferings.

A woman named Kathryn suffered the effects of a stroke she experienced after surgery. She struggled with some success to overcome these physical and emotional sufferings, yet her troubles remained. As she was praying over the passion of Jesus, she had the following experience:

> I contemplated Jesus right after Pilate had condemned him to death and washed his hands of the whole affair. I saw Jesus dragged off by those who wanted him dead. The moment of terror I felt as his final walk through Jerusalem began, was excruciating. I prayed many hours holding that terror in my heart, desiring to comfort Jesus, to tell him I was there for him and that I would not leave him alone.[6]

Kathryn's compassion deepened as the days went on:

> One day in prayer I stood beneath the cross and sank to the ground at its foot after he had died. I had told Jesus I would not leave him alone, and so I stayed there keeping watch. I kept the cross before my eyes for hours, feeling the sorrow Mary must have felt, as I asked for the courage to stay near the

5. See Edward Sri, *Walking with Mary*, 100.

6. Timothy N. Gallagher, *Meditation and Contemplation* (New York: Crossroad, 2008), 20.

> cross. It was at this point that my retreat director pointed out to me that perhaps God was bringing together Jesus' experience and my own. I began to cry when I returned to prayer. For several hours, in prayer . . . scenes of my hospital stay after my stroke so many years before alternated with scenes of Jesus' passion and death. It was like watching a movie. My moments of loneliness and fear alternated with Jesus' loneliness and fear. I cried inconsolably for hours—seventeen years-worth of tears. God was truly embracing me tightly and saying, "Do not be afraid even of this. I am holding you tightly and nothing can hurt you."[7]

Kathryn experienced Christ's passion in her own passion. Her suffering became the point of connection between his life and hers. She had faithfully endured her suffering in participation with his and was now experiencing the healing effects of that union. Christ was pleased with her willingness to suffer for his sake and strengthened her to do so by the grace of his own passion, death, and resurrection.

Mary collaborated in her son's redemption in a very direct and immediate way. Arnulf of Chartres, a disciple of Saint Bernard, speaks of Mary's sacrifice in her heart as being in communion with Christ's sacrifice of his body. "Christ sacrificed his flesh, Mary her soul. She wanted to die with her son, but the death on the cross was the privilege of the high priest, a dignity which Christ could not share with anyone. . . . The Mother's affection moved Jesus, so that Christ and Mary were one in will, and the two, in like manner, offered but a single holocaust: she in the blood of the heart, he in the blood of the flesh. As a result, Mary obtained with Christ a shared effect, the salvation of the

---

7. Ibid., 20–21.

world."[8] Like the bride of the Song, she was willing to be struck and wounded as she searched for her Bridegroom (see Song 5:7). In this she had no regard for herself but only desired to seek her beloved. Mary's union with the heart of Christ and her compassion for him were so great that she felt in her soul everything he felt in his body and emotions. The insults cast upon him fell upon her heart. The scourges that tore his flesh tore her heart and the crown that cut his head penetrated her mind. The sword fully penetrated Mary's heart as she watched the soldier pierce Jesus' side. "Blood no longer flowed from the Lord's wounds, nor did the Virgin's eyes weep tears; and the heart of Mary was buried with the dead body of Jesus."[9] Just as Christ gave the blood of his heart to the last drop, so Mary completely gave of her heart, broken in compassion. Mary's yes to God, her vocation to motherhood, her purpose in life, all seemed to be extinguished. She would naturally have cause for the deepest possible despair, and yet she was given supernatural hope. She abandoned herself to the Father's will and trusted his plan. Her *fiat* was then realized in a completely new way and offered with Christ in those ignoble circumstances.

We too are called to co-offer Christ's sacrifice. Christ is the one Redeemer and his ransom is all-sufficient for our salvation. Our role is to accept the gift he offers and to extend it by our cooperation with his sacrifice. We are called to be co-redeemers with Christ. Paul speaks of being co-workers with Christ in our apostolic activities toward establishing his kingdom. Christ sends us to proclaim the Gospel and to cooperate in bringing

---

8. In Lombardi, 190.

9. Charles Drelincourt, cited in Thurian, *Mary, Mother of All Christians* (New York: Herder and Herder, 1960), in Lombardi, 190–191.

about the life of grace in others. We accomplish this in union with Christ through our striving for holiness, our witness, and our apostolic activities. Christ has made us a kingdom of priests to offer sacrifice. Our lives become one with him as *alter Christus,* "other Christs," in his sacrifice for the sake of others. Paul writes," I am now rejoicing in my sufferings for your sake, and in my flesh I am completing what is lacking in Christ's afflictions for the sake of his body, that is, the church" (Col 1:24). The only thing that could be lacking in Christ's perfect sacrifice is my participation in those sufferings. By accepting our share of suffering for the Gospel we become Christlike and extend his kingdom to the world. Our suffering is truly efficacious when it is united with Christ's one ultimate sacrifice. The life of Dietrich Bonhoeffer gives us an example of this kind of suffering.

On July 7, 1939, the young German theologian and pastor arrived safely in Hoboken, New Jersey. He was known to be a relentless and outspoken anti-Nazi, and because of this his life was in danger. Union Theological Seminary in New York offered to rescue him and give him a position on their faculty. Bonhoeffer prayed about it and answered that he could not accept the position but would return to Germany. He said that unless he shared in the sufferings of the German people he would not have the right to go back after the war to help reconstruct Christian life there.[10] He returned to Germany where eventually he was arrested by the Nazis and put to death in April 1945. He insisted that there is only one leader to whom absolute allegiance can be given, and that leader is Jesus Christ.

10. See Pettinger, Tejvan. "Dietrich Bonhoeffer Biography," https://www.biographyonline.net/spiritual/dietrich-bonhoeffer.html.

The fruit of his beautiful example won him many disciples. While suffering for his convictions, Bonhoeffer wrote about what he called "cheap grace." He wrote, "Cheap grace means grace sold on the market like cheapjacks' wares. The sacraments, the forgiveness of sins, and the consolations of religion are thrown away at cut prices. Grace is represented as the Church's inexhaustible treasure, from which she showers blessings with generous hands, without asking questions or fixing limits. Grace without price, grace without cost! The essence of grace, we suppose, is that the account has been paid in advance; and because it has been paid, everything can be had for nothing."[11]

Bonhoeffer's point is that we can take God's grace for granted, believing God has done it all and there's nothing more for us to do. While there is nothing we can do to earn our redemption, we have to live by the implications of Christ' sacrifice. We cannot receive the grace of God in vain (see 2 Cor 6:1). Jesus said that whoever would be his disciple must deny himself, take up his cross, and follow him (see Mt 16:24). We cannot remain passive observers, but must be active participants in our own salvation, imitating Christ by his grace. In so doing, we must prepare to die to self in daily sacrifice for the sake of Christ and others. "Very truly, I tell you, unless a grain of wheat falls into the earth and dies, it remains just a single grain; but if it dies, it bears much fruit" (Jn 12:24). Like Mary, and like the bride, our willingness to die to self and suffer in union with Christ will bear much fruit in the salvation of souls.

---

11. Dietrich Bonhoeffer, *The Cost of Discipleship* (New York: SCM, 1959), 6.

Questions for Reflection and Discussion

1. Have you ever had an experience in prayer or in life in which you felt as if you had lost Jesus? What was this experience like, and how did you continue to search for him? Did you find him or did he find you?
2. When have you lost Jesus in a familiar way only to find him in a new and greater way?
3. In what sense is God hidden in your life? How does a hidden God reveal himself to you?
4. Have you ever desired to suffer for anyone else? For Jesus? Do you feel closer to God in suffering, or further from him?
5. How well do you offer your sufferings in union with Jesus? Have you ever felt like a "co-redeemer" or participant in his redemption?

Prayer Exercises

1. Consider Mary's tribulation at losing Jesus (pp. 129–130). Pray with Luke 2:41–52 and ask for the grace to persevere in seeking Jesus.
2. Consider the bride's loss of familiar ways of knowing her Beloved (p. 130). Pray with Song 3:1–5 and ask for the grace to grow to new levels of relationship with Jesus.
3. Consider Joseph Ratzinger's description of the hidden nature of God (pp. 133–134). Pray with Colossians 3:1–17 and ask for the grace to discover your life hidden with Christ.
4. Consider the quote from Thérèse, and Mary's utter devastation at the foot of the Cross (pp. 134–136). Pray

with John 19:25–27 and ask for the grace to accept your losses in anticipation of greater gain in grace.

5. Ponder Kathryn's experience of prayer with Jesus crucified (pp. 136–137). Pray with Matthew 27:32–55 and ask for the grace to remain united with Christ in his suffering.
6. Reflect on Bonhoeffer's quotations about the cost of discipleship (p. 140). Pray with John 12:20–36 and ask for the grace to die with Christ in order to live with him.

Chapter 8

Beauty's Persuasion

On the third day there was a wedding in Cana of Galilee, and the mother of Jesus was there. Jesus and his disciples had also been invited to the wedding. When the wine gave out, the mother of Jesus said to him, "They have no wine." And Jesus said to her, "Woman, what concern is that to you and to me? My hour has not yet come." His mother said to the servants, "Do whatever he tells you." Now standing there were six stone water jars for the Jewish rites of purification, each holding twenty or thirty gallons. Jesus said to them, "Fill the jars with water." And they filled them up to the brim. He said to them, "Now draw some out, and take it to the chief steward." So they took it. When the steward tasted the water that had become wine, and did not know where it came from (though the servants who had drawn the water knew), the steward called the bridegroom and said to him, "Everyone serves the good wine first, and then the inferior wine after the guests have become drunk. But you have kept the good wine until now." Jesus did this, the first of his signs, in Cana of Galilee, and revealed his glory; and his disciples believed in him. (Jn 2:1–11)

[D] What is that coming up from the wilderness,
    like a column of smoke,
perfumed with myrrh and frankincense,
    with all the fragrant powders of the merchant?
Look, it is the litter of Solomon!
Around it are sixty mighty men
    of the mighty men of Israel,
all equipped with swords
    and expert in war,
each with his sword at his thigh
    because of alarms by night.
King Solomon made himself a palanquin
    from the wood of Lebanon.
He made its posts of silver,
    its back of gold, its seat of purple;
its interior was inlaid with love.
    Daughters of Jerusalem,
    come out.
Look, O daughters of Zion,
    at King Solomon,
at the crown with which his mother crowned him
    on the day of his wedding,
    on the day of the gladness of his heart.
[G] How beautiful you are, my love,
    how very beautiful!
Your eyes are doves
    behind your veil.
Your hair is like a flock of goats,
    moving down the slopes of Gilead.
Your teeth are like a flock of shorn ewes
    that have come up from the washing,
all of which bear twins,
    and not one among them is bereaved.
Your lips are like a crimson thread,
    and your mouth is lovely.

Your cheeks are like halves of a pomegranate
    behind your veil.
Your neck is like the tower of David,
    built in courses;
on it hang a thousand bucklers,
    all of them shields of warriors.
Your two breasts are like two fawns,
    twins of a gazelle,
    that feed among the lilies.
Until the day breathes
    and the shadows flee,
I will hasten to the mountain of myrrh
    and the hill of frankincense.
You are altogether beautiful, my love;
    there is no flaw in you.
Come with me from Lebanon, my bride;
    come with me from Lebanon.
Depart from the peak of Amana,
    from the peak of Senir and Hermon,
from the dens of lions,
    from the mountains of leopards.
You have ravished my heart, my sister, my bride,
    you have ravished my heart with a glance of your eyes,
    with one jewel of your necklace.
How sweet is your love, my sister, my bride!
    how much better is your love than wine,
    and the fragrance of your oils than any spice!
Your lips distill nectar, my bride;
    honey and milk are under your tongue;
    the scent of your garments is like the scent of Lebanon.
    (Song 3:6–4:11)

I once read a story about a woman named Nancy who was intrigued by a painting of the Madonna and Child. She bought it, and after some research she discovered that the icon was called "Our Lady of Perpetual Help." Nancy thought the title was perfect, since perpetual help was just what she needed. It had been a rough year for Nancy's family, and she was feeling totally overwhelmed. Her family had moved to a smaller house, and she was expecting their fourth child only half-heartedly, because of the difficult things then happening in her life. Nancy's father was close to death. Her husband was on the verge of losing his job. Her oldest son was hyperactive and couldn't sleep through the night. Two of her three children were frequent bed-wetters, and, to top it off, the dog had just died. Nancy loved God and her family, but she felt overwhelmed because she couldn't manage so much happening at once. It was difficult to admit that she couldn't handle things herself. She knew she needed help but didn't know where or how to look for it. As she gazed at the icon, the words "Our Lady of Perpetual Help" soothed her. She clung to those words and repeated them to herself when things got too difficult. Gradually she developed a close relationship with Mary. Nancy discovered that Mary, like an earthly mother or friend, is a sympathetic listener, and offers a comforting hug. It took a careful ear and a peaceful heart for Nancy to hear her gentle voice. But Mary is eternally patient, and repeats her words as many times as needed. She always has a loving suggestion. Just as Nancy sometimes intercedes for her children when they need a little extra help, Mary will also intercede for her to her son. Eventually Nancy's fourth child was born healthy and strong. Her husband found a new and more secure job, and they moved to a bigger house. Nancy made peace with her father before he died. She slowly learned not to carry the world on her shoulders. Over time, Mary's place in her heart expanded and grew deeper.

Nancy knew that her friendship with Mary helped her in many ways. She became more patient, more concerned with loving and raising her children than with cleaning the house, and more relaxed when unforeseen events interfered with her plans. She learned how to ask for help, learning the limits of her endurance. Now Nancy can lighten up, knowing that she won't have to carry on past her strength.

Mary Intercedes for Us

Mary was not only a good model for Nancy, but a confidant and intercessor with her son. Mary notices what we lack and obtains it from Jesus. At the wedding feast at Cana, she recognized a tragic situation and took the newlyweds' problem to heart. They had no wine. Wine was essential to properly celebrate a wedding feast. Mary was concerned about this couple. Their problem became her problem. The couple would have been terribly embarrassed by the lack of wine, and the celebration might even have come to a halt without it. In Mary's deep compassion, their embarrassment became hers. Mary shows us how to boldly go to Jesus, putting everything in his hands, trusting that he will provide for our needs. Even though Jesus did not tip his hand as to what he would do, Mary showed complete confidence that it would be the right thing. She asked Jesus no questions. With complete trust Mary directed the servants: "Do whatever he tells you."

When Mary told Jesus "they have no wine," he seemed put off and reluctant to act. "What concern is that to you and to me? My hour has not yet come" (Jn 2:4). Actually, as often happens in John's Gospel, Jesus took an event presented at a very human level of understanding and elevated its meaning to the supernatural level. Jesus suggested that this moment was not just about ordinary wine running out, but about what he would provide at the level of divine grace. Jesus was aware that this first miracle, which manifested his divinity, would launch him into his public ministry. It would also lead to the "hour" of his passion, death, and resurrection. By changing water into wine, Jesus performed the first of his miraculous signs at Cana, a somewhat flashy one. Because of it many would come to believe in him. But his final sign would be more sobering and powerful. He would change Passover wine into his blood on Calvary, leading to the miracle of his resurrection from the dead. Now at Cana he showed Mary the full import of her request. Life would change dramatically for him and for her. Although Mary knew that her intervention would ultimately lead to Jesus' death and her own tragic loss, she did not step back from her request but proceeded to usher in Jesus' miracle.

It was the bridegroom's role to provide wine for the wedding feast. By providing the wine, Jesus showed himself to be the true Bridegroom.[1] His marriage is to his people, the Church. Jesus as the Bridegroom and King will marry his bride and spiritually unite with her in his death and resurrection. Adam was cast into a deep sleep when the Lord formed Eve from his side to be his bride and helpmate. So too, as Jesus slept the sleep of death on the cross, his side was opened and his bride, the Church, was formed, symbolized by Mary standing beside him. As Jesus rose from the dead he beheld his bride. In the Song of Songs, the divine Bridegroom is manifest in a dramatic way on his wedding day. He sits on his throne wearing the crown of his kingship, surrounded with dozens of mighty warriors. The column of

1. For further reflections on this theme, see Brant Pitre, *Jesus the Bridegroom: The Greatest Love Story Ever Told* (New York: Image Books, 2014).

perfumed smoke suggests a theophany or revelation of God. The Lord accompanied Israel through the desert as a column of fire. At Sinai, the Lord revealed the Law to Moses in thunder and smoke. Fulfilling the role of the Bridegroom, Jesus rose from the dead in the greatest revelatory event, manifesting his divinity. He is the warrior who has conquered the greatest enemy of human nature, death. Jesus wears his crown of kingship and sits upon his throne, ruling at the right hand of the Father. His death and resurrection are the consummation of his wedding with his bride the Church, symbolized by Mary. His covenant is eternal, symbolized by the wedding banquet.

The New Creation

Jesus' death and resurrection happened at the end of the Sabbath rest and symbolized the beginning of a new creation. The wedding at Cana happened on the seventh day in John's numbered days,[2] suggesting that Jesus was ushering in a new creation. In this new creation, Jesus is the new Adam and Mary is the new Eve. Of course, Adam and Eve had both been disobedient to God and his covenant. Now Jesus and Mary are the obedient ones. Mary as the new Eve will become the "bride" of Christ.

2. "Some scholars have noted how John's Gospel continues this creation theme by setting up a series of days, which establish a new creation week. After the phrase 'In the beginning,' John then demarcates a second day in 1:29 with the words, 'The next day.' He then uses the same phrase to note a third day in 1:35 ('The next day') and a fourth day in 1:43 ('The next day'). Finally, after these first four days, the story of the wedding at Cana is introduced as taking place three days later: 'On the third day there was a marriage at Cana' (2:1). The third day after the fourth day would represent the seventh day in the Gospel of John. Consequently, the wedding at Cana takes place at the climax of the new creation week, the seventh day." Sri, *Walking with Mary*, 123–124.

Renowned German theologian Matthias Scheeben explains the "bridal motherhood" of Mary: "Mary is as much anointed and made the Mother of God as the flesh taken from her is made the flesh of God, for the Logos is so taken up in her that she herself is taken up in him in an analogous way as the flesh taken from her. Consequently, the relation of the Mother to her divine son appears as a marriage with this divine person. Here now the Bridegroom gives himself to the Bride as her son and dwells in her in virtue of this gift."[3] The annunciation reveals a kind of spiritual marriage between the Son of God and human nature. Mary's consent was sought on behalf of the whole human race.[4]

Mary as the new Eve will become the mother of all the living in Christ. Just as she bore Christ, so all the members of Christ's body are born in her and in the Church as our mother. God said in Eden that the woman's son would crush the serpent's head (see Gen 3:15). Now, in bearing Christ, Mary, together with Christ, crushes the head of Satan. At Cana, Jesus calls his mother "woman," a term no son would ever use to refer to his mother unless he was making a point. Eve was the "woman" of Genesis who became the "mother of all [the] living" (Gen 3:20). In bringing about the new creation, Jesus designates Mary as the woman, the new Eve, and mother of all the living in Christ.

The springtime of the wedding in the Song of Songs captures the sense of the new beginning of creation emerging from the dead of winter. The bride symbolizes the beauty of the earth and symbolizes in her person all creation wedded to God. The Bridegroom is now held captive by the beauty of the bride,

3. M. J. Scheeben, *Mariology I*, trans. Rev. T. L. M. J. Guekers (London and St. Louis: B. Herder, 1946), 162f.

4. See *ST III*, 30, 1.

describing her in relation to the created beauty of the land of Israel. The spiritual significance of the characteristics of the land can be applied to Mary, who is the figure of the bride. Mary's eyes are doves (4:1), filled with the Holy Spirit (see Lk 1:28, 35), shining forth with liveliness, innocence, and charm. Mary's long, silky black hair is like a flock of Syrian goats surging down Mount Gilead (4:1), symbolizing her vivacity and freedom in the Holy Spirit to serve Christ in every detail of her life. We can imagine Mary smiling, showing the whiteness of her teeth (4:2), which feed on the word of God, allowing her to assimilate its meaning and be nourished. The ewes that bear twins (4:2) symbolize the fruitfulness of the God's word in Mary's life. Jesus said, "Blessed . . . are those who hear the word and obey it" (Lk 11:28). No one ever kept the word as well as Mary did.

Mary's lips and cheeks are scarlet (4:3) from the blood of Christ's redemption as she stood beneath the cross. Saint Catherine of Siena invites us to press our lips to the wounded side of Christ, which is like a mouth that breathes a blaze of love, flowing with blood to wash away our sins.[5] Graciousness is poured upon Mary's lips and the words of her mouth proclaim the praise and glory of God (see Lk 1:46–55). Mary's neck is the Tower of David (4:4), vigilant in the Lord's service, strong and protective as a fortress. In Christian tradition, Mary is spoken of as the neck that connects Christ the head to his body, the Church. Though Israel was a stubborn, stiff-necked people, Mary is pliant and yielding to God's will. As Mary is Queen of All Saints, her neck is a tower layered with the shields (4:4) of heroes "who through faith conquered kingdoms, administered

5. See Catherine of Siena, in "Catherine of Siena," in *Dictionnaire de spiritualite*, vol. 2 (Paris: Beauchesne), 329.

justice, obtained promises, shut the mouths of lions, quenched raging fire, escaped the edge of the sword, won strength out of weakness, became mighty in war, put foreign armies to flight" (Heb 11:33–34). Her strong, protective motherly nature reflects her inner peace. Finally, in her twin breasts (4:5) Mary sums up the Old and New Testaments of Sacred Scripture, between which she is the bridge.

Do Whatever He Tells You

The splendor of the bride has ravished her lover's heart (4:9). He is disarmed by her beauty and caught under her spell, willing to do whatever she asks. Mary as the true bride at the wedding feast of Cana requested and obtained favors from her son. While Jesus seemed reluctant to respond, he could not refuse his mother. Mary turned to the servants at the celebration and directed them to "do whatever he tells you" (Jn 2:5), echoing the faith of the Israelites in the Exodus. When the Lord made his covenant with the Israelites at Sinai, Moses proclaimed to them the responsibilities and vocation of being God's elect. The people responded, "All that the LORD has spoken we will do, and we will be obedient" (Ex 24:7). God's people renewed their promise to obey and serve the Lord when they conquered Canaan (Josh 24:24) and centuries later when they rebuilt the Temple in Jerusalem (Neh 5:12).[6]

Mary exemplifies the true and faithful servant of the Lord. She invited the servants to obey Jesus' commands. He told them to fill six stone jars with water. Each jar contained about twenty gallons. We can imagine the servants protesting, "What's the

6. See Sri, 163–164.

use? All the guests have already arrived and performed the customary washings. We don't need more water—we need wine!" But the servants did not question Jesus or hesitate to fulfill his command. Without understanding his order, these faithful servants simply went and did as he instructed. They filled the jars to the brim and took some of the water-turned-wine to the steward.

Mary invites us to do whatever Jesus tells us. When we come to serve the Lord, we first listen to what Jesus is asking of us. We put aside our agenda and our preconceived notions of what we think is best. We ask, "Lord, what do you want me to do?" (see Acts 22:10). We seek to conform our will to that of the Lord, willing to do whatever he asks, whatever the sacrifice, bother, or humiliation. As servants of Christ and others, we are willing to be available and inconvenienced in offering people our practical and substantial help. We allow ourselves to be interrupted by people crossing our paths and overturning our plans with their claims and petitions. Often our superiors and subordinates will demand things that seem unreasonable. We should prayerfully consider what God is asking in each situation.

When I was assigned to my first parish after ordination, I had my own ideas about what I wanted to do in my ministry. I had just completed my thesis on the *Spiritual Exercises of Saint Ignatius* and wanted to offer a form of the retreat on a parish level. While the pastor was not impressed, he allowed me to begin the group retreat in daily life. After a few weeks, interest fizzled, and I sensed this was not God's will. Meanwhile I was being assigned more and more ministries that I would not have chosen for myself. I began ministry in two prisons practically in the backyard of our parish. One was a sex-offenders prison and the other a maximum-security prison, neither of which seemed desirable places to visit. There I began offering catechism classes and weekly confessions. The biggest sacrifice was to forego Mass in the parish with all the wonderful families in order to offer Mass in the prisons on Saturday evenings and Sunday mornings. Then I was placed in charge of the Saint Vincent de Paul Society, which had nearly died out in the parish. I began to welcome poor and needy people at the rectory door, listening compassionately to their plight. I offered food vouchers and material assistance with rent and utilities. Sometimes I even moved furniture to people's apartments. God sent many volunteers to work at the food pantries, clothing centers, and hot-meal kitchens. We began a friendly visitor program for the homebound and their caregivers. Soon the Society was growing with enthusiastic new members and attracting people willing to lead. Finally, I was made the chaplain of our parish ministry to the mentally and physically disabled in the Developmental Center. Our ministry thrived as we taught catechism on the most elementary level imaginable, singing songs, playing games, and celebrating liturgies every week. As I said yes to these and many other ministries assigned to me, God made me much more fruitful and fulfilled than if I had chosen to do what I wanted. I was beginning to understand Mary's words, "Do whatever he tells you."

Mary believed in advance that Jesus would perform a miracle for the newlyweds. The servants and disciples had to see the miracle to believe. Jesus performed the first of his signs in changing the water into wine to reveal his glory. While Jesus' signs capture people's attention and bring about a rudimentary faith, they more importantly demonstrate Jesus' true character. As John's Gospel progresses, Jesus' signs increasingly reveal who he is as the Son of God. By the end of the Gospel, Jesus' greatest sign will be his death and resurrection, which completely reveal his glory: "The hour has come for the Son of Man to be glorified" (Jn 12:23). The resurrection is the cornerstone of our faith.

Jesus' transformation of water into wine in this first sign prefigures his transformation of wine into his blood at the Last Supper. In his resurrection, he will transform his death into everlasting life. Jesus then ascends to the right hand of the Father, where he intercedes before the Father for us.

Jesus' intercession for us does not annul our need to be intercessors; rather, we participate in his intercessory power. We are called upon to intercede for others. By the merits of Christ, our prayers go up like incense before the Father who hears and grants our petitions made in the name of Jesus. In the Book of Revelation, prayers are associated with incense, rising as a pleasing scent to God: "Another angel with a golden censer came and stood at the altar; he was given a great quantity of incense to offer with the prayers of all the saints on the golden altar that is before the throne. And the smoke of the incense, with the prayers of the saints, rose before God from the hand of the angel" (Rev 8:3–4). The bride's perfumes, more fragrant than all other spices, are pleasing to the Bridegroom and symbolize our intercessory prayers on behalf of others (see Song 4:10–11). The perfumes call to mind the incense of the Temple that rose with the prayers and sacrifices of the people. God has given Mary a special intercessory power with her son, efficacious because of his glorification. Mary's compassion for us and her intercessory role with Jesus are highlighted in the wedding feast at Cana.

Mary has interceded with her son to bring about great numbers of physical and spiritual healings throughout the centuries. Many of these have happened at Lourdes, where Mary appeared to Saint Bernadette Soubirous in 1858. A miraculous spring emerged at the grotto where Mary appeared, and it became the source of cures for many sick people who visited. The Medical Bureau of Lourdes has documented over 7,000 cures since 1858 and declared dozens of them as official miracles. The cures have been confirmed by an elite international team of twenty physicians of several faiths from many countries. The story of Lourdes was made into a movie called *The Song of Bernadette*, based on a book with the same title by a famous Jewish author, Franz Werfel. During World War II he and his wife escaped from the Nazis and crossed the German border. As the Nazis pursued them, they fled through France and hoped to cross the Spanish border and take a boat to America. However, the Spanish border patrol rejected them. Franz and his wife took refuge in nearby Lourdes at the famous shrine of Our Lady, which Franz visited that evening. As he stood alone in the dark, he bargained with the Lord through Mary: "I am not a believer, and I must be honest and say so. But in my extreme need, and on the chance that I could be wrong about God, I ask him for help for me and my wife. See us safely to the United States and I promise to write the story of this place for all the world to read."[7] Then Werfel returned to the village. Later, he related to a friend that he felt an inexplicable peace of mind that he had never felt before. Days later, Werfel and his wife discovered a pathway to cross the border into Spain. Not long after, they boarded a ship and sailed safely to America. When Franz arrived there the first thing he did was to write the story of Our Lady of Lourdes. His book is a testament to Mary's concern and intercession for him in dangerous times. She will intercede for us too.

Questions for Reflection and Discussion

1. How have you found Mary to be not only a model of discipleship, but also an intercessor and confidante?

---

7. Mark Link, *Sunday Homilies*, Years A, B, C/Series 1, Immaculate Conception, 5–6.

2. Mary was sure that Jesus would do what was necessary for the newlyweds. How confident are you that the Lord will do what is best for you and others?
3. How do you relate to Christ as your divine Bridegroom? How does Mary help bring about this "marriage" in you?
4. Do you intercede much for others in prayer? Do you sense your intercessory prayer to be effective?
5. Have you ever felt that what God is asking of you is futile? Do you question his plans for you and grow discouraged?

Prayer Exercises

1. Consider Nancy's experience with Our Lady of Perpetual Help (pp. 146–147). Pray with John 2:1–11 and ask for the grace to have a closer relationship with Mary.
2. Ponder the ravishing beauty of the bride (p. 151). Pray with Song 3:6–4:8 and ask for the grace to know your ability to capture Jesus' heart.
3. Reflect on Father Greg's experience in his first parish assignment (pp. 153–154). Pray with Isaiah 49:1–7 and ask for the grace be open to do whatever the Lord asks.
4. Consider Mary's intercessory role (pp. 147–148). Pray with Ephesians 3:14–21 and ask for the grace to participate in Christ's intercessory role.
5. Ponder Franz Werfel's escape to America (p. 156). Pray with Isaiah 43:1–13 and ask for the grace to know the Lord's protection.

Chapter 9

Enclosed Garden, Concealed Spring

[G] A garden locked is my sister, my bride,
    a garden locked, a fountain sealed.
Your channel is an orchard of pomegranates
    with all choicest fruits,
    henna with nard,
nard and saffron, calamus and cinnamon,
    with all trees of frankincense,
myrrh and aloes,
    with all chief spices—
a garden fountain, a well of living water,
    and flowing streams from Lebanon.
Awake, O north wind,
    and come, O south wind!
Blow upon my garden
    that its fragrance may be wafted abroad.
[B] Let my beloved come to his garden,
    and eat its choicest fruits.
[G] I come to my garden, my sister, my bride;

I gather my myrrh with my spice,
I eat my honeycomb with my honey,
I drink my wine with my milk.
[D] Eat, friends, drink,
and be drunk with love. (Song 4:12–5:1)

Then they returned to Jerusalem from the mount called Olivet, which is near Jerusalem, a sabbath day's journey away. When they had entered the city, they went to the room upstairs where they were staying, Peter, and John, and James, and Andrew, Philip and Thomas, Bartholomew and Matthew, James son of Alphaeus, and Simon the Zealot, and Judas son of James. All these were constantly devoting themselves to prayer, together with certain women, including Mary the mother of Jesus, as well as his brothers. . . .

When the day of Pentecost had come, they were all together in one place. And suddenly from heaven there came a sound like the rush of a violent wind, and it filled the entire house where they were sitting. Divided tongues, as of fire, appeared among them, and a tongue rested on each of them. All of them were filled with the Holy Spirit and began to speak in other languages, as the Spirit gave them ability. (Acts 1:12–14; 2:1–4)

An article appeared in a national magazine about a Catholic marketing representative named Rachel. Though she was thriving in her work, she felt a certain hollowness and futility in her life. One day, amid a breakfast meeting with her business advisor, she acknowledged that void in her life.

"Do you want to fill it?" her associate inquired.

"Of course I do," she said.

He looked at her and answered, "Then start every day with an hour of prayer."

She stared at him and said, "Don, you've got to be kidding. If I tried that I'd go off my rocker!"

He grinned and replied, "That's exactly what I said twenty years ago."

At that point he said something more that made her ponder. He told her, "You're trying to fit God into your life. Instead, you should be trying to fit your life around God."

Rachel left the diner in a state of unrest, thinking, "start each day with prayer?—for an hour? Totally not feasible!" However, the following day she ended up doing precisely that. Furthermore, she continued to do it from then on. Rachel is the first to concede that it's been challenging. On some mornings she's been completely at peace and full of delight. On other mornings she's been completely the opposite, totally fatigued.

On these tired mornings she recalled something more that her consultant had said:

"There will be times when your mind just won't go into God's sanctuary. That's when you spend your hour in God's waiting room. Still, you're there, and God appreciates your struggle to stay there. What's important is the commitment."[1]

Remaining in God's waiting room tests our commitment to prayer. After Jesus ascended into heaven, Mary and the disciples were in God's waiting room of prayer, preparing to enter the sanctuary of the Holy Spirit. They were committed to a life of prayer over nine days in the Upper Room—the same room

1. Mark Link, *Illustrated Sunday Homilies*, Years A, B, C/Series I, Year C, 78.

where Jesus had shared the Last Supper, and where Jesus had appeared to the disciples on the first Easter evening. If Jesus had manifested himself in such a powerful way in that place before, he would surely do it again. Every time Jesus departed, Mary and the disciples experienced their own poverty of spirit. The disciples felt close to Jesus in the first Eucharist, then felt the pain of losing him in the crucifixion. Jesus had appeared to them throughout the forty days of Easter, and now he had ascended to the right hand of his Father in heaven. As Jesus ascended into heaven, he reminded his apostles, "I am with you always" (Mt 28:20). Though Jesus disappeared into heaven, he became more interiorly present to his Church through the gift of his Holy Spirit. Mary taught the disciples to open themselves to the presence of the Spirit interiorly, in their "inner being" (Eph 3:16). Prayer opened their spirits to the gift of God's Spirit within. Like Rachel, they had to step back from their busy lives and make room in their hearts for the Spirit.

Overcoming Resistance to Grace

The Holy Spirit came upon Mary and the disciples with the sound of a roar of mighty wind. The bride in the Song of Songs calls upon the wind: "Awake, O north wind, and come, O south wind! Blow upon my garden" (Song 4:16). The Hebrew word *ruah* means "breath" or "wind," and is used to refer to the Holy Spirit as the wind or breath of God. Wind is powerful and overwhelming, like love, and a good symbol for God, who is love. There is no escaping a wind, which penetrates every nook and cranny of a landscape. God's wind penetrates the secret depths of our hearts. Jesus spoke of the Spirit as mysterious and unpredictable: "The wind blows where it chooses, and you hear the sound of it, but you do not know where it comes from or where it goes. So it is with everyone who is born of the Spirit" (Jn 3:8). Though we don't see the Spirit, we observe the effects of his sanctifying work in the Church and in people's lives. The saints performed marvelous works and even miracles, not by themselves, but by the power of the Holy Spirit blowing through their being. The power of the Holy Spirit changes hearts. For example, as an avowed atheist, C. S. Lewis resisted grace for years. Yet he finally felt forced to his knees by the Holy Spirit and was moved to accept Jesus Christ as the Lord of his life. If no resistance is offered, the wind will move objects like they are feathers. Persons who offer no obstruction to the movements and inspirations of the Spirit will quickly be transformed to think and act like Jesus in their daily life and gain an intimate union with God. Sinless and unselfish, Mary was completely available to the divine will and able to be moved by the Spirit. She teaches us how to be open to the Spirit and overcome our many resistances.

Unfortunately, we do offer many impediments to the Holy Spirit. Saint Ignatius of Loyola, though a great saint, was aware of the many ways he resisted the Lord's grace. He wrote: "The creature often poses obstacles to the effects our Lord wishes to produce in the soul. Not only does man set up these obstacles *before* receiving [transforming] graces, gifts, and consolations of the Holy Spirit, but even *after* he has received them. . . . There is no one who during this mortal life can properly judge how far he is an obstacle and to what extent he resists the workings of God's grace in his soul."[2] These impediments are often interior ones.

2. Saint Ignatius of Loyola, Letter to Saint Francis Borgia, in *Letters of Saint Ignatius of Loyola*, Selected and Translated by William J. Young, S.J. (Chicago: Loyola University Press, 1959), 84–85.

When we open our hearts to the Lord in prayer, we can expect to find wounds and brokenness, based on a lifetime of painful experiences. We need to open our hearts to the Spirit's healing power, to be strengthened in the "inner man." When we are healed and strengthened interiorly by the Spirit, we are less easily upset by the external circumstances of life (see Cor 4:8–12). The first work of the Spirit is to bring about interior healing of our spirits.

The Outpouring of the Holy Spirit

Breath is fundamental to life and symbolizes the supernatural life of God that is breathed into human beings. As we breathe, vital oxygen is transported through our bloodstream to every cell of our body. When I was young I enjoyed playing tackle football with my brothers and friends, which was always a bit risky without pads. Being the youngest, I was the smallest member of our family and would sometimes get the wind knocked out of me, especially if I was gang tackled. It was a horrible feeling, gasping for air, feeling like I might die for lack of breath. I felt lifeless, motionless, and disoriented, and would usually take a time-out to recover. The disciples might have felt like they had the wind knocked out of them when Jesus ascended into heaven. They might have felt purposeless, directionless, and lifeless. At this crucial moment, Mary taught them how to wait on the Lord in prayer. Jesus had once breathed the Holy Spirit upon the disciples in the Upper Room on Easter evening. He would breathe a fuller outpouring of the Spirit upon them on Pentecost.

In holy Baptism the Spirit bestows supernatural life upon us so that, by his gifts of faith, hope, and love, we participate in the very life of God. It is up to us to cooperate with the Spirit in bringing that gift to fruition. As we open ourselves to the Spirit in prayer, compassion, and charity, the Lord bestows his gifts and fruits of the Spirit upon us to bring us to spiritual maturity. Saint John of the Cross explains how the Holy Spirit both breathes in and through the soul, as through a garden: "To breathe in the soul is to infuse graces, gifts, and virtues. To breathe through the soul is to touch and put in motion the virtues and perfections already given, renewing and moving them in such a way that they of themselves afford the soul wonderful fragrance and sweetness as when you shake aromatic spices and they spread their abundant fragrance, which prior to this was neither so strong nor so highly perceptible."[3] The bride in the Song desires the wind to blow upon her garden to stir up the spice trees and fruits of her garden, making them pleasing to her beloved and wafting them abroad. As the fulfillment of the bride, Mary has the fullness of virtues and perfections. These are stirred up by the wind of the Spirit at Pentecost and made available to the Church. The Spirit enkindles the fire of his love in her and spreads that love to the disciples of Christ. The Holy Spirit engenders within us the power to love. Jesus gave his new law of love before he demonstrated that love on the cross. He said, "No one has greater love than this, to lay down one's life for one's friends" (Jn 15:13). Before Pentecost, the disciples could only learn about this kind of love, without being able to achieve it. With the sending of the Holy Spirit, the disciples received the power to imitate Jesus in this kind of love. Later, they did lay down their lives in martyrdom for Jesus and one another.

The Spirit gave the apostles a supernatural language that enabled them to convert hearts. By contrast, the Spirit created

---

3. John of the Cross, *Spiritual Canticle*, Stanza 17, in *The Collected Works of Saint John of the Cross* (Washington, D.C.: ICS Publications, 1991), 544.

new depths of quiet in Mary, leading her to a solitary and hidden life as Mother of these witnesses. Mary experienced a new desire for contemplative prayer wherein she could remain completely hidden and given to God for the sake of his Church. She almost seemed to disappear as the apostles grew more prominent in their public evangelization. God communicated his personal love to Mary in secret, in a richer and more intense way. The Holy Spirit was fully given to her, not only in his gifts, but in his very Person. The Spirit, who is the bond of love between Father and Son, united her more personally and intimately to Jesus and to the Father. The Holy Spirit permeated her with greater love as he reminded her of everything Jesus had taught her (see Jn 14:26).

Saint Thérèse of Lisieux discovered a vocation like Mary's in her own life as a cloistered, contemplative sister. She was praying over 1 Corinthians 12 in which Paul speaks of the various members of the body having different gifts of the Spirit. Thérèse desperately desired to know what her own special gift was. She longed to understand her role in the Church. Besides being a bride of Christ and a mother to souls as a Carmelite sister, she felt an intense desire to be an apostle, a warrior, a martyr, a missionary, and a priest. Thérèse described her prayer at that moment as a veritable martyrdom, because while she could not recognize herself as fulfilling those vocations, she still saw herself in each one. As she pondered Paul's teaching on the greater gifts, the greatest being love, it dawned on her that her unique vocation was to be love in the heart of the Church. The heart, Thérèse realized, was the most important part of the body, the seat of love and the silent, hidden force behind all human activity. She reckoned that without love, the apostles would not have preached the Gospel, and the martyrs would not have shed their blood. She realized that love was eternal and comprised all vocations in all times and places. Thérèse became delirious with joy in discovering her place in the Church.[4] Her experience parallels Mary's, who conceived the love of God in her heart and allowed love to incarnate itself in her womb for the world. After Pentecost, the Spirit would continue to beat with love in the heart of Mary on behalf of the apostles who proclaimed the Gospel and the martyrs who shed their blood.

Mary's Garden

Mary is truly the "garden locked" of the Song of Songs, enclosed by the Spirit for his own cultivation and enjoyment. Eve had sinned in the garden of Eden, while Mary offered her gift of self in obedience to God in her garden. Her garden is enclosed by the Lord's protective love, which admits no destructive foxes, lions, or leopards, symbols of evil. Mary as the bride is enclosed in the garden of her heart for mystical union with her Beloved. The Spirit makes her supremely fruitful. She becomes an orchard of trees, fruits, and spices. As the Spirit blows upon her garden, the scent is wafted abroad to faraway places. As the Spirit blew upon Mary's garden and upon the apostles, the aroma of Christ was fanned to the ends of the earth. Saint John of the Cross relates that "the soul means by this wind the Holy Spirit and says that it awakens love because when the divine wind breathes over it, it sets it afire, recreates it and animates it.... Breathing with its Divine Spirit over her flowery garden, it thus opens all the buds of virtue, discovers the perfumes of these

4. See Saint Thérèse of Lisieux, *Story of a Soul: The Autobiography of Saint Thérèse of Lisieux*, trans. John Clarke, O.C.D. (Washington, D.C.: ICS Publications, 1996), 193–195.

gifts, the perfections and riches of the soul; and opening this treasure and this inner domain, it unveils all its beauty."[5] The bride's external, virtuous actions are like a fragrance emanating from her inner life of union with her beloved, just as Mary's life was a fragrant offering to the Lord. Saint Paul states that "Christ always leads us in triumphal procession, and through us spreads in every place the fragrance that comes from knowing him. For we are the aroma of Christ to God among those who are being saved . . ." (2 Cor 2:14–16).

The bride prays for both the chilling north wind of trials and sorrows, and the fiery south wind of comfort and delights to blow upon her garden (Song 4:16). The Spirit comes within both experiences to season the soul, making all things work for the good in the soul that loves God. Mary experienced both joys and sorrows in the mysteries of her life with her son. Now at Pentecost and beyond, she will continue to make a fragrant offering to God amidst her contemplative life. The mystic, Saint Macarius the Egyptian, describes mature souls at prayer and provides insight into the type of prayer Mary likely experienced at this stage of her journey:

> At times they are sunk in sadness and tears for mankind and praying ceaselessly for all men, they dissolve into tears because of the ardent love they nourish for mankind. At other times, instead, they are inflamed by the Holy Spirit to great joy and love, and, if it were possible, they would hold everyone, good and bad, without distinction, in their hearts. And yet, at other times, their humility makes them feel they are beneath all others. . . . Often, the soul rests in a mystic silence, in tranquility and peace and relishes all spiritual delights and perfect

5. John of the Cross, *Spiritual Canticle*, Stanza 27, par. 6, in *The Collected Works of Saint John of the Cross* (Washington D.C.: ICS Publications, 1991).

> harmony. It receives special gifts of intelligence, ineffable wisdom, and an inscrutable knowledge of the Spirit. And grace instructs them on things that language cannot explain, nor words express. At other times they behave like any normal person.[6]

Mary would likely have experienced such a full range of experiences of union with God in the fertile garden of her heart.

The Fountain of Living Water

Mary is also the "fountain sealed" (Song 4:12). Having imbibed the living water of her son, she becomes a fountain of living water to others. Jesus said that whoever comes to him and drinks of him will become a river of living water. John tells us that Jesus was speaking about the Spirit, whom his disciples were to receive (see Jn 4:14; 7:37–39). When we come to Christ, our thirst for union with God is quenched. The grace of his Spirit flows into our hearts and fills us with the very life of God. The very water of the Spirit flows through Mary to us as she becomes a source of life. Mary and the disciples persevered in prayer to remain united with the Lord and to intercede for the whole Church. Prayer is the one thing necessary to receive the gift of salvation. In prayer we express our faith, hope, and love toward the Lord in response to his gift of self to us. Without prayer, we more easily fall into sin. Jesus exhorted his disciples to "keep awake and pray" lest they be put to the test and fail, because

---

6. Saint Macarius the Egyptian, 18, 7 f. (*PG* 34, 649). In Pseudo Macarius the Egyptian, *Fifty Spiritual Homilies of St. Macarius the Egyptian* (New York: Macmillan, 1921), 155, https://archive.org/details/fiftyspiritualho00pseuuoft/page/154.

"the spirit indeed is willing, but the flesh is weak" (Mk 14:38). Saint Paul reminds us to "Pray in the Spirit at all times in every prayer and supplication. To that end keep alert and always persevere in supplication for all the saints" (Eph 6:18). We must be committed to prayer not just in a given moment, but throughout our entire lifetimes, clinging to the Lord with dogged determination. Otherwise, the streams of living water of the Spirit will dry up within us.

This point is illustrated by the spiritual counselor John Sandford. He describes his life as a boy in an old farmhouse acquired by his family in New Hampshire. The home was over 150 years old and had never been modernized with plumbing or electricity, because they didn't have enough money. The family drew water from an old well located near the front of the house. Its water was icy cold and delightful to drink, and never ran dry. Even during the driest summers, when others had to draw water from the lake, their family well continued to produce cold, clear water. Eventually, when the family finances improved, they modernized the house, installing electricity and plumbing which brought in running water from a deep artesian well. The old well was no longer needed. It was sealed and kept in reserve, in case a future need for it ever arose. Out of curiosity and nostalgia several years later, John decided to open the old well and inspect it. He expected to see the deep, cold water still intact. He was stunned to discover that the well was completely dry. After much research, John learned that this kind of well is fed by hundreds of small subterranean rivulets that seep along a continuous water supply. As water is drawn from the well, more flows in through the rivulets, keeping these small openings clear. But when the well lies dormant and water is not constantly taken, the small rivulets dry up. The well went dry, not for lack of water, but because it had not been used.[7] The same thing can happen within our hearts if we do not pray. Prayer is like those clear rivulets that enable God to not only be present, but to flow into our hearts. We might sometimes feel as if God has abandoned us, but often we are the ones who have abandoned him, covering our hearts, failing to draw up into our souls what is present in the inner depths. Mary teaches us the importance of persevering in prayer as the only way to receive the living waters of the Holy Spirit.

Mary's Life in the Spirit

The hidden contemplative life of Mary in the Spirit gave a great impetus to the disciples' evangelizing power. In the Upper Room the disciples learned from Mary how important it is to pray to become open to the Spirit's power. It might appear that the water spilling over the top of a dam provides the power, but in reality, what is seen is only froth. Deep within the dam, turbines and generators transform the force of tons and tons of water to electricity quietly and without any fanfare. We enter the silent depths of contemplative prayer in imitation of Mary, waiting for the Holy Spirit's power to generate the forces of faith, hope, and love in our lives. Too often we are running about trying to accomplish our own works on behalf of God, without relying on the inspiration and power of the Spirit to motivate us. Instead we need to plug into the power of the Spirit, which we experience first and foremost in prayer. Without a firm connection with God in prayer, we might work very hard, look very

---

7. See John Sandford, *The Kingdom Within* (San Francisco: HarperOne, 2009), 15–16.

busy, and speak verbosely, all the while missing the life and power of God. When we are "plugged into" the Holy Spirit, we experience a divine power and cooperation with all our actions.

Because of her perfect union and cooperation with God, Mary is often called the spouse of the Holy Spirit. Saint John Eudes proclaims that the Holy Spirit was united to Mary as the Spirit of her spirit, the soul of her soul, the heart of her heart.[8] Spousal union on the human level is a mere analogy to the greater union of the Holy Spirit with the human person, but it's still the best image we have to convey such a bond. The Holy Spirit overshadowed Mary at the annunciation and spiritually conceived Christ in her womb, as a divine Spouse. Marriage implies living together in a stable union with lifelong commitment. Mary, full of grace, became the dwelling place of the Spirit, as we all do through baptism. "Do you not know your body is a temple of the Holy Spirit within you?" (1 Cor 6:19). The Holy Spirit accompanied Mary throughout her life. At the visitation she was filled with the Spirit and uttered her Magnificat. Mary was committed to the Holy Spirit from the moment of the annunciation, to the hour of her standing faithfully at the foot of the cross. At Pentecost, the Spirit came upon her in a fuller outpouring of his gifts. In marriage there is a union of mind that implies good communication, mutual acceptance, and efforts to understand one another. A spouse must open the hidden recesses of one's mind and heart and share one's deepest self with the other spouse. Mary was totally transparent to the Holy Spirit in her thought, expressing her concerns, needs, and praise of God. In prayer, and in all of life as Christians, we communicate with

8. See Saint John Eudes, *The Admirable Heart of Mary*, Part IV, ch. 3, https://www.devoutlifelibrary.org/uploads/9/5/5/9/95598946/jeudes_admirable_heart_mary_8-30-16.pdf.

the Holy Spirit and grow in wisdom, knowledge, and understanding of the things of God.

Marriage also demands a commitment to the same goals and ideals in a union of wills. Spouses make a covenant to accept the best and most beautiful in the vision and idealism of the other, rising upward in response to each other. Mary accepted the lofty purposes of the Spirit in being willing to conceive Christ in her womb and cooperate in the Spirit's mission to form the Messiah. In continual conversion, we also surrender to the ideals and values of the Holy Spirit to experience greater union and freedom. Dominic Bertetto posits that the Holy Spirit and Mary acted in perfect collaboration of wills with one another. The Spirit actuated Mary's powers of mind and will, as he does with each of us, in connection with his own supernatural power, becoming one in action (not being) with Mary in seamless cooperative energy. As a result, two persons, one divine and one human, move in such unison that we can at once attribute the same act to both the Spirit and Mary. For instance, Mary's prayer was at once her prayer and that of the Spirit. The Spirit prayed through the faculties of Mary, who united herself with him and became his dwelling place, his temple. In her he lived his intimate relationship with the Father and the Son.[9] Mary is transparent to the Holy Spirit, radiating his fire and light. As spouses, the work of one is attributed to the other. At Pentecost Luke singles out Mary's presence because she is intimately associated with the Holy Spirit's presence.

Even in her humanity, Mary was changed into an expression, almost a personification of the Holy Spirit. One of the key

9. See Dominic Bertetto, "La Sinergia dello Spirito Santo con Maria. Approfondimenti teologici," in *Maria e lo Spirito Santo,* 291–299, in Lombardi, 230.

names and roles of the Holy Spirit is Paraclete, which in Greek means "an attorney," or someone who stands beside a client to advise and defend. A paraclete is also a coach who instructs and corrects us, encourages and motivates us when we are down, and challenges us and inspires us to be our best. Mary, one with the Spirit, acts as our advocate and defender, encouraging us when we are down. I once visited the first church in the world dedicated to Mary, Our Lady of the Pillar, in Saragossa, Spain. According to tradition, Saint James preached the Gospel in that ancient Roman city in 40 A.D. But he became disheartened at the failure of his mission because the people did not accept the Christian message. As he was praying with his disciples one night on the banks of the Ebro, the Mother of God, who was still living at the time, appeared to him on a column of jasper wood. She commanded him to erect an oratory in that place. Mary also left him a miraculous image of herself with the child Jesus on a pillar of marble. The apostle immediately set to work obeying her directive, and, with the assistance of his disciples, soon constructed a small chapel. Over time a larger church was built and dedicated to what became known as Our Lady of the Pillar. Through the intercession of Mary, city dwellers and pilgrims visiting the church came to faith in Christ, and James was once again encouraged in the Spirit. He remained strong in his faith to the point of martyrdom. He was beheaded by Herod Agrippa in Jerusalem in 44 A.D. Mary not only taught the apostles at Pentecost to remain disposed to the Spirit in prayer, but by her deep union with the Spirit in contemplation she became their advocate. She strengthened them to persevere in their ministry of proclaiming the Gospel to the point of shedding their blood.

Questions for Reflection and Discussion

1. What has been your experience of waiting on the Lord in prayer and in life? How patient, persevering, and trusting are you that the Spirit will come?
2. In what ways do you resist the Spirit? How has the Spirit overcome your obstacles to his grace? Where in your life has the Spirit healed you?
3. What gifts of the Spirit are most operative in you? In what ways has the Spirit stirred up supernatural virtues in your life?
4. Do you identify the Spirit's presence and work more in your deep contemplative prayer experiences, or in your active life and ministry?
5. How have you, in the past, relied more on your own power to live the Christian life? Have you learned to depend more on the power of the Holy Spirit? How have you experienced a synergy of your efforts with those of the Spirit?

Prayer Exercises

1. Consider Rachel's commitment to pray a daily holy hour (pp. 160–161). Pray with Acts 1:12–14; 2:1–4 and ask for the grace of fidelity to prayer.
2. Reflect on Mary as the garden locked and the fountain sealed (pp. 167–169). Pray with Song 4:12—5:1.
3. Reflect on John Sandford's visit to the old family well (p. 170). Pray with Luke 18:1–8 and ask for the grace to persevere in prayer.

4. Consider Mary as the Spouse of the Holy Spirit (p. 172). Pray with Acts 1:12–14; 2:1–4 and ask for the grace to be one with the Spirit in vision and will.
5. Ponder Mary's appearance to Saint James the Apostle (p. 174). Pray with John 14:15–31 and ask to know the Holy Spirit as your Advocate.

Chapter 10

Valiantly Victorious

[B] I slept, but my heart was awake.
Listen! my beloved is knocking.
"Open to me, my sister, my love,
    my dove, my perfect one;
for my head is wet with dew,
    my locks with the drops of the night."
I had put off my garment;
    how could I put it on again?
I had bathed my feet;
    how could I soil them?
My beloved thrust his hand into the opening,
    and my inmost being yearned for him.
I arose to open to my beloved,
    and my hands dripped with myrrh,
my fingers with liquid myrrh,
    upon the handles of the bolt.
I opened to my beloved,
    but my beloved had turned and was gone.
My soul failed me when he spoke.
I sought him, but did not find him;

I called him, but he gave no answer.
Making their rounds in the city
the sentinels found me;
they beat me, they wounded me,
they took away my mantle,
those sentinels of the walls.
I adjure you, O daughters of Jerusalem,
if you find my beloved,
tell him this:
I am faint with love. (Song 5:2–8)

A great portent appeared in heaven: a woman clothed with the sun, with the moon under her feet, and on her head a crown of twelve stars. She was pregnant and was crying out in birth pangs, in the agony of giving birth. Then another portent appeared in heaven: a great red dragon, with seven heads and ten horns, and seven diadems on his heads. His tail swept down a third of the stars of heaven and threw them to the earth. Then the dragon stood before the woman who was about to bear a child, so that he might devour her child as soon as it was born. And she gave birth to a son, a male child, who is to rule all the nations with a rod of iron. But her child was snatched away and taken to God and to his throne; and the woman fled into the wilderness, where she has a place prepared by God, so that there she can be nourished for one thousand two hundred sixty days. . . . Then the dragon was angry with the woman, and went off to make war on the rest of her children, those who keep the commandments of God and hold the testimony of Jesus. (Rev 12:1–12, 17)

When I was a newly ordained deacon in my first parish assignment, I assisted at a retreat on the Blessed Virgin Mary and her relationship to Jesus Christ. Though I was one of the speakers leading the retreat, the Lord had a special grace in mind for me. Using our imaginations in prayer according to the method of Saint Ignatius, we reminisced about being in a special peaceful place, where we had somehow experienced God's grace. Then we invited Mary to join us in that place in order to experience her presence and perhaps even engage in dialogue with her. My prayer immediately went to the backyard of our summer cottage in Wisconsin, where we used to vacation as children and still visited as adults. I was sitting in a lawn chair watching the sunlight come in through the trees in the late afternoon, a time of quiet repose. Mary entered the place. A dialogue ensued. I admitted to her that I was suffering. I now focused on my present feelings. I felt very alone and homesick. I was still in transition over the past few months from my seminary life in Boston to this parish life in New Jersey. I missed my religious brothers, friends, and classmates. I had not yet felt at home in my new community or close to any of my new religious brothers in the parish. In fact, a couple of those relationships were strained. While I was making new acquaintances in the parish, they had not yet developed into friendships. It felt as if my heart were broken into pieces. Mary looked at me with love. She understood my painful emotions. She took my broken heart in her hands, holding it together for me. I especially remember how much she cherished me, showing me how precious I was in her eyes as she held my heart. God had a special grace in mind for me even as I led that retreat, a love that sustained me through a difficult time. Since then I have never forgotten how Mary is the virgin of compassion for me.

Mary and Rachel

Soon after my first year in the parish, I visited Israel on a Holy Land pilgrimage. I was deeply impressed with Rachel's tomb, which is located just outside the city of Bethlehem. I learned that Rachel is honored by Jews and Muslims alike. The site of Rachel's tomb is visited by devout Jews who believe in the power of her prayers of intercession. Rachel's role as the sorrowful mother of Israel is fulfilled in Mary, the compassionate mother of the Church. Eminent Scripture scholar Brant Pitre's groundbreaking research in his book *Jesus and the Jewish Roots of Mary* has made clear the connections between the two matriarchs.

Rachel was the beloved wife of Jacob, the father of the twelve tribes of Israel (see Gen 29:28–30). Rachel was "graceful and beautiful" and Jacob truly loved her (see Gen 29:17–20). Rachel's marriage was filled with sufferings from the beginning. Her father Laban tricked Jacob into marrying her older sister, Leah. Once Rachel was finally married to Jacob, she found out she was barren. Finally she was able to conceive and bore Jacob's final two sons, Joseph and Benjamin. Pitre explains that Jacob favored Joseph because he was the firstborn son of Rachel, the wife he had always loved. Of course that made the ten older brothers envy Joseph (see Gen 37:3–4).[1] Rachel died while giving birth to Benjamin, travailing in hard labor. As she died, she named her second child "benoni," which means "son of my sorrow." But Jacob changed it to "Benjamin," a more positive name that means "son of my right hand." Rachel was not buried with the other

---

1. See Brant Pitre, *Jesus and the Jewish Roots of Mary* (New York: Image Books, 2018), 164–165.

matriarchs of Israel, Sarah and Rebecca, in the family tomb, but along the road near Bethlehem (see Gen 35:19).

Rachel is not only the mother of Joseph and Benjamin, she is also the mother of all Israel. She somehow suffers with them and weeps for them, even after her death. Rachel is described by Jeremiah as weeping for her "children" who have been killed and driven out of the Promised Land and into exile:

> Thus says the LORD:
> A voice is heard in Ramah,
> lamentation and bitter weeping.
> Rachel is weeping for her children;
> she refuses to be comforted for her children,
> because they are no more. (Jer 31:15)

Pitre notes that Rachel's tomb was located near the place where the exiles were taken captive by the Babylonians. The spirit of Rachel is still living, witnessing the suffering of her descendants, mourning and interceding for them as her children. Her intercession succeeds in moving the heart of God.[2] In the next verse, God tells Rachel not to cry anymore because her work will be rewarded, and her children will come back to the Promised Land (see Jer 31:16–17). One later rabbinic tradition actually says that Jacob buried Rachel at that particular spot because he foresaw that the exiles would move forward from that place. He entombed her there so that she might obtain mercy for them.[3] Jews, Christians, and Muslims have come to regard the traditional site of Rachel's tomb near the city of Bethlehem as a holy place of prayer. In the twentieth century, there are records of

---

2. Ibid., 167.

3. See Genesis Rabbah 82:10 in H. Freedman and Maurice Simon, eds., *Midrash Rabbah* (10 vols.; London: Soncino, 1983), 2:761.

Jews visiting Rachel's tomb to light candles and ask for her prayers.

In the ancient rabbinic commentaries, Rachel is portrayed not just as the matriarch of her people, but as the most powerful intercessor on behalf of Israel. For example, in one rabbinic tradition, both Abraham and Moses come to God weeping and pleading for Israel after the destruction of the Temple in Jerusalem, but God does not answer their prayers.[4] It is only when the matriarch Rachel intercedes with God on behalf of the sinful people that his mercy is stirred and he responds that for Rachel's sake he will restore Israel to their land.[5] Rachel's pleading is efficacious with God when all other intercession fails, because she expresses love and not empty sacrifices.[6]

The first and most obvious link between Rachel and Mary comes in the well-known story of King Herod's massacre of the innocent infant children in Bethlehem. After he kills them, Matthew tells us that Jeremiah's prophecy was fulfilled, "A voice was heard in Ramah, wailing and loud lamentation, Rachel weeping for her children, she refused to be consoled because they are no more" (Mt 2:18). The massacre of the infants occurred near Rachel's tomb, on the road to Bethlehem. Jewish scholar David Flusser notes that Rachel and Mary are counterparts of each other. In Matthew, Rachel is a symbolic figure for the suffering Jewish mother. And Rachel's pain for the dead children also represents the travail of Mary with regard to her glorious son.[7]

---

4. See Lamentations Rabbah 24; in Ibid., 2:43–49.

5. See Lamentations Rabbah, in Ibid., 7:49.

6. See Jacob Neusner, "Can People Who Believe in Different Religions Talk Together?" Journal of Ecumenical Studies 28 (1991): 89–100.

7. See Flusser, Pelikan, and Lang, *Mary: Images of the Mother of Jesus* (Minneapolis: Fortress Press, 2005), 11–12.

The second link between Rachel and Mary takes place in John's vision of the woman clothed with the sun:[8]

> A great portent appeared in heaven: a woman clothed with the sun, with the moon under her feet, and on her head a crown of twelve stars. She was pregnant and was crying out in birth pangs, in the agony of giving birth. Then another portent appeared in heaven: a great red dragon, with seven heads and ten horns, and seven diadems on his heads. (Rev 12:1–3)

Scholars widely recognize that the vision of the woman in heaven is directly based on the dream of Joseph in which the sun, moon, and stars symbolize Jacob, Rachel, and Joseph's eleven brothers:

> He had another dream, and told it to his brothers, saying, "Look, I have had another dream: the sun, the moon, and eleven stars were bowing down to me." But when he told it to his father and to his brothers, his father rebuked him, and said to him, "What kind of dream is this that you have had? Shall we indeed come, I and your mother and your brothers, and bow to the ground before you?" So his brothers were jealous of him, but his father kept the matter in mind. (Gen 37:9–11)

In Joseph's dream, the "moon" very clearly stands for Rachel his mother. In the Hebrew Bible, putting something or someone "under one's feet" is often an image for royal dominion (see Pss 8:6; 110:1–4). The implication of John's vision of a woman clothed with the sun, standing on the moon, and wearing a crown of twelve stars seems to be that the heavenly Mother of the Messiah is exalted above all Israel, including the patriarchs and matriarchs of old.[9]

---

8. See Pitre, 172.

9. Ibid., 173.

The Sufferings of Rachel and Mary

Moreover, Pitre explains that the image of a woman crying out in the pangs of birth with great anguish (Rev 12:2) recalls the one woman whose anguish in childbirth is explicitly described in the Jewish Bible: Rachel. Rachel suffered "hard labor" and her pain was so severe that she died in childbirth (see Gen 35:16–19). The woman clothed with the sun is not just the mother of the Messiah. She is also the mother of all the children of God. John is very explicit about this: "Then the dragon was angry with the woman, and went off to make war on the rest of her children, on those who keep the commandments of God and hold the testimony of Jesus" (Rev 12:17). Just as Rachel was regarded in a special way as mother of all God's persecuted children in the Old Testament (see Jer 31:15), so the heavenly woman clothed with the sun is a mother to all those who believe in Jesus but are persecuted by the forces of evil.[10]

Finally, Pitre elucidates that just as Rachel gave birth to her second son, Benjamin, through suffering and dying in childbirth, so Mary spiritually "gives birth" to her second son—the beloved disciple—by her interior suffering and "dying" at the foot of the cross. Recall that Simeon prophesied Mary's sufferings at the cross as having her soul pierced by a sword, a kind of spiritual death (see Lk 2:35). Just as Rachel's soul departed as she died giving birth to Benjamin (see Gen 35:18), so Mary's soul is slain by the sword of the suffering she experiences at the foot of the cross. Like Rachel's, Mary's suffering is not futile but fruitful. For it is precisely through her interior dying that she becomes the mother of another child: the apostle John. At the foot of the

10. Ibid., 174.

cross Jesus tells Mary, "Woman, here is your son" (Jn 19:26). The Church is born at the cross through the passion and death of Jesus and Mary's labor pains of suffering. When Jesus died physically, Mary died spiritually (like Rachel) in childbirth.[11]

Mary experiences the severe spiritual labor pains of being present at her son's death on the Cross. During the Last Supper, Jesus described his own impending passion and death in terms of labor pains and birth, obviously for himself, but also for his apostles: "When a woman is in labor, she has pain, because her hour has come. But when her child is born, she no longer remembers the anguish because of the joy of having brought a human being into the world. So you have pain now; but I will see you again, and your hearts will rejoice, and no one will take your joy from you" (Jn 16:21–22). Jesus speaks of the short time of pain. For him it consists of his arrest, trial, imprisonment, condemnation to death, scourging, crowning with thorns, and three-hour crucifixion. Similarly, the apostles' anguish after losing Jesus to death would become a lasting joy only three days later when Jesus rose from the dead.

Women have an enormous capacity to endure pain, especially in childbirth. Most women think of labor as the hardest, most exhausting work of their lives. But as the baby is placed in a mother's arms, she sees the pain as suffering with purpose. She is transformed in a moment from exhibiting visceral and primitive strength to becoming single-focused and nurturing. Through the incredible pain of childbirth, a woman's body is convulsed and her blood is shed in order to give life, just as Jesus' body is broken and his blood shed for our life in the Eucharist and on the cross. Jesus' self-gift is mirrored in Mary's gift of her own

11. Ibid., 175–176.

flesh in conceiving and bearing Christ, which becomes a model of Christian discipleship. As Mary stood faithfully by the foot of her son's Cross, she participated in his bitter sufferings.[12] She endured extreme pain in her compassion for her dearly beloved son. Her suffering had tremendous purpose and meaning. This was the moment of the birth of the Church from the side of Christ. Just as Mary is called the new Eve, the Church too as the bride is the new Eve, the mother of all the living.

It is possible for one to suffer in compassion for a loved one as much as, or even more than, the loved one himself suffers. Ask any parent who watches a child suffer how much pain he or she feels on behalf of the child. As the soldier pierced Jesus' heart with a lance the sword prophesied by Simeon passed at length through Mary's soul (see Lk 2:35). We also consider how the apostles in the newly-born Church experienced Christ's sufferings.[13] As members of his body, they were willing to labor and suffer for the extension of Christ's kingdom to Rome and the ends of the earth. Saint Paul the Apostle sums it up well: "We are afflicted in every

---

12. According to Church tradition, due to her preservation from sin, Mary did not experience labor pains in childbirth (which are a consequence of sin in Genesis 3:16). Mary's labor pains were experienced at the Cross and are associated with cooperating in giving birth to the Church. For more on this see Pitre, *Jewish Roots of Mary*, 141–158.

13. James the Greater was beheaded in Jerusalem by Herod Agrippa in 44 A.D. Peter and Paul experienced Nero's persecution in Rome, resulting in Peter's upside-down crucifixion and Paul's imprisonment and beheading. For the others, tradition holds that Andrew was crucified by order of the Roman governor of Patras, Greece. Philip was crucified in Hierapolis, Turkey. Bartholomew was flayed and crucified in Armenia. Thomas was killed in Southern India, Matthew in Ethiopia, James in Egypt, Jude Thaddeus in Syria, and Simon the Zealot in Armenia, all toward the end of the first century. The Romans attempted to poison and boil John, but neither killed him. He was exiled to hard labor on the prison island of Patmos, Greece.

way, but not crushed; perplexed, but not driven to despair; persecuted, but not forsaken; struck down, but not destroyed; always carrying in the body the death of Jesus, so that the life of Jesus may also be made visible in our bodies. . . . So death is at work in us, but life in you" (2 Cor 4:8–10, 12). Just as the bride is willing to be beaten by the watchmen in going out to search for her beloved (see Song 5:7), the apostles are willing to endure every kind of suffering to proclaim the Gospel of Jesus Christ.

The Call of the Bridegroom

In the Song of Songs, the Bridegroom stands at the door of the bride and knocks, begging her to open (see Song 5:2). Immediately we recall Jesus' words in the Book of Revelation: "Listen! I am standing at the door, knocking; if you hear my voice and open the door, I will come in to you and eat with you, and you with me" (Rev 3:20). The Bridegroom's head is wet with dew, a sign of blessing for the Jews, as manna was like the dew of heaven. We recall Jesus' Body and Blood given at the Last Supper as the true Manna from heaven. The Bridegroom's locks are also wet with the drops of the night and he appears to be in distress as he seeks his bride. We recall the great drops of blood, resulting from extreme stress, that oozed from the skin of Jesus during his agony. Now the bride seems surprised at his desperate condition as he seeks to enter. She is being called to a new level of acceptance of her Bridegroom, to join in his distress as she loses and seeks him anew. As she eventually searches for him, she endures the beatings of the watchmen who seem to have no sympathy for her (Song 5:7). We are reminded of Mary, who in the passion and death of her son was called to a new level of commitment and surrender. She was called to seek him in suffering. Knowing the cruelty of the Romans, she naturally recoiled as she imagined Jesus' extreme suffering. Yet through the gift of supernatural fortitude Mary embraced his anguish, just as the bride opens to her lover and goes out seeking him in his hour of tribulation.

The bride's hands are dripping with myrrh (5:5), the symbol of death to self in sacrifice for another. On the cross Jesus was offered myrrh mixed with wine (see Mk 15:23) and he was anointed with myrrh at his burial (see Jn 19:39). Myrrh is the main ingredient in the anointing oil of priests who would enter the sanctuary. Myrrh is a symbol of Christ, the great high priest who, through his death, brings us into God's innermost heart. The bride's hands' dripping with myrrh symbolize her participation in her lover's suffering and sacrifice. She is now called to a greater surrender that will demand the giving of her entire self, even her body to be beaten and wounded in imitation of her beloved.

As Mary experienced deep compassion for her son in his sufferings, so too she experiences compassion for the suffering members of his body the Church. We pray in the Salve Regina, "turn then O most gracious advocate, thine eyes of mercy toward us," knowing Mary's compassionate gaze. The Hebrew word for compassion, *rahamin,* expresses the instinctive attachment of one person for another, especially a parent for his or her child. God's compassion is rooted in his covenant with his people, whom he has borne as his children. This feeling of compassion is also linked to the root word *raham,* meaning "maternal womb" and "bosom." A woman who has carried her child in her womb feels a deep attachment for the child and keenly feels her child's suffering. Similarly the Lord felt deep compassion for Israel in her exile. In Jeremiah 31:20, the Lord laments the loss of the northern kingdom of Israel, destroyed by the Assyrians in 722 BC. According to Scripture scholar Ellen Davis, the literal rendering of the Hebrew is "my guts heaved/churned for him." This remarkable expression of God's visceral attachment to his people has become an established figure of prophetic speech. An astonishing transformation occurs here in the Song when the bride repeats these words, reciprocating the Lord's compassion for Israel. In the Song (5:4), the bride's "guts are churning." She is yearning in her inmost being for her beloved as she goes out in search of him.[14] She shares the same sense of dread at her bridegroom's suffering as her very life is drained out of her: "My soul failed me when he spoke" (5:6). Mary felt her very life drained as she stood compassionately at the cross of Jesus. As the woman who gives birth to Christ and "the rest of her children" (see Rev 12:17) who are persecuted by the dragon, Mary feels the Lord's same compassion, especially for their vulnerability and suffering. Mary in her glorified humanity continues to experience compassion and weeps for her children. Her compassion also leads her to alleviate that suffering through her intercessory prayer to her son. Symbolically, the woman is carried into the desert, the place of contemplative and intercessory prayer.

In our compassion, we not only share in one another's pain; we also do whatever we can to alleviate that pain. The French philosopher and mystic Simone Weil is a contemporary woman who embodied compassion for her suffering compatriots. Her strong concern for deprived persons started when she was a child, stemming from the distress she felt when her father was absent from home, fighting in World War I. At age six Simone refused to eat sugar in solidarity with the troops entrenched along the Western front who had none. She became involved in political activism during her teenage years out of concern for the

14. See Davis, *Proverbs, Ecclesiastes, and the Song of Songs*, 277–278.

working class. In her mid-twenties she took a leave of absence from teaching and worked incognito at an auto factory to protest wage cuts. She also wanted to endure the mental impact of heavy industrial labor on workers. Though her health was poor, she became a cook on the Catalonian front during the Spanish Civil War, enduring the mental and emotional ravages of war. Simone worked with the French Resistance in England during World War II, asking to be parachuted into Nazi occupied France. She later limited her food intake to the small amounts her French compatriots were given during the German occupation, because she wanted to share the privations of those she had left in France. After a lifetime of battling sickness and frailty, Weil died in August 1943 of cardiac failure at the age of 34.

Philosopher Donald de Marco sums up Weil's teaching that love eliminates distances and inequalities. Loving compassion can overcome the gap between the powerful and the weak, the healthy and the sick. Through compassion, love identifies with those who are afflicted; through generosity, love gives of itself to them. Christ is the model for this self-giving love in creation and in his passion. Christ commiserates with us as he enters our suffering, showing divine compassion through our humanity.[15] Experiencing Jesus' misery to an extreme degree, Mary also commiserates with us in such a way as to give us comfort and strength. In her experience of pain and loss, she can understand and share our own misery. When we are received by compassionate friends, our sorrows are divided. We sense that they are sharing our burden with us, making it lighter to bear. When a person who suffers witnesses the love his friends have for him in

15. Donald de Marco, *The Heart of Virtue* (San Francisco: Ignatius Press, 1996), 36–37.

kindly words and deeds, he experiences a pleasure that mitigates his sorrow and assuages his pain.[16] Mary's kind, motherly presence and compassion bring us sweetness in the midst of our sufferings.

Mary is compassionate toward her children in the Church and intercedes for their protection. In the Book of Revelation, the dragon seeks to devour her child as he is born, and the child is snatched away to safety. War breaks out in heaven between Saint Michael the Archangel and the dragon, who is now identified as Satan, the great deceiver. After Satan is defeated and cast down to earth, he continues to pursue the woman and make war against her offspring, the Church. The nascent Church was severely persecuted by the Roman empire, especially under Nero, as well as by some Jews under Herod (see Acts 12:1–3). The persecution of the Church did not end with the Roman empire or the legalization of Christianity. The Church in every age undergoes persecution. Jesus once told the disciples: "If the world hates you, be aware that it hated me before it hated you. If you belonged to the world, the world would love you as its own. Because you do not belong to the world, but I have chosen you out of the world—therefore the world hates you. . . . If they persecuted me, they will persecute you; if they kept my word, they will keep yours also" (Jn 15:18–20). Members of the Church who undergo great persecution (see Rev 12:17) look to Mary for compassion, help, and protection.

Mary bore labor pains at the foot of the cross in giving birth to the Church as its mother. She is the most compassionate of mothers who assuages our pain and tribulation by her loving presence and through her powerful intercession with her son.

16. See Saint Thomas Aquinas, *Summa Theol.*, I–II, q. 38, a. 3.

Our suffering is turned to great joy as we give birth to Christ in the members of his body, the Church, and as we are born again to eternal life. We can echo Saint Paul's words, "I consider that the sufferings of this present time are not worth comparing with the glory about to be revealed to us" (Rom 8:18).

Questions for Reflection and Discussion

1. Mary helps to win the victory over Satan by conceiving and bearing Christ. How do you participate in Christ's victory as a co-redeemer?
2. What are the labor pains you endure in giving birth to Christ? Is your suffering meaningless or full of purpose? How do you experience the joy of childbirth in your life?
3. In what way have you experienced the compassion of Jesus and Mary in your suffering? Have you sensed them drawing close to you? Has their compassion given you joy?
4. When are you moved to show compassion to others, whether distant suffering members of the Church and the world, or those close to you?

Prayer Exercises

1. Ponder Rachel's efficacious prayers for her people Israel as a prefiguring of Mary and her compassion for us (pp. 180–182). Pray with Revelation 12:1–12 and ask for the grace to appreciate the birth pangs of Mary at the foot of the cross in giving birth to the Church and each of us as her children.

2. Reflect on the labor pains of women (p. 185). Pray with Revelation 12:1–17, John 15:18–20, or 2 Corinthians 4:8–12, asking for the grace to realize the spiritual meaning of your sufferings.
3. Consider how the Bridegroom knocks at the bride's door and how she goes out in search of him (p. 187). Pray with Song 5:2–8 and Revelation 3:20, asking for the grace to bear your share of suffering with Christ, and to intercede on behalf of the persecuted and suffering members of the Church.
4. Ponder the compassion of God and Mary, and the life of Simone Weil (pp. 189–190). Pray with Song 5:2–8 or Jeremiah 31:10–20, asking for the grace to understand Jesus and Mary's compassion for you.

Chapter 11

I Am His and He Is Mine

[G] You are beautiful as Tirzah, my love,
    comely as Jerusalem,
    terrible as an army with banners.
Turn away your eyes from me,
    for they overwhelm me!
Your hair is like a flock of goats,
    moving down the slopes of Gilead.
Your teeth are like a flock of ewes,
    that have come up from the washing;
all of them bear twins,
    and not one among them is bereaved.
Your cheeks are like halves of a pomegranate
    behind your veil.
There are sixty queens and eighty concubines,
    and maidens without number.
My dove, my perfect one, is the only one,
    the darling of her mother,
    flawless to her that bore her.
The maidens saw her and called her happy;
    the queens and concubines also, and they praised her.

"Who is this that looks forth like the dawn,
fair as the moon, bright as the sun,
terrible as an army with banners?"
[B] I went down to the nut orchard,
to look at the blossoms of the valley,
to see whether the vines had budded,
whether the pomegranates were in bloom.
Before I was aware, my fancy set me
in a chariot beside my prince.
Return, return, O Shulammite!
Return, return, that we may look upon you.
Why should you look upon the Shulammite,
as upon a dance before two armies? (Song 6:4–13)

Then God's temple in heaven was opened, and the ark of his covenant was seen within his temple; and there were flashes of lightning, rumblings, peals of thunder, an earthquake, and heavy hail. A great portent appeared in heaven: a woman clothed with the sun, with the moon under her feet, and on her head a crown of twelve stars. (Rev 11:19–12:1)

Blessed Duns Scotus (1266–1308) was a holy Franciscan priest and theologian who ably asserted the doctrine of Mary's Immaculate Conception and laid the groundwork for what would eventually become the Church's dogmatic teaching. A profound moment occurred in the midst of the debates. After Scotus answered the crucial objections, his opponents advanced one final argument they thought would clinch the debate. It was presumed in the Latin Church that Mary experienced death in perfect imitation of Christ before she was assumed into heaven (as opposed to the Eastern Church's view that she merely "fell asleep"). Since death is a consequence of original sin, they demanded, how could Mary have died if she had been conceived without original sin? Scotus answered that there is another cause of death, referring to passages in the Song of Songs in which the bride attests that she is "faint with love" (Song 2:5; 5:8). He explained that if one can be sick with love, one can also die of this lovesickness, be it great enough.[1] After Jesus' ascension, Mary's love for him grew to such an intensity that she could only desire to die to be in more perfect union with him forever.[2] Jesus had been her sole desire throughout her life. Now that he was ascended, she longed to enter a union with him that could only be accomplished by sharing in his death and resurrection. Bishop Fulton Sheen relates: "Love is the secret of the Ascension of one and of the Assumption of the other, for love craves unity with its beloved. The Son returns to the Father in the unity of Divine Nature, and Mary returns to Jesus in the unity of human nature. Her nuptial flight is the event to which our whole generation moves."[3]

---

1. As referenced in the movie *John Duns Scotus: Defender of the Immaculate Conception* (San Francisco: Ignatius Press, 2018).

2. While feeling this deep desire, Mary would nevertheless remain completely indifferent and surrendered to God's will as to whether she be in heaven or on earth for a longer time. Her attitude would mirror Saint Paul's: "For to me, living is Christ and dying is gain. If I am to live in the flesh, that means fruitful labor for me; and I do not know which I prefer. I am hard pressed between the two: my desire is to depart and be with Christ, for that is far better; but to remain in the flesh is more necessary for you" (Phil 1:21–24). Mary did in fact live many years of faithful service to Christ and his Church after the Lord's death.

3. Fulton Sheen, *The World's First Love: Mary, Mother of God* (San Francisco: Ignatius Press, 2011), 139.

Saint Francis de Sales eloquently describes the intensity of Mary's passage of love:

> The Virgin-Mother, having collected in her spirit all the most beloved mysteries of the life and death of her Son by a most lively and continual memory of them, and together with this, ever receiving directly the most ardent inspirations which her Child, the sun of justice, has cast upon human beings in the highest noon of his charity; and besides, making on her part also, a perpetual movement of contemplation, at length the sacred fire of this divine love consumed her entirely as a holocaust of sweetness, so that she died thereof, the soul being wholly delighted and transported into the arms of the love of her Son.[4]

Mary received new graces and blessings that transformed her powers of intellect and will to perceive the divine essence by new favors and light. Divinity revealed itself in this new light of unveiled beatific vision intuitively and in an exalted manner.

Mary at her death enters the beatitude of union with the most holy Trinity, the goal of all her desiring on earth. By the light of glory her soul beholds God himself, "face to face," and not merely an image or likeness of God. Mary beholds the divine essence directly, intuitively. Her intellect is pervaded with the boundless fulfillment of the essential truth of God as Holy Trinity. The Father of lights interiorly takes hold of her intelligence and reveals himself in full light. As the Psalmist relates, "For with you is the fountain of life; in your light we see light" (Ps 36:9). Mary contemplates the Word present in the

---

4. St. Francis de Sales, *Treatise on the Love of God*, book 7, chapter 13, Christian Classics Ethereal Library (slightly edited), https://www.ccel.org/ccel/desales/love.viii.xiii.html.

innermost depths of her heart. Beholding the Word, she also beholds the Father and the Spirit in Trinitarian contemplation. As she gazes upon the Word Incarnate, she witnesses the totality of the love of the Father for the Son, feasting upon this love with the Father and the Spirit. She beholds all the splendor of this love in Christ's soul and risen body, and the bonds of love that tie her to her son. The mystery of Mary's own life is more fully revealed. She understands the mercy of God in the unique privilege of her Immaculate Conception, her union with her son in the Incarnation, and her cooperation with him in redemption. Saint John Damascene comments:

> It was fitting that she, who had kept her virginity intact in childbirth, should keep her own body free from all corruption even after death. It was fitting that she, who had carried the Creator as a child at her breast, should dwell in the divine tabernacles. It was fitting that the spouse, whom the Father had taken to himself, should live in the divine mansions. It was fitting that she, who had seen her Son upon the cross and who had thereby received into her heart the sword of sorrow which she had escaped when giving birth to him, should look upon him as he sits with the Father. It was fitting that God's Mother should possess what belongs to her Son, and that she should be honored by every creature as the Mother and as the handmaid of God.[5]

The Dominican theologian Fr. Bernard explains how Mary's noblest activity in the beatific vision is evidently to see God and to love him. Presently the Blessed Virgin is so essentially a Mother that she can only see every one of her children in God and care for them in him. This is her transcendent motherhood

5. John of Damascene, *Homily 2 On the Dormition of Mary* (PG 96, 741).

in its most elevated form, for here we see a woman who is empowered to see those whom she generates as God sees them, and to carry them always in her heart as God himself carries them. We cannot imagine anything more beneficial for us than being penetrated and held by her loving gaze.[6] In sublime contemplation of her Son, Mary is given a share in his vision.

The Symbolism of the Temple

The bride in the Song of Songs, like Mary, is wholly focused on a magnificent vision of her Bridegroom. She is asked: what makes him her most beloved among others? She replies by describing his physical stature using images of the Jerusalem Temple (Song 5:10–16).[7] The Temple is a symbol of Christ, especially in his resurrection. Jesus had said to the money changers, "Destroy this temple, and in three days I will raise it up" (Jn 2:19). John adds that Jesus was speaking about the temple of his body (see Jn 2:21).

Though the Romans would destroy Jesus' body in his crucifixion, he would rise again, bodily, in three days. The precious materials of the Temple speak to us of the dignity and goodness of the human body. The Temple of Jerusalem was one of the most awesome structures of ancient times. By the time of Jesus, it had been expanded to twice its original size. It was surrounded by a gigantic wall to enclose the whole area of about thirty-six acres. Some 150,000 men of Israel constructed the Temple with

---

6. See Pere Rogatien Bernard, O.P., *The Mystery of Mary*, trans. M. A. Bouchard (St. Louis: Herder, 1960), 243.

7. See Cleveland, *Awakening Love*, chapter 25, p. 278 for a detailed explanation of how these images of the Temple apply to the risen Christ.

local stone and adorned it with carved wood, white marble, cast bronze, hammered gold, and other precious metals. The Temple reflected the beauty of God and inspired prayer and worship. The Temple represents the Lord and Bridegroom of Israel throughout the Song of Songs. Christ, as the Bridegroom, referred to the Temple as an image of his body.

Saint Paul calls our bodies temples, because we are truly God's work of art, created in Christ Jesus for the good works that God has chosen for us (see 1 Cor 3:16; Eph 2:10). Our bodies are the means by which we feed the hungry, clothe the naked, visit the sick, and shelter the homeless. Our bodies mediate the love of God to others. God took flesh in the person of Jesus and exalted our human nature, including our bodies. Saint Paul exhorts us to realize that we are temples of God's Spirit living within us. Therefore, we shouldn't abuse our bodies through intemperance and violence, but instead glorify the Lord in our bodies (see 1 Cor 6:19–20). While we experience death in the body, we also experience bodily resurrection. Our bodies will take on a glorified character, after the pattern of Christ's resurrection. "Beloved, we are God's children now; what we will be has not yet been revealed. What we do know is this: when he is revealed, we will be like him, for we will see him as he is" (1 Jn 3:2). Paul likens the body to a seed that is buried in the ground and emerges as a plant. It is the same seed, but transformed into something more glorious.

In C. S. Lewis' book, *The Great Divorce*, the narrator (who is Lewis himself) in a dream boards a bus on a rainy afternoon and embarks on a journey through hell to heaven. The narrator meets a host of supernatural beings in heaven who converse with those visitors from hell, most of whom, through their own choices, prefer to reign in hell rather than serve in heaven. It is interesting that in heaven, everything is solid and thus painful to the visitors from hell. A blade of grass penetrates the feet. An apple is as heavy as a bowling ball. Water is solid even as it cascades down a river. The radiant people in heaven are solid, real, human beings made whole by the Lord of heaven. They have solid muscles, radiant skin, and a youthful agelessness. Those in hell are miserable, disintegrated souls—ghosts who in living for self have lived for small things, shriveling up in the process.[8] Lewis' images help us to realize the awesome nature of the human body destined for the glory of eternal life, reunited with and illumined by the soul, through God's power.

The Assumption of Mary

The assumption of Mary teaches us the goodness of the human body. It is integral to the human person and destined for eternal life and glorification. God created man and woman and affirmed their goodness in soul and body as made in the image of God. When the Word became flesh, bodily human nature was assumed by God himself and meant to share in the glory of the Lord. Throughout history, the human body, considered apart from God and his revelation, has been either denigrated or exalted. False ideologies such as Manichaeism considered material and bodily nature to be evil, something to be escaped. Gnostic heresies during the time of the early Church considered human beings to be spiritual substances trapped in physical bodies in which they could do nothing but sin. Salvation meant escaping the bondage of material existence and returning home to one's merely spiritual origins. On the other hand, modern ideologies such as Communism consider only the material as real, and deny the reality of the immaterial soul and spirit.

---

8. See C. S. Lewis, *The Great Divorce* (New York: Macmillan, 1946).

Our modern culture has exalted the human body apart from the higher faculties and virtues of the soul, resulting in materialism and hedonism. While maintaining physical health is a good thing, many become obsessed with body image and what they eat, as though the body is all that matters. Vatican II's *Gaudium et Spes* sums up well the union of body and soul in the human person: "Though made of body and soul, man is one. Through his bodily composition he gathers to himself the elements of the material world; thus they reach their crown through him and through him raise their voice in free praise of the Creator. For this reason man is not allowed to despise his bodily life; rather, he is obliged to regard his body as good and honorable since God has created it and will raise it up on the last day."[9] Mary's assumption teaches us we are to regard our body as good in union with our spiritual souls, as temples of God, destined for union with him for all eternity.

Even the finest earthly temples cannot compare with Mary's glorified body. The Taj Mahal has been described as a love song in marble, an attempt to immortalize another human being. Finished in 1645, the stunning marble burial chamber was constructed at the order of Indian ruler Shah Jahan in remembrance of his most loved spouse, Mumtaz Mahal, a Persian princess. The emperor adored her profoundly, calling her his "Taj Mahal," or "Crown of the Palace." But Mumtaz died giving birth to their fourteenth child, leaving the Shah in deep grief. He called upon a great architect from Persia to construct a monument to her, telling him that it must be the one ideal masterpiece on earth. After seventeen years, the architect completed the magnificent structure of sparkling white marble, bejeweled with glittering gems such as lapis lazuli, jade, crystal, and amethyst. It remains a

---

9. *GS* 14 § 1; see Dan 3:57–80.

lasting testament to love that continues to inspire sightseers, poets, and artists throughout the world. Such a lovely story offers some insight into the Lord's love for Mary. The emperor could not bear the death of his beloved and could only build a shrine to remember her. By contrast, God raised his beloved Mary body and soul into heaven, closer to himself in a more beautiful and perfect union. There is no need to build a Taj Mahal to immortalize Mary, and there is no tomb on earth where one might venerate her body.[10] In her risen and glorified body she is a resplendent temple of the Holy Spirit. The Lord, who took his flesh from her, is forever bonded spiritually and corporally to her. He completes this union by assuming Mary's soul and body to himself in heaven. Mary is aware of being possessed by her son in eternal union through bodily death and resurrection. Like the bride, she can exclaim in a quite definitive way, "I am my beloved's and my beloved is mine" (Song 6:3).

The Beauty of Mary

No human being ever resembled Jesus in his physical features more than Mary. No human being ever resembled Jesus more spiritually than Mary in her discipleship. She perfectly conformed her life and her heart to his heart. Mary's body, now glorified by the light of Christ, resembles her son's risen and glorified body. Jesus delights in the glorified physical presence of his mother, just as in the Song of Songs the Bridegroom extols the bodily features of the bride, using metaphors from the land of Israel.

10. Of course, we build churches to honor Mary in her glorified state in heaven.

The bride is now "beautiful as Tirzah" and "comely as Jerusalem," the capital cities of Israel, symbolizing Israel in her glory. She is "terrible as an army with banners" ready for battle. Just as the king had arrived surrounded by his warriors (Song 3:7–8), she now resembles him as a formidable army in the intensity of her presence, before which he is filled with awe. He tells her to "turn away your eyes from me," for her beautiful eyes assault him. The bride's hair, the glory of a woman (see 1 Cor 11:15), is an energetic "flock of goats" frisking down the slopes. Her teeth are a "flock of ewes" that each "bear twins," another sign of the abundance of life given by the Spirit. In her glory, the bride now resembles her warrior king. Just as he emerged in the wilderness surrounded by a great number of skilled swordsmen (Song 3:7–8), she appears as an army in battle array, surrounded by queens, concubines, and maidens without number. She is full of life as the goats frisking down the slopes, the ewes that bear twins and the trees that give forth fruit. She so resembles him in her beauty that he calls her "my perfect one" who is "flawless." Just as the bride resembles her Bridegroom, so Mary, glorified, resembles her son.

Just as the bride is compared to the beauty of the earth and all creation, so too the glorified body of the Virgin Mary is a synthesis of the created world, formed from its elements. The universal destination of all creation to be set free and recreated by the Spirit of the risen Lord is realized in Mary. Saint Paul speaks of the redemption not only of our bodies, but of all creation: "We know that the whole creation has been groaning in labor pains until now; and not only the creation, but we ourselves, who have the first fruits of the Spirit, groan inwardly while we wait for adoption, the redemption of our bodies" (Rom 8:22–23). Rosa Lombardi explains how Mary's assumption, participating in the power and triumph of Christ's resurrection, is the finality of all creation: "It is as it were an enthronement of creation within the final glory of God. Because of her Assumption, Mary anticipates and preludes the ultimate destiny not only of human beings but of the cosmos as well: the entire material universe has begun its resurrection in her. In her and through her the whole of creation has been led into the sacred space of trinitarian love. The entire creation, purified and clearly manifesting God, is symbolically contained in the glorified Virgin."[11] All nature is set free in the Spirit, who creates and renews the face of the earth (see Ps 104:30). Mary's glorified body in heaven is a sign of the new heavens and new earth (see Rev 21:1).

Though from the earth in her humanity, Mary is elevated by grace to the heavenly realms and becomes an icon of our eternal destiny. Her role as our heavenly mother is to lead us to heaven to be with her son for all eternity. As the heavens are opened in the Book of Revelation and the Ark of the Covenant is seen, it is a Woman clothed with sun who appears with the moon at her feet, wearing a crown of twelve stars.

This heavenly figure calls to mind a certain perspective on human life from the pagan religions of ancient Greece and Rome. The heroes of their extraordinary legends from past ages would fight physically or match wits mentally with the gods. When a hero won such a fight, he would be spared from death and hell. He was changed into a celestial body, accomplishing a sort of everlasting status, since the ancients thought the heavenly stars were unchanging. As constellations, the heroes would enlighten and direct generations to come, just as the stars guided navigators on the sea.[12] This enchanting ancient perspective, though

11. Lombardi, 215–216.

12. See Epriest, Solemnity of the Assumption (ABC) Homily Pack, https://www.epriest.com/homily_packs/illustrations/view/638 (requires subscription).

mythical, inspired authors and heroes for ages to come. It revealed a truth about human nature, our impulse for paradise and that we need help to arrive at our destination.

With the arrival of Christianity, these stories from pagan mythology found their realization. Mary, as a true heroine, is engaged in a spiritual battle. Through her obedience to God, in her laboring to give birth to her son, she conquers Satan, the dragon (see Rev 12:1–9). The Lord desires her for himself and raises her up to the heavenly realms as an icon for all of humanity seeking eternal life. From her place in heaven she guides us as we voyage on the waves of distress in this world. In this vein, ancient Christians began to refer to Mary as *Stella Maris,* or "Star of the Sea." She guides us on the way of following Christ amid the darkness and tempests of life. Pope Benedict XVI harkens to this ancient tradition:

> With a hymn composed in the eighth or ninth century, thus for over a thousand years, the Church has greeted Mary, the Mother of God, as "Star of the Sea": *Ave Maris Stella.* Human life is a journey. Toward what destination? How do we find the way? Life is like a voyage on the sea of history, often dark and stormy, a voyage in which we watch for the stars that indicate the route. The true stars of our life are the people who have lived good lives. They are lights of hope. Certainly, Jesus Christ is the true light, the sun that has risen above all the shadows of history. But to reach him we also need lights close by—people who shine with his light and so guide us along our way. Who more than Mary could be a star of hope for us? With her "yes" she opened the door of our world to God himself; she became the living Ark of the Covenant, in whom God took flesh, became one of us, and pitched his tent among us (see Jn 1:14).[13]

13. Benedict XVI, *Spe Salvi,* 49.

Our Lady of Guadalupe

Finally, in this passage of the Song, the bride is described as being observed as one would watch a dance performed before two armies. The bride's dance represents the hope for reunion among the tribes of Israel and Judah, who had long been divided since the end of Solomon's reign. Mary is the bride of God, who, by conceiving Christ, brings about reconciliation between God and man. Christ brings reconciliation among Jews who accept him, and between Jews and Gentiles. In her co-extensive role with Christ in heaven, and by his merits, Mary cooperates in his mission of reconciliation. When Our Lady of Guadalupe appeared to Juan Diego on the hillside at Tepeyac in Mexico City, the Aztec Indians and the Spaniards were edging toward war. Their cultures were very different. The Aztecs offered human sacrifices as worship to their gods, often killing 50,000 people per year.[14] The Catholic Spaniards were appalled by this. However, they were brutal and vindictive toward the Aztecs, treating them like beasts and at times slaughtering them without justification. If war were to break out between them, it would be extremely fierce, and the Spaniards and the Church would likely be eradicated. By appearing to Juan Diego, Mary altered that destructive course of history. She enabled the Aztecs to accept Christ, and she taught the Spaniards to treat the Indians with dignity in accord with their humanity. In just seven years, six million Indians became Catholic Christians, the single greatest number of baptisms in Church history![15] Mary's appearance also ended pagan worship and ceremonial human sacrifice.

---

14. See *The Story of Guadalupe*, Archdiocese of Baltimore, https://www.archbalt.org/wp-content/uploads/2017/05/gTHE-STORY-OF-OUR-LADY-OF-GUADALUPE.pdf.

15. Ibid.

As we examine the image[16] Mary left on Juan Diego's *tilma*, or cloak, we see her hands joined in prayer. She is also in the Aztec posture of prayer: dance. For these natives, the whole body expressed prayer, not only in their hallowed celebrations, but also in their extravagant sacrifices and sacred ceremonies. Early missionaries to Mexico noted that the Aztec solemnities were extravagant events with numerous roses and green and brilliant things. The people engaged in solemn chants and dances of intense emotion and significance as their main form of prayer. The emperor himself would join with his people in supplication, singing, and dancing for their deities. Our Lady of Guadalupe appears in the image on the *tilma* in a dancing prayer position, her knee bent in movement. One can observe signs of her prayer in the gold-hued design of nine heart-shaped flower blossoms adorning her clothing. Examined from different angles, these blossoms resemble various characters of the Indian codices. The characters show that Mary is offering her heart in her hands in a gesture of love and sacrifice in prayer to God. The native leaders taught their descendants that their elders offered their hearts to God to bring about peace in their lives. This Woman showed them that, without tearing them out, they should place their hearts in her hands so that she might present them to the one, true God.

In conclusion, by appearing in the image of Guadalupe as the woman dancing in a prayer offering to God, Mary spoke to the hearts of the native peoples. Their worship was redirected toward the Holy Trinity. Embracing Christianity, they were reconciled with the Spaniards. Just as the bride of the Song danced for peace before the opposing armies, Mary's dance brought about reconciliation. As we contemplate Mary's bodily assumption into

---

16. See *Secrets of the Image: Our Lady of Guadalupe*, 2018, Knights of Columbus, http://www.secretsoftheimage.org/en/secret/hands.html.

heaven, we reflect on the beauty of her glorified body and its manifestation in dance. Mary's dance of joy is in the presence of and in union with the Holy Trinity, which seizes her entire being in love. She is clothed with the sun, an image of the Eternal Son who now radiates his light through her. Mary's destiny is our destiny as she draws us toward eternal beatitude, back to paradise, which we had lost with Eve. Francis Thompson eloquently addresses Mary:

> The celestial traitress play,
> And all mankind to bliss betray;
> With sacrosanct cajoleries,
> And starry treachery of your eyes,
>   Tempt us back to Paradise.[17]

Questions for Reflection and Discussion

1. How do you imagine the beatific vision? What will it be like to be completely one with God, with your desire for love and knowledge fulfilled? Can you imagine bodily resurrection and the transformation of your physical being and sense knowledge? Do you view the afterlife as a ghostly existence or a more solidly real experience?
2. How do you view your bodily existence? Do you fall into either extreme of a negative view of the body, or an overly exalted view of the body? How much time in your life do you give to bodily care vs. soul care?

---

17. Francis Thompson, "The After Woman," in *The Complete Poems of Francis Thompson* (New York: Modern Library, 1913), 233–235. https://archive.org/details/completepoemsoff00thomiala/page/233.

3. How do you experience your bodily existence in union with all of creation? How do you understand it as being, in a sense, the sum and height of material creation?
4. How is Mary assumed into heaven a star of hope for you? In what ways have you experienced her guiding help?
5. Have you ever experienced Mary as a unitive influence on your life and relationships? Has she ever brought harmony to a difficult situation?

Prayer Exercises

1. Consider Mary's experience of the beatific vision (pp. 198–199). Pray with Psalm 45 or 1 Corinthians 15:20–27 and ask for the grace to desire eternal life more fervently.
2. Reflect on the story of the building of the Taj Mahal (p. 203). Pray with Song 6:4–12 and ask for the grace to appreciate bodily resurrection.
3. Consider the Rosa Lombardi quote about Mary and all of creation (p. 206). Pray with Romans 8:18–26 or Revelation 21:1–8 and ask for the grace to hope for a transformed creation.
4. Ponder Pope Benedict XVI's statement on Mary, Star of the Sea (p. 207). Pray with Revelation 12:1–9 and ask for the grace to look to Mary as a sign of hope and guidance.
5. Reflect on the image of Our Lady of Guadalupe in a dancing position (p. 209). Pray with Song 5:9–6:12 and ask for the grace to experience harmony and to celebrate your life in the Spirit.

Chapter 12

Queenly Maiden

[G] How graceful are your feet in sandals,
O queenly maiden!
Your rounded thighs are like jewels,
the work of a master hand.
Your navel is a rounded bowl
that never lacks mixed wine.
Your belly is a heap of wheat,
encircled with lilies.
Your two breasts are like two fawns,
twins of a gazelle.
Your neck is like an ivory tower.
Your eyes are pools in Heshbon,
by the gate of Bath-rabbim.
Your nose is like a tower of Lebanon,
overlooking Damascus.
Your head crowns you like Carmel,
and your flowing locks are like purple;
a king is held captive in the tresses.
How fair and pleasant you are,
O loved one, delectable maiden!

You are stately as a palm tree,
    and your breasts are like its clusters.
I say I will climb the palm tree
    and lay hold of its branches.
O may your breasts be like clusters of the vine,
    and the scent of your breath like apples,
and your kisses like the best wine
    that goes down smoothly,
    gliding over lips and teeth.
[B] I am my beloved's,
    and his desire is for me.
Come, my beloved,
    let us go forth into the fields,
    and lodge in the villages;
let us go out early to the vineyards,
    and see whether the vines have budded,
whether the grape blossoms have opened
    and the pomegranates are in bloom.
There I will give you my love.
The mandrakes give forth fragrance,
    and over our doors are all choice fruits,
new as well as old,
    which I have laid up for you, O my beloved. (Song 7:1–13)

Then God's temple in heaven was opened, and the ark of his covenant was seen within his temple; and there were flashes of lightning, rumblings, peals of thunder, an earthquake, and heavy hail. A great portent appeared in heaven: a woman clothed with the sun, with the moon under her feet, and on her head a crown of twelve stars. She was pregnant and was crying out in birth pangs, in the agony of giving birth. Then another portent appeared in heaven: a great red dragon, with seven heads and ten horns, and seven diadems on his heads. His tail swept down a third of the stars of heaven and threw

> them to the earth. Then the dragon stood before the woman who was about to bear a child, so that he might devour her child as soon as it was born. And she gave birth to a son, a male child, who is to rule all the nations with a rod of iron. But her child was snatched away and taken to God and to his throne; and the woman fled into the wilderness, where she has a place prepared by God, so that there she can be nourished for one thousand two hundred sixty days. (Rev 11:19–12:6)

I met author Roy Schoeman in 2004 at Saint Clement Eucharistic Shrine in Boston when I was rector of our Oblate seminary. He has remained a friend of our Oblate congregation over the years and has captivated us with his conversion story. Roy was raised as a devout conservative Jew. But in his young adult life he fell away from his faith into the hippie, "free-love" culture of his day. Eventually he became a stellar student at both M.I.T. and Harvard. But as he began to pursue a doctorate and teach on the tenure track at Harvard Business School, he found only emptiness in his life with the professors there. Roy would find solace in long walks in nature. One weekend while hiking the beach on Cape Cod, he had an experience of "falling into heaven." He was in the presence of God and aware of the immensity of God's love. The mysterious figure of God led him through a review of his life, as might happen upon one's death. Roy realized that everything in his life had a reason, especially suffering, and that God had provided for everything he needed. Every action of his life had a moral quality. Roy regretted many of the frivolities he had pursued apart from God. He also regretted worrying about whether he was loved, for he realized that God's love was more immense than the ocean. He received all the answers to his questions about life. He had only one question that God would not answer. He wanted to know God's name, whether it be Buddha, Krishna, or even Apollo. The only name Roy would refuse to acknowledge was Jesus Christ, whom he considered a perversion of the Jewish religion. The Lord respected Roy's antipathy and withheld his name.

Roy took up a new eclectic religious path and followed some New Age practices. Exactly one year to the day after his initial revelation, he fell asleep and found himself wide awake, as it were, in the presence of a beautiful woman, whom he immediately recognized as the Blessed Virgin Mary. She lovingly answered all his questions. He felt the purity and intensity of her love and felt ecstatic in her presence. When he awoke from his sleep, he knew that the God he had met on the beach the preceding year was Jesus Christ. Roy then wanted to be as perfect a Christian as possible. Soon he visited a Carthusian monastery in the French Alps. There he felt Mary's central, penetrating presence in the Catholic Church. Distressed at not being able to receive Holy Communion, he was drawn to the baptismal font and eventually received the sacraments of initiation into the Catholic Church.[1] Mary's love, beauty, and compassionate, penetrating gaze conquered Roy's obstinate heart and brought him into union with Christ and his Church.

Roy had the privilege of "falling into heaven" in the presence of a magnificent woman, Mary. In the Book of Revelation we are

1. Roy Schoeman, *Salvation Is from the Jews* (San Francisco: Ignatius Press, 2004), 367–372.

given a glimpse into the opened heavens. The Ark of the Covenant (the place of God's presence) is seen, in the figure of a powerful woman. Since she gives birth to a son, who is destined to rule the human race with a rod of iron, it would be impossible for this woman not to be the Blessed Virgin Mary.[2] She now appears in glory as a royal figure, clothed with the sun, with the moon at her feet and on her head a crown of twelve stars.[3] As in Psalm 110:1, where the Lord's enemies are under his feet, Mary's queenly power is symbolized by the moon positioned under her feet.

The Queen Mother

For Israel, the queen was not the king's wife but his mother. She was referred to as the "queen mother." As a ruler, the queen mother's power was always secondary to that of the king, but she held great moral sway. She was a privileged guide who often spoke for specific political interests of persons and the community before the king. In 1 Kings 2:19, Bathsheba, the queen mother, enters the presence of her son, King Solomon, on a mission of intercession for Adonijah. The king stands up to meet her and bows down to her in homage. She then sits on a throne at the right of his throne, where she rules alongside him. Though

---

2. Recall that John's Gospel highlights that Jesus had called Mary "woman" (Jn 2:4; 19:26), which no son would call his mother unless it signified something more. Eve was referred to as the "woman" in Genesis (2:23) who became the "mother of the living." As the New Eve, Mary is simply referred to as "woman" by Jesus at Cana and at the foot of the Cross.

3. In Joseph's dream in Genesis, he tells his father, "the sun, the moon, and eleven stars were bowing down to me" (37:9). These heavenly bodies symbolize the royal authority Joseph would have over his parents (symbolized by the sun and moon), and brothers (symbolized by the eleven stars and tribes of Israel).

he is the primary ruler and authority figure, he bows to his mother and takes her as his co-ruler. During one crisis in Judah's history, Athaliah, queen mother of the slain King Ahaziah, ruled in his place for six years (2 Kgs 11:1–3). A woman became queen mother as soon as her son became king. She retained the title until her death, even if a new king came to the throne.

Judean rulers always took counsel from wise men, prophets, and priests, and the senior advocate was the king's mother. Amazingly, in Proverbs 31:1–9, the queen mother instructs the king on how to rule the kingdom. She counsels him to shun wives who would harm the kingdom, to avoid strong drink, and to care for the poor who have no voice. In no other ancient culture do we find instructions for the king given by his own mother. As a King, Jesus would fulfill the Hebrew tradition of honoring his mother as queen. He would share his rule with her and grant the requests of her heart aligned with his own heart (see Jn 2:1–11).

Mary is the fulfillment of the queen prefigured by Esther in the Old Testament.[4] She was a Jewish queen of the Persian king Ahasuerus. The evil advisor Haman hated the Jews and was plotting to have them all killed. Queen Esther was exempt from the decree of condemnation to death of all her people. This prefigured Mary, conceived without sin and full of grace, who was the only human being preserved from the sentence of death imposed upon humanity as a result of original sin. Esther cooperated with God in his plan to save her people from the decree of annihilation that Haman's deceitful plotting had brought about. Mary humbly and courageously cooperated in God's plan to save

4. See Stefano Manelli, "The Mystery of the Blessed Virgin Mary in the Old Testament," in *Mariology*, 32–33.

his people from Eden's condemnation by giving birth to the Savior. Finally, Esther's beauty was so exceptional that King Ahasuerus chose her to be his spouse and queen. The Holy Spirit chose Mary in her resplendent beauty to be his spouse and Queen alongside Christ our King. The Church extols Mary as the "All Beautiful" glory of Jerusalem and joy of Israel in the fourth century Christian hymn, *Tota Pulchra Es*. As with Mary, Esther's beauty was primarily an interior reality. "All glorious is the princess within" (Ps 45:14, NIV).[5]

Esther tried to hide her body, hoping the king would not be attracted to her. But he was especially attracted to the depth of spiritual beauty within her. Proverbs teaches that "Charm is deceitful, and beauty is vain, but a woman who fears the Lord is to be praised" (Prov 31:30). When a person is interiorly beautiful in grace and wisdom, it will be manifest exteriorly in the holiness and virtue of one's actions. The king was most attracted to Esther's interior depth of wisdom and grace. Queen Esther remained behind the scenes, yet she was the woman who was really changing the world. Mary is a lot like Esther in that she remained mostly hidden throughout her life while helping to bring about the salvation of the human race. Her sublime beauty and intercessory power with her son, the king, are finally revealed in heaven for us all to see (Rev 12).

The bride in the Song has already emerged in queenly glory, bright as the sun, fair as the moon, terrible as an army set in battle array (6:10). She is now described as a royal maiden who is filled with grace in her joyful dance (6:13—7:9). As a queen she exhibits majestic qualities. Her neck is like the tower of

---

5. Saint Jerome interprets this psalm as referring to Mary's beauty as grace from within. See Saint Jerome, *Letter 107*, 7 (PL 22,874).

David, suggesting queenly courage and strength. The bride's navel and belly are a storehouse of nourishment, wine, and wheat, which nourish her people. The eyes of the queen are deep as the pools of Heshbon, demonstrating queenly wisdom and compassion. Her nose is an imposing sentinel like the tower of Lebanon that faces Syria, instilling imperial fear and challenging her enemies. She rises stately as a palm tree in grace and mature stature. The queen's very head is like a crown to her body, as Mt. Carmel crowns the beauty of the land of Israel. By her association with the king, the bride takes on the purple color of royalty in the locks of her hair. The king is held captive by the beauty of her tresses. He takes complete possession of her being in heavenly beatitude. The bride exclaims, "I am my beloved's, and his desire is for me" (7:10). The contemplative knowledge of heaven, imbued with love, will be a penetrating and experiential knowledge. We will enjoy the Lord's eternal embrace and savor his goodness, just as the Psalmist invites us to taste and see that the Lord is good (see Ps 34). These images of touch and taste in the Song capture the immediacy of union of the soul and God in heaven, and the savoring of that union in expanded contemplative awareness.

The Kingship of Christ

The bride has been transformed by the king's love into his very likeness. By union with the king, she has become the queen. By conceiving Christ her King, Mary takes on his kingly stature and becomes the queen. Christ's kingship is revealed especially in his ascension to his throne in heaven. Mary's queenship is revealed as she is assumed or taken up into heaven to be united with Christ and to rule at his side. Mary is exalted as the fairest honor of our race, yet her destiny is our destiny, both as individuals and collectively as the Church. Jesus had promised the apostles who stood by him in his trials, "and I confer on you, just as my Father has conferred on me, a kingdom, so that you may eat and drink at my table in my kingdom, and you will sit on thrones judging the twelve tribes of Israel" (Lk 22:29–30). The apostles were given authority to rule in his Church, and, in a moral capacity, to rule the world. Having fought the good fight in keeping the faith, Saint Paul knew that "from now on there is reserved for me the crown of righteousness, which the Lord, the righteous judge, will give me on that day, and not only to me but also to all who have longed for his appearing" (2 Tim 4:7–8). Paul suggests that all of us who persevere in keeping the faith will be crowned with the Lord's glory (see Rev 2:10; 1 Pet 5:4). Mary has the most exalted position as queen of the Church and the twelve apostles (who sit ruling the twelve tribes of Israel) who form her crown.

Mary's destiny is our destiny, since as children of God we share in Christ's kingship. Christ gives us the gift of royal freedom in self-control so that, by denying ourselves in striving for holiness, we win victory over the reign of sin in our flesh.[6] Saint Ambrose explains, "That man is rightly called a king who makes his own body an obedient subject and, by governing himself with suitable rigor, refuses to let his passions breed rebellion in his soul, for he exercises a kind of royal power over himself."[7] We also extend Christ's kingship to the temporal affairs of this world, ordering them toward eternal values. Vatican Council II urges: "Let the laity also by their combined efforts remedy the customs and conditions of the world, if they are an inducement

6. See *Lumen Gentium*, 36.

7. Saint Ambrose, *Psalm 118*:14: 30, in CCC, no. 908.

to sin, that they all may be conformed to the norms of justice and may favor the practice of virtue rather than hinder it. By so doing they will imbue culture and human activity with genuine moral values."[8] Christ extends the blessings of salvation in and through us as we care for one another in self-sacrificing love. As human beings are healed and freed from oppression and come to enjoy the fullness of life in Christ, his kingdom is extended in the world.

All human beings are meant to be kings and queens in their own unique and often humble way. Everyone has a basic need to establish right order through wise ruling of one's life and affairs. Kings and queens traditionally provide fertility and blessing, bearing children and blessing their kingdom's children. Kings and queens symbolize the energy and balance of life. When they are models of virtue, they can serve as wise counselors to others. As the woman in Revelation 12, Mary gives birth to her children in the Church and nurtures them with her life. Through her son's kingship, she crushes the head of the serpent, Satan, and protects her children from evil. The bride in the Song, now as queen beside her king, goes forth with him into the fields and villages where their royal reign is extended to the universe (Song 7:11). In their royal capacity they are not removed from their people, but instead draw near to them.

Queen Saint Elizabeth of Hungary is an example of a compassionate and kind queen who remained close to her people in their need. She was born on July 7, 1207 to the Hungarian King Andrew II and Gertrude of Merania. When Elizabeth was very young, her father arranged for her to be married to Ludwig IV of Thuringia, a German nobleman. Because of this plan,

8. *Lumen Gentium*, 36, 3.

Elizabeth at age four was sent for education to the court of the Landgrave of Thuringia. Elizabeth's mother, Gertrude, was murdered in 1213, when Elizabeth was just six years old. The murder was carried out by Hungarian noblemen due to the conflict between some Germans and the Hungarian nobles. This tragedy dramatically changed Elizabeth's perspective on life and death and she sought peace with prayer. Happiness was returned to her young life in 1221 when she married Ludwig, whom she deeply loved. The couple had three beautiful children. Two of them became members of the nobility and the third entered religious life, becoming abbess of a German convent. Elizabeth continued to live an austerely simple life, full of prayer, penance, and service to the poor. Ludwig, who was now one of the rulers of Thuringia, supported all of Elizabeth's religious endeavors even though she was part of the royal court. She used her royal position to advance her mission for charity. In 1223, Franciscan friars arrived in Thuringia and taught Elizabeth about Francis of Assisi's ideals. From that point on, she decided to live her life mirroring his. She wore simple clothing and set aside time every day to take bread to hundreds of poor people in her land.

When disease and floods struck Thuringia in 1226, Elizabeth cared for the victims. It is said she even gave away the royal clothing and goods to the afflicted people. Elizabeth had a hospital built and provided for almost a thousand poor people daily. Her life was full of love and faith. However, tragedy struck when Ludwig passed away from illness in 1227. Upon hearing the news, she said it felt as if the whole world had died. Elizabeth vowed to never remarry and to live a life similar to a nun, despite pressure from relatives. Her vows included celibacy and an agreement of complete obedience to her confessor and spiritual director, Master Conrad of Marburg. Having received her dowry in 1228, Elizabeth joined the Third Order of Saint Francis. She founded a hospital in his honor where she ministered to the sick and provided support to the poor. Elizabeth's life was consumed by her devotion to God and her charitable labor.

One of Saint Elizabeth's greatest known miracles occurred when she was still alive, the miracle of roses. It is said that during one of her many secret trips to deliver bread to the poor, she encountered her husband Ludwig. He questioned her in order to silence those who suspected that she was stealing treasures from the castle. Ludwig asked Elizabeth to show him what she was carrying under her cloak, and as she lifted the cloak a vision of white and red roses appeared. To Ludwig, this was a sign of God's evident pleasure and protection. Another miracle occurred when Elizabeth placed a leper in the bed she shared with her husband. Her mother-in-law discovered this and, enraged, informed Ludwig. Greatly annoyed, Ludwig pulled back the bedclothes. Instead of a leper, lying there was the figure of Jesus crucified.

After Elizabeth's death, miraculous healings began to occur at her graveside near the hospital she had founded. Examinations were held for those who had been healed from 1232 to 1235. These investigations, along with testimony from Elizabeth's handmaidens and companions and her immense popularity, led to her canonization by Pope Gregory IX on May 27, 1235. Saint Elizabeth is often depicted with a basket of bread to illustrate her devotion to the poor and hungry. She is also depicted in art in scenes representing the "Miracle of Roses" and the "Crucifix in the Bed." Saint Elizabeth has been praised by Pope Benedict XVI as "a true example for all who have roles of leadership," demonstrating that "the exercise of authority, at every level, must be lived as a service to justice and charity, in the constant search for the common good."[9] Elizabeth extended the reign of Christ's justice to her nation, and his mercy to those most in need: the sick and the hungry. Her queenship did not separate her from her people, but instead drew her closer through her greater power and heightened compassion.

Like Elizabeth of Hungary, Mary's queenship affords her the opportunity to do more good for each of us. Her influence in the universe is intensified as she is more disposed to serve us. Jesus said "whoever wishes to be great among you must be your servant" (Mt 20:26). Mary was the greatest woman of all, whom all generations would call blessed. Yet she characterized herself as the humble maidservant of the Lord from the moment God called her. She continues her service to us as she stoops to draw close to us. In her glorified nature she can better sympathize with all our earthly sorrows and bring them to Christ for our comfort. Often, her comfort will be encouragement to accept our sufferings and trials for our growth in holiness and to participate with Christ in his redemption of souls.

Mary's Presence in the Church

In his ascension to the Father, Jesus Christ became more powerfully present to us through his greater extension in space and time, leaving us with the words, "Remember, I am with you always" (Mt 28:20). Now transformed like her risen Lord by his grace, Mary is able to be more present to us in the Church.

9. Benedict XVI, General Audience, Oct. 20, 2010, http://w2.vatican.va/content/benedict-xvi/en/audiences/2010/documents/hf_ben-xvi_aud_20101020.html.

Indeed, she is revealed in Revelation as the true Ark of the Covenant, the dwelling place of God's presence among us. In his homily on the dormition of Mary, the patriarch Saint Germanus of Constantinople explains that though Mary has been assumed from this earth, she has not distanced herself from us. On the contrary, she is close to those who call upon her:

> Still desiring that you might dwell bodily in our midst, the eyes of our souls are compelled to look toward you daily. Indeed, as you were a fellow citizen of our ancestors, even so you dwell with us spiritually, and your ample protection in our regard is like a sign that you are with us. We all hear your voice, and all our voices reach your ears. Through the protection you offer us, we are known by you. We, in our turn, recognize your ever-wonderful assistance. Nothing, not even death, can come between you and your servants. . . . You see everyone, and your vigilance, O Mother of God, extends to all. Yes, our eyes are prevented from seeing you, O Most Holy One, but still you delight to remain in our midst, manifesting yourself in various ways to those who are worthy. Truly, the flesh cannot impede the power and ability of your spirit, because your spirit blows where it wills, being a spirit pure and immaterial, incorruptible and immaculate, a companion spirit of the Holy Spirit, the favorite spirit of the Godhead of the Only-begotten.[10]

Immersed in Christ, Mary fervently desires that the Holy Spirit create in us a new heart (see Ps 51:10). As Christ's kingdom is established in our hearts, she is given reign as queen of our hearts.

As a cooperator in her son's incarnation and redemption, the Blessed Virgin Mary now shares in the kingly rule that Christ

10. Germanus of Constantinople, *Homily 1 on the Dormition*, PG 98, 344B–345A.

exercises over the hearts and minds of human beings. In addition to all the other graced means he uses for our salvation, he also imparts the fruits of redemption to us through the role and work of his most holy Mother. Christ has given Mary to us as our mother and she exercises a queenly rule over us. She is, as Saint Bernard says, "the royal way" by which Christ came to us, and by which we can go to him. The apostle of Marian consecration, Saint Louis de Montfort, writes:

> Mary received from God a far-reaching dominion over the souls of the elect. Otherwise she could not make her dwelling-place in them as God the Father has ordered her to do, and she could not conceive them, nourish them, and bring them forth to eternal life as their mother. She could not have them for her inheritance and her possession and form them in Jesus and Jesus in them. She could not implant in their heart the roots of her virtues, nor be the inseparable associate of the Holy Spirit in all these works of grace. None of these things, I repeat, could she do unless she had received from the Almighty rights and authority over their souls. For God, having given her power over his only-begotten and natural Son, also gave her power over his adopted children.[11]

We should all rejoice in being subjects of Mary our queen, "who, while wielding royal power, is on fire with a mother's love."[12]

A couple years after my ordination, I led a pilgrimage to the great Marian shrines of Fatima in Portugal, and Lourdes in France. The crowning moment of our journey was our visit to

---

11. Saint Louis de Montfort, *True Devotion to Mary* (Bay Shore, NY: Montfort Publications, 1984), par. 37, p. 15.

12. Pius XII, *Ad Caeli Reginam*, 43.

the great city of Paris, where we completed our pilgrimage. There I beheld the architectural symphony that is Notre Dame Cathedral, dedicated to our Blessed Mother. As I entered the magnificent and holy structure, hallowed by centuries of devotion and worship, I trembled in awe. I actually felt my skin prickle ,and shivers ran down my spine. I walked up to the front, around the altar and into the sanctuary, where I saw the centerpiece of the cathedral, a breathtaking sculpture. It was the statue of the Virgin of Compassion (which miraculously survived the devastating 2019 fire). Our Blessed Mother, who had stood faithfully at the foot of the cross until her son's death, now opened her arms to receive his corpse. I imagined the feelings she had endured watching her son die, and how she felt now holding the only remnant of his life—his body. It was the body of the same son she had cradled in her arms at Bethlehem, the same son she had raised at Nazareth, the same son she had watched fulfilling his role as Messiah. What greater suffering could a mother endure than to hold the body of her dead son? As she held Jesus' body, the sword of sorrow pierced her heart, as prophesied by Simeon. I pondered, has anyone besides our blessed Lord known such suffering? If Mary has suffered so greatly, is she not sensitive to the sufferings of our life?

My eyes were distracted by another figure to the right of the Virgin of Compassion. It was King Louis XIII, kneeling before Mary and offering her his scepter and crown, the symbols of his own sovereignty. He was consecrating himself to her as the servant of his queen. What great humility for a king to surrender his power to this lady. He surrendered not only his power, but also his weakness. Mary's open arms receive the king's offering and gather the nation of France as a whole. She offers it together with the death of her Son, the sacrifice for our salvation, the sacrifice pleasing to the Father.

We place our lives in the arms of Mary, confident that she will offer us together with her son to our heavenly Father. We place at Mary's service all our gifts and talents, good works and acts of love. We know that she can purify them and make them a holy sacrifice in union with Jesus. We turn over to Mary not only our goodness, but also our poverty and weakness, our struggles and limitations. How many sins and failings we have. We feel inadequate as we seek to follow the example of our blessed Lord; often discouraged, we might be tempted to give up. Tossed about by the wind and the waves on the ocean of this life and its trials, we grow afraid. And so we turn to Mary, our most gracious queen and advocate, in the prayer *Hail, Holy Queen*. We ask her to turn her eyes of mercy toward us, to look upon us with love and compassion. We ask her to see what we lack, to make up for our weakness with her strength, to fill our sadness with her joy, to change our selfishness into her purity of heart. Mary's Immaculate Heart is like an altar on which all that we are is transformed into a pleasing incense offered to God. She purifies and enriches it with her fullness of grace and virtue in the Holy Spirit.

Our encounter with Mary will always lead us to Jesus. She is one with Jesus in the desires of his heart. Her only desire is that we share the same life of heavenly beatitude that she enjoys. Mary is the queenly maiden of the Song of Songs, who nourishes us with the wine and wheat of Christ's body and blood, which she conceived and bore for the world. As queen, the bride is the tower of David and tower of Lebanon, who protects us from evil and instills fear in her enemies. By the birth of her son, Mary has crushed the head of the ancient serpent, Satan, who is the beast of Revelation. We entrust our lives to her as our exceedingly beautiful queen, knowing that she will guide us to Christ our King.

Questions for Reflection and Discussion

1. Do you acknowledge Mary as queen? If so, how do you relate to her? What elements of her queenship stand out for you?
2. What elements of the description of the bride in her glory as the queenly maiden are attractive to you? How do you see these characteristics embodied by Mary?
3. How do you experience the kingship of Christ and the queenship of Mary in your own life as a Christian? How is Christ King in your life? How do you live and exercise kingship or queenship?
4. In what ways does your kingship or queenship draw you closer to others and enable you to help them? How do you use your power to serve? How are you tempted to lord your power over other people?
5. How do you experience Mary as a queen who is close to you? How do you experience her loving presence and compassionate gaze?
6. Have you ever made a consecration to Jesus through Mary? Can you entrust yourself to the Lord by placing your life in her hands? How can you serve Mary as your queen?

Prayer Exercises

1. Consider Roy Schoeman's conversion story (pp. 215–216). Pray with Revelation 12:1–9 and ask for the grace to see Mary's inner beauty and to love her more.
2. Reflect on the role of the queen mother in Israel's history (pp. 217–219). Pray with Proverbs 31:1–9 or John

2:1–11 and ask for the grace to know Mary's queenly reign, help, and advice.

3. Ponder the description of the bride as the queenly maiden (pp. 219–220). Pray with Song 7:1–13 and ask for the grace to appreciate Mary's characteristics as queen.
4. Consider the story of Saint Elizabeth of Hungary (pp. 222–224). Pray with Revelation 12:1–9 and ask for the grace to exercise Christ's kingship and Mary's queenship in your life (see also 2 Timothy 4:7–8; Revelation 2:10; 1 Peter 5:4).
5. Ponder the quotes of Saint Germanus (p. 226) and Saint Louis de Montfort (p. 227). Pray with Revelation 12:1–9 and ask for the grace to know Mary's love and tenderness.

Chapter 13

Maternal Presence

[B] O that you were like a brother to me,
    who nursed at my mother's breast!
If I met you outside, I would kiss you,
    and no one would despise me.
I would lead you and bring you
    into the house of my mother,
    and into the chamber of the one who bore me.
I would give you spiced wine to drink,
    the juice of my pomegranates.
O that his left hand were under my head,
    and that his right hand embraced me!
I adjure you, O daughters of Jerusalem,
    do not stir up or awaken love
    until it is ready!
[D] Who is that coming up from the wilderness,
    leaning upon her beloved?
[B] Under the apple tree I awakened you.
    There your mother was in labor with you;
    there she who bore you was in labor.
Set me as a seal upon your heart,

as a seal upon your arm;
for love is strong as death,
passion fierce as the grave.
Its flashes are flashes of fire,
a raging flame.
Many waters cannot quench love,
neither can floods drown it (Song 8:1–7a).

A great portent appeared in heaven: a woman clothed with the sun, with the moon under her feet, and on her head a crown of twelve stars. She was pregnant and was crying out in birth pangs, in the agony of giving birth. . . . And she gave birth to a son, a male child, who is to rule all the nations with a rod of iron. But her child was snatched away and taken to God and to his throne; and the woman fled into the wilderness, where she has a place prepared by God, so that there she can be nourished for one thousand two hundred sixty days. . . . Then the dragon was angry with the woman, and went off to make war on the rest of her children, those who keep the commandments of God and hold the testimony of Jesus. (Rev 12:1–2, 5–6, 17)

When Saint John Bosco began his school and orphanage for the poor boys of Turin in 1846, he soon discovered something was missing—a maternal presence. With urgency, he begged his mother Margaret to come and live with the boys. Though she had struggled to raise her boys on her own as a widow, and had now reached a comfortable time in her life at age fifty-eight, she was inspired by Mary's *fiat* to immediately accept his invitation. She left her home with a few necessities and took up residence in poverty at the orphanage, bringing her feminine and motherly presence. John often consulted her for advice and relied on her motherly wisdom in making decisions. If he had to be away, he felt secure in knowing that Margaret would take charge of the boys. He even left her to greet important visitors and benefactors. She also helped him keep his teaching down to earth when he tended toward excessive intellectualism. By 1854 there were 110 lads. With poor means, she took care of the boys' meals and lodging, preparing meals of hearty soup and polenta (an Italian dish of boiled cornmeal). She tended the vegetable garden, fed the chickens and rabbits, laundered, mended, and ironed the children's clothing. Margaret often worked well into the night while the children slept. She cared for them while they were ill. Her greatest challenge lay in dealing with the unruly boys. She showed tremendous patience with the bad manners and carelessness of the street orphans. The children would do things such as trample her garden or knock down the clothes drying in the sun. One evening her patience wore thin and she broke down in tears while talking to her son. She said that four years were enough, and she could take no more of this life. Each day the boys tried her patience with something new. She only desired to return home to a life of peace. John listened to his mother with compassion and then lifted his eyes to the crucifix on the wall. His mother followed his eyes to Jesus and began to weep, knowing that John was right in inviting her to embrace the cross. After that, Margaret never again complained. She was always present to her orphan children throughout each day. The children loved to speak with her, finding in her words advice, exhortation to virtue, correction, and comfort. She offered wise sayings and taught them to pray and receive the sacraments fervently. Her influence was so great that she has been called the co-founder of the oratory of Saint John Bosco and the Salesian order of priests.[1]

Mother of the Church

Knowing the tremendous influence his mother Mary had had on him throughout his life, Jesus desired his Church to have her as her mother. As Mary and John stood at the foot of the Cross, Jesus said to his mother, "Woman, here is your son" (Jn 19:26). Like Momma Margaret, Mary would maternally watch over members of the Church. She would care for their spiritual needs, teaching them to pray and receive the grace of God. She would show them how to cultivate an interior relationship with her son, in order to make their apostolate fruitful. In cooperation with the Holy Spirit, Mary would remind them of all that her son said and did, helping them to imitate Jesus.

Mary is the new Eve, the "woman" who is "mother of the living." She mothers all who come to life in Christ. As the body of Christ, the Church was conceived with the conception of Christ at the annunciation. Everything Christ did throughout his life was to establish his kingdom, which is present in his Church. Motherhood involves birth. The Church was born on the Cross from the side of Christ. Just as Adam was cast into a deep sleep and Eve was formed from his side, so too, as Christ slept the sleep of death, his bride, the Church was formed from his open

1. See Joseph Aubrey, *Mamma Margaret, Don Bosco's First Collaborator*, http://www.bosconet.aust.com/pdf/MAMMA-MG.pdf.

side. As his side was opened with a lance, blood and water flowed forth, the source of the sacramental life of the Church. We are born again of water and the Spirit in holy Baptism. We are nourished by the flesh and blood of Christ in the Holy Eucharist, the same flesh and blood he took from his mother.

Mary's motherhood is extended to all the faithful who are born through the paschal mystery of Jesus' death and resurrection. In the Book of Revelation, the "woman" gives birth in labor pains. These labor pains for Mary were not at the birth of Jesus at Bethlehem, but at his death on the Cross. That was when she became the mother of the Church. Jesus had spoken of his own death in terms of enduring labor pains, for himself, and for his disciples (see Jn 16:20–22). Christ chose to become man and save us through Mary's cooperation at the foot of the cross. At Calvary Mary was totally dependent on her son and strengthened by his passion. At that point of total surrender, crushed by the death of Jesus, she was given a new role to be mother of the Church. It would again demand complete abandonment to the will of God as she expanded her heart to include all of God's children. It is completely by grace that she will assume this role of universal motherhood. Mary teaches us first and foremost to depend on God's grace, to lean on our beloved (Song 8:4), to receive God's gift of self in our hearts.

The grace bestowed upon us in Christ Jesus has come to us through Mary and continues to do so. Vatican II teaches:

> The maternal duty of Mary toward men in no wise obscures or diminishes this unique mediation of Christ, but rather shows his power. For all the salvific influence of the Blessed Virgin on men originates, not from some inner necessity, but from the divine pleasure. It flows forth from the superabundance of the merits of Christ, rests on his mediation, depends

> entirely on it and draws all its power from it. In no way does it impede, but rather does it foster the immediate union of the faithful with Christ.[2]

Mary's presence at the birth of the Church from the Cross as the new Eve, the mother of all the living in Christ, accentuates her maternal role in the birth of grace in our hearts.

The entire Church shares in the motherhood of Mary. Mary is first and foremost a member of the Church, receiving saving grace from the merits of her son. She is the holiest and most excellent member of the Church, serving as a model of the Church in the way of faith, charity, and perfect union with Christ.[3] Joseph Ratzinger proclaims: "Everything said about the *ecclesia* in the Bible is true of her, and vice versa: the Church learns concretely what she is and is meant to be by looking at Mary. Mary is her mirror, the pure measure of her being, because Mary is wholly within the measure of Christ and of God, is through and through his habitation. And what other reason could the *ecclesia* have for existing than to become a dwelling for God in the world?"[4] As the perfect disciple of Christ, Mary conceived him in the dwelling place of her heart before conceiving him in her womb. She becomes for us a model of discipleship and shows us the one thing necessary—to conceive and bear Christ in our lives. Saint Augustine writes: "Did, perhaps, the Virgin Mary not do the Father's will, she who in faith believed, in faith conceived, who was chosen so that man's salvation would

---

2. *Lumen Gentium*, 60.

3. See Saint Ambrose, quoted by Saint Augustine, in *Sermons,* 72a, in Cantalamessa, 124.

4. Joseph Ratzinger, *Mary, the Church at the Source* (San Francisco: Ignatius Press, 2005), 66.

be born of her and who was created by Christ before Christ was created in her? Certainly, the holy Mary did the Father's will and therefore, it is a higher thing for Mary to have been Christ's disciple than to have been Christ's Mother."[5] Mary is the first-born child of the Church as a perfect disciple, having been full of grace from her conception and bearing Christ in her heart and womb in the Incarnation.

The bride of the Song of Songs is a daughter of her mother who conceived her (8:2). Mary is the Daughter of Sion representing the best of the Old Covenant with Israel, who was the daughter of the Lord. Mary is also the first and most exemplary daughter of the Church, born of Christ at the Cross. The bride of the Song brings the Bridegroom to the place where her mother conceived her, that is, Calvary in Jerusalem. She compares her Bridegroom to an apple tree (8:5), the most fruitful of trees. The Cross of Jesus is the most fruitful of trees, bearing members of his body, the Church. By grace we are adopted sons and daughters of our heavenly Father, truly made brothers and sisters of Christ. This happens in the Church, the mother who conceives and bears us. The bride now speaks of her desire to be as a sister to her Bridegroom. By consenting to God's will, Mary helped to bring about the Incarnation whereby the Word of God became flesh and Jesus became one of us as our brother. Mary, by grace, as an adopted daughter of the Father, is also sister to Christ, as we all are his brothers and sisters. She totally depends on Christ her son for the grace of her entire life, just as the bride completely depends on her Bridegroom. The bride exclaims: "O that his left hand were under my head, and that his right hand embraced me!" (8:3).

---

5. Saint Augustine, *Sermons*, 72a in Cantalamessa, 61.

The Role of the Holy Spirit

Jesus tells us that "whoever does the will of my Father in heaven is my brother and sister and mother" (Mt 12:50). Mary is the one who did the Father's will, hearing the Word of God and obeying it (see Lk 11:28). Mary had waited upon the Lord for his grace at the annunciation and was filled with the Holy Spirit also at the visitation, uttering her Magnificat of praise. At Pentecost, she taught the disciples how to wait upon God until the Spirit came to clothe them from on high (see Lk 24:49; Acts 1:6–8). It was not by their own efforts, but in the power of the Spirit that they praised God and served as his witnesses. Throughout the Acts of the Apostles, the same dynamic is repeated. After being released from prison, Peter and John pray with the community. They are shaken and filled with the Holy Spirit (see Acts 4:31). They are sent to Samaria to pray for the new disciples so that they might receive the Holy Spirit (see Acts 8:15). When Saul prays, the Lord sends him Ananias so that he will regain his sight and be filled with the Holy Spirit. Clearly, the star player of the Acts of the Apostles is not Peter or Paul or any of the others, but the Holy Spirit who comes upon them to accomplish the works of God. From the beginning of Acts we learn from Mary to give priority to prayer and to wait for the Spirit to act in and through us. If we do not follow Mary's example in this, we are acting on our own, as one author notes:

> Without the Holy Spirit: God is far away, Christ stays in the past, the Gospel is a dead letter, the Church is simply an organization, authority a matter of domination, mission a matter of propaganda, liturgy no more than an evocation, Christian living a slave morality. But with the Holy Spirit: the cosmos is resurrected and groans with the birth-pangs of the kingdom, the risen Christ is there, the Gospel is the power of life, the

> Church shows forth the life of the Trinity, authority is a liberating service, mission is a Pentecost, the liturgy is both memorial and anticipation, human action is deified.[6]

By the power of the Spirit, the Church becomes a tender mother by her preaching, sacraments, and instruction as she brings forth and nurtures God's children for eternal life.

A priest involved in formation work once overheard two seminarians talking about which Bible translations they liked best. One said, "I enjoy the New American Bible. It's plainer and easy to decipher." The other said, "I prefer the New Jerusalem Bible. It's more lyrical and lends itself better to prayer." The priest felt inspired to pipe up: "I love my mother's interpretation. She translates the text into action. It's more vibrant and you can comprehend it really well!"[7] He was speaking about his own biological mother putting the word of God into action, but how much more true this would be of our heavenly mother Mary's example.

Mary shows us how to become mothers by obeying the word of God: "Here am I, the servant of the Lord; let it be with me according to your word" (Lk 1:38). Her response to the Angel Gabriel characterized her whole life with Jesus. Filled with the Spirit, her life became an imitation of Jesus to the point of following him to the Cross. Her final words in the Gospel, "do whatever he tells you" (Jn 2:5), are a testament to her life of practicing that dictum. The Holy Spirit leads the Church to the

---

6. Ignatius of Latakia, Goodall, Norman and World Council of Churches. Assembly Uppsala, Sweden, 4th: 1968 *The Uppsala report 1968: Official Report of the Fourth Assembly of the World Council of Churches, Uppsala July 4–20, 1968*. World Council of Churches, Geneva, 1968.

7. See Mark Link, *Vision 2000, Praying Scripture in a Contemporary Way*, Cycle A (Allen, TX: Tabor Publishing, 1992), 356.

same obedience, conforming our hearts to Jesus so that we might imitate him. Jesus had said, "the one who believes in me will also do the works that I do" (Jn 14:12). In Acts we see the Church, in obedience to the Spirit, imitating Jesus in doing his works. As Jesus proclaimed the word, so too do the disciples. As Stephen is dying, he forgives his persecutors as Jesus did from the Cross. The disciples heal the sick, cast out demons, and raise the dead in imitation of Jesus. They are completely available to do the works of God. The Church becomes the very seal of Jesus Christ, just as the bride says: " Set me as a seal upon your heart, as a seal upon your arm" (8:6). The seal was the mark of the owner that became the guarantor of his approval. The Church, sealed with the Spirit, becomes the identifying mark of the presence and action of Jesus Christ.

Mary as Teacher

As mother, the Church is also our teacher. As the most noble and exemplary member of the Church, Mary shows us how to exercise our teaching role. She does not merely offer us doctrine, which is important, but she gives us the very person of Jesus Christ, the Word made flesh in her womb. The Church continues to give this same living Word preached by the apostles to human beings. Henri de Lubac explains: "The transmission of this Word by those who are its 'servants' is not simple teaching, mere 'catechesis.' It is, for the one who really wants to open his heart to it, the communication of the life of Jesus Christ, Word of the Father."[8] Saint Hippolytus adds: "The Church never

8. Henri de Lubac, *The Motherhood of the Church*, trans. Sr. Sergia Englund, O.C.D. (San Francisco: Ignatius Press, 1982), 60. www.ignatius.com. Used with permission.

ceases to give birth to the Word from her heart . . . and because she ceaselessly gives birth to Christ, God and man, she teaches all peoples."[9] No one gave us Christ better than the Virgin Mary. We are all called to imitate her in transmitting Jesus to others through our lives and witness. We imitate Mary in conceiving Christ when we contemplate his word in prayer and receive him in the sacraments. We are then able to transmit Christ to the world primarily by the testimony of our lives and then through speaking the truth in dialogue. The world values witnesses who authentically live out their faith, more than mere instructors. The Church continuously gives birth in the preaching of the word, the administration of Baptism, prayers, various works: everything is the activity of the Church giving birth to, developing, and carrying to completion in the heart of believers this gift from God which is eternal life.[10]

A wonderful example of this ministry is found in the life of Saint Peter Claver, who preached the Gospel with actions that spoke louder than words. A native of Spain, the young Jesuit left his homeland forever in 1610 to be a missionary in the colonies of the New World. He sailed into Cartagena, a rich port city on the shores of the Caribbean. He was ordained there in 1615. By this time the slave trade had been established in the Americas for nearly 100 years, and Cartagena was its major hub. Ten thousand slaves poured into the port each year after crossing the Atlantic from West Africa. They suffered such foul and inhuman conditions that an estimated one-third of them died in

9. Saint Hippolytus, *De Antichristo*, c. 61 (GCS, Hipp. Vol. I, 2:41–42), in Henri de Lubac, *The Motherhood of the Church*, 64.

10. See Karl Delahaye, *Ecclesia Mater* (Paris: Editions du Cerf, 1964), 120 in de Lubac, *The Motherhood of the Church*, 65.

transit. As soon as a slave ship entered the port, Peter Claver climbed into its infested hold to minister to the ill-treated and exhausted passengers. One entry in his diary reads:

> Yesterday . . . the day of the Most Holy Trinity, a huge ship of black people of the rivers appeared on land. We went there loaded with two baskets of oranges, lemons, sponge cakes and other things. We boarded and . . . passed many people until we reached a large group of sick people who were lying on the floor. They were wet and muddy, and were using a mound of tiles and bricks as a bed, even though they were naked with not a thread of clothing to protect themselves. We threw blankets out and went to bring tables from another cellar, and we established a place to take care of them. We carried the very infirm in our arms, and built a ramp to transport the others. . . . Their renewed spirits and the gratitude on their faces when they looked at us was wonderful to see! We spoke with them, not with words, but with hands and deeds. . . . Words were not needed. We stood next to them or knelt with them, and we washed their faces and bodies with wine. . . . And made every effort we could to bolster the spirits of those who were sick.[11]

Peter Claver testified to Christ first by his heroic works of charity, and only afterward with instruction. He then administered the sacraments in which he became a parent to souls born again in Christ. With the help of interpreters, he gave basic instructions and assured his brothers and sisters of their human dignity and God's love. During the forty years of his ministry, Claver instructed and baptized an estimated 300,000 slaves. Father Claver's apostolate extended beyond his care for slaves.

11. Peter Claver, *Letter to His Superior,* May 31, 1627 (author translation).

He became a moral force, indeed, the apostle of Cartagena. He preached in the city square and gave missions to sailors and traders. He also gave missions in the country, during which he avoided, when possible, the hospitality of the planters and owners and lodged in the slave quarters instead.

The Church as Mother

Peter Claver shows us how the Church herself becomes a mother by her charity, preaching, and sacraments. In these "she brings forth to a new and immortal life the sons who are born to her in baptism, conceived of the Holy Spirit and born of God."[12] Saint Paul exclaims to the Galatians, "My little children, for whom I am again in the pain of childbirth until Christ is formed in you" (4:19). The Church as a collective exercises motherhood, and so does each individual soul that believes, conceives, and brings forth the Word of God after the pattern of Mary. The medieval theologian Blessed Isaac of Stella combines these truths:

> Mary and the Church are one mother and many mothers; one virgin and many virgins: both mother, both virgin. Both one and the other conceive without concupiscence by the same Spirit; both one and the other give God a progeny without sin. One, without any stain of sin, brought forth the Head of the body; the other, in the remission of sin, brings forth the body of the Head. Both are the mother of Christ, but neither one brings forth the whole without the other. That is why, in Scripture divinely inspired, what is universally said of the Virgin Mother Church, is said, in a special way, of the Virgin

12. *Lumen Gentium*, 64.

> Mother Mary; and what is said in a special way of Mary is intended, in a general sense, of the Virgin Mother Church.... Finally, every faithful soul, spouse of the Word of God, mother, daughter, and sister of Christ, is seen to be, in her own way, a fertile virgin. God's Wisdom itself, which is the Father's Word, therefore applies to the Church what is especially said of Mary and individually of every soul that believes.[13]

Blessed Isaac helps us to understand why the Church has always understood that the woman of Revelation is at once the Blessed Virgin Mary and the whole Church. She is giving birth to Christ and to her children in Christ. The bride desires to be awakened in the house of her mother. She represents Mary, united to Christ in the midst of her mother, Israel, which will become the Church. Saint Augustine taught that Mary is blessed and holy, but that the Church is more important than she. Mary is a member of the whole body, and the whole body is more important than a member of the body.[14] Mary's motherhood will result in the motherhood of the greater collective Church.

As children of God within the Church, our mother, we receive the life of grace. Mary teaches us this fundamental receptivity. Before we give, we must learn how to receive, since we cannot give what we don't have. A mother teaches us receptivity as our fundamental stance toward life. I think of how my own mother received and conceived the life of each one of us her children. We receive the gift of our own existence from God and through our parents. The first thing we realize as children is that

13. Blessed Isaac of Stella, *Sermons, PL* 194, pp. 1862–1863, 1865.

14. See Saint Augustine, Sermons, 72 A (Denis 25), 7, in Cantalamessa, 88.

our existence comes from someone else. Hopefully we never forget that our existence comes from God. This truth is the essence of remaining a child before God. Our mother is there for us to secure and affirm our existence. My family was blessed in that our mother was always there for us as children and affirmed our own existence with her love and constant care. We receive the life of grace from God in the Church. Faith itself is a gift from God. The content of our faith does not come from ourselves, but from the Church. We must fundamentally receive all of this from God.

Jesus' fundamental stance and attitude toward life was receptivity, which he learned from Mary. Humanly, he received life from his mother. Mary received Jesus in saying her yes to God in order to conceive and bear him. Jesus received life eternally as generated from the Father. Jesus continued to receive his identity and mission from his Father. His food was to do the Father's will. He received his mission at his mother's instigation. At Cana she invited him to step forth as Bridegroom to provide wine for the wedding feast. Eventually Jesus would provide his Blood in the form of wine at the Last Supper and in dying for us on the Cross. He received and accepted suffering and death from the Father, trusting it would lead to greater life for himself and for us all. Mary taught Jesus this fundamental receptivity in his humanity and teaches us as a Church how to receive so that we can give to others.

Mary as a Model Disciple

Mary, who taught Jesus how to receive in his humanity, then became the disciple of Christ. She is the bride who desired to be taught by her lover, Christ. Henri de Lubac explains how Mary was the most understanding and responsive disciple: "And finally, on Calvary through the three long hours, holding the Church's place at the foot of the cross, she received from her son the definitive teaching—a teaching not of words but of act, through which all words are illuminated."[15] Paul Claudel reflects that rather than weep at the foot of the cross, Mary was learning her catechism lesson on behalf of the whole Church, which had just been established in her person. Mary bridged the gap between the Old and the New Testaments. Everything she had learned from her mother, including the teachings of Moses and the prophets, and the promise to Abraham and David, was being fulfilled as she stood beneath the cross of her son, Jesus.[16]

Like the bride who desired to be taught by the Bridegroom in the house of her mother, Mary was being taught by her son within the newly formed Church. At the foot of the cross, Mary was the best of pupils, able to comprehend and receive Jesus' total outpouring of love. In response she completely poured herself out in compassion. She was willing to abandon herself totally to her son's will in assuming the motherhood of the Church. As mother to us all, she will instruct us in Jesus' teaching to love one another as he has loved us. Mary wholly received Jesus' gift of redemption and sanctification from the cross and communicates it to us as our mother in the order of grace. She teaches us how to receive the Lord's grace and to convey it to others.

Some Christians quite happily receive God's gifts with gratitude, while doing nothing to share those gifts with others. Other Christians not only receive God's gifts, but also respond in

15. Henri de Lubac, *The Splendor of the Church*, trans. Michael Mason (San Francisco: Ignatius Press, 1986), 344. www.ignatius.com. Used with permission.

16. See Paul Claudel, *L'Epee et le miroir* (Paris: Éditions Gallimard, 1939), 74–75, in de Lubac, *The Splendor of the Church*, 345.

gratitude. They energetically transmit those graces to others in dedicated service to the Lord. In so doing, they are enriched all the more with God's grace. When I was in Israel, I visited two great bodies of water, the Sea of Galilee and the Dead Sea. The famous Dead Sea is located in the Mediterranean basin. It is called the Dead Sea because there is absolutely no life in it, even though it is forty-two miles long, eleven miles wide at its widest point, and 1,237 feet deep. It is one of the saltiest bodies of water on earth, almost nine times saltier than normal ocean water. This high density of salt never allows even the slightest hint of marine flora or fauna to survive and flourish. The Dead Sea is so salty because it never flows out. It receives water from the River Jordan but keeps it all to itself. It is so much below the mean sea level that the water has no outlet. Some water gets evaporated leaving the salts behind, and in the process creates the lifeless, most uninhabitable environment.

To the north of this Dead Sea is the Sea of Galilee. It is only thirteen miles by eight miles—rather small in comparison to the Dead Sea—but it holds great treasures. It is rich with the most exotic flora and fauna. It is home to at least twenty different types of fish. In fact, this sea has supported the lives of many for over two millennia through the flourishing fisheries of the region and the plentiful harvest of crops in the lands surrounding its waters. Although very tiny as compared to the huge Dead Sea, the Sea of Galilee is bursting with life because it shares its waters. The same River Jordan flows into this sea too, but the Sea of Galilee allows its waters to flow out. And this is precisely what makes it so healthy, vibrant, and brimming with life. It is the same with God's grace, which is not only given for us, but is meant to overflow to others. God didn't pour love into our hearts to remain stagnant for ourselves alone; his grace is meant flow out in love to others.

The bride has been awakened by love and gives completely of herself to her beloved, offering him pomegranates and spiced wine to drink. She understands that her mother's labor pains were necessary for her birth, and is willing to endure the same in conceiving and giving birth to others. The Woman of Revelation, symbolizing both Mary and the Church, conceives not only Christ (12:5), but her other children (12:17). She is in continuous labor, giving birth to new members of the body of Christ through her apostolic labors. Each Christian shares in these labors as we imitate Mary in the one thing necessary, to conceive Christ in our hearts and to bear him to the world.

Questions for Reflection and Discussion

1. How have you experienced God as a motherly presence, in your family, in the Church? How do you relate to Mary as a mother? Do you perceive the motherhood of God revealed through her?
2. Are you aware of sharing in the spiritual motherhood of the Church, conceiving and bearing Christ to the world? Have you experienced labor pains in giving birth to God's grace?
3. How do you experience dependence on God; how much are you able to surrender to him? What does Mary teach you about how to be obedient to the Lord?
4. How has the witness and teaching of others helped you to come to Christ? How do you teach Christ to others by your being, actions, and words?
5. How well do you pass on to others the gift you have received? How do you find yourself enriched by giving the love of Christ to others?

Prayer Exercises

1. Ponder the story of Saint John Bosco's mother Margaret (pp. 234–236). Pray with Song 8:1–7 and ask for the grace to know Mary's maternal presence in your life.
2. Reflect on Joseph Ratzinger's quote about Mary as the mirror of the Church (p. 238). Pray with Revelation 12:1–17 and ask for the grace to imitate Mary in her motherhood.
3. Consider Christ crucified as the apple tree bearing the fruit of redemption (p. 239). Pray with John 19:17–30 and ask for the grace to wholeheartedly receive the gift of salvation.
4. Ponder the story of Saint Peter Claver serving the slaves (p. 244). Pray with Galatians 4:1–20 and ask for the grace to bear witness to Christ by your presence, deeds, and words.
5. Reflect on the image of the Sea of Galilee vs. the Dead Sea (p. 249). Pray with James 2:14–26 and ask for the grace to express your faith in works of charity.

Chapter 14

Beauty Unveiled

[B] Set me as a seal upon your heart,
 as a seal upon your arm;
for love is strong as death,
 passion fierce as the grave.
Its flashes are flashes of fire,
 a raging flame.
Many waters cannot quench love,
 neither can floods drown it. (Song 8:6–7a)

And I saw the holy city, the new Jerusalem, coming down out of heaven from God, prepared as a bride adorned for her husband.... Then one of the seven angels ... came and said to me, "Come, I will show you the bride, the wife of the Lamb." And in the spirit he carried me away to a great, high mountain and showed me the holy city Jerusalem coming down out of heaven from God. It has the glory of God and a radiance like a very rare jewel, like jasper, clear as crystal.... But the throne of God and of the Lamb will be in it, and his servants will worship him; they will see his face, and his name will be on

their foreheads. And there will be no more night; they need
no light of lamp or sun, for the Lord God will be their light,
and they will reign forever and ever. . . .
The Spirit and the bride say, "Come."
And let everyone who hears say, "Come."
And let everyone who is thirsty come.
Let anyone who wishes take the water of life as a gift.
(Rev 21:2, 9–11; 22:3–5, 17)

Douglas Hyde was once a committed socialist and former publishing supervisor of Britain's socialist paper. As its editor, he began to study the Catholic Church in order to destroy it in his articles. But he was surprised as he studied. The more he examined the Church, the more mentally convinced he became of its truth. Yet something was keeping him from embracing the faith. He was riding to work in London one day on the passenger train. When it reached its destination at the Ely Place station, he looked up at a sign he had seen countless times before. It read, "Saint Etheldreda's Catholic Church." He felt inspired to get off the train and visit the church. When he went in, he sat in the back, wondering what peculiar force had directed him there. Then a young lady entered the church. She ambled down the main aisle and headed directly toward a statue of Mary. As she passed him, Hyde noticed the agitated expression on her face. The girl knelt at Mary's feet for quite a while. Then she stood up and headed for one of the exits. As she passed him once more, Hyde saw that her agitation was gone. She appeared absolutely serene. He now knelt down and gazed upward to the Virgin's countenance, wondering how one petitioned Mary. In his book *I Believed,* he wrote: "How did one pray to Our Lady? I did not know. . . . At last I heard myself mumbling something which seemed appropriate enough when I began it, but petered out, becoming miserably inappropriate. But it did not matter. I knew my search was at an end. . . . Outside the church I tried to remember the words I had said and almost laughed as I recalled them. They were those of a dance tune . . . 'Oh, sweet and lovely lady, be good, Oh, lady, be good to me.'"[1]

Mary, Our Advocate

Mary desires the best for us, and she knows the needs of our hearts. She is the mediatrix of all graces that come to us from her son through his incarnation and redemption. Christ did not choose to come to us only once through Mary; he continues to choose to come to us through her. Before she died, Saint Thérèse of Lisieux wrote: "I feel that my mission is soon to begin—my mission to make others love God as I love Him . . . to teach souls my *little way* . . . I will spend my heaven in doing good upon earth."[2] Saint Thérèse describes well our Lady's mission, magnified to a much greater degree, as intercessor on our behalf. While she was still on earth, Mary showed her intercessory power with Jesus when she asked him for a favor at the wedding feast of Cana. She asked on behalf of the married couple and even

1. Mark Link, *Illustrated Sunday Homilies,* Years A, B, C/Series I, Year A, Assumption, 92.

2. Saint Thérèse of Lisieux, *Novissima Verba* (July 17, 1897). http://www.gutenberg.org/cache/epub/16772/pg16772-images.html.

overcame Jesus' seeming reluctance. It seems that Mary can command her son because her will is perfectly aligned with his in desiring our good. Jesus told us, "If in my name you ask me for anything, I will do it" (Jn 14:14). When Saint Catherine of Genoa asked the Lord for something in prayer, she would sometimes hear her Beloved say to her, "Command, for love can do it."[3] In our love for our mother we can also boldly command her, knowing she desires what is best for us for our salvation and sanctification. In his *Memorare* prayer, Saint Bernard reminds Mary that "never was it known that anyone who fled to your protection, implored your help, or sought your intercession was left unaided." Then he adds, "O Mother of the Word Incarnate, despise not my petitions, but in your mercy hear and answer them." In the ancient hymn *Ave Maris Stella*, we command Mary according to her essential intercessory role: "Show yourself to be a Mother: Take the prayers we offer you to him, who was born for us, so that he accepts them as yours."

In union with the Holy Spirit Mary is truly our advocate. She reveals the truth of God who is not only a transcendent, provident father, but is also at our side as a maternal, nurturing presence. Eve was created as the final masterpiece of God's creation. She was meant to be not just a "helpmate" of Adam, but a companion and a kind of saving presence. Hebrew scholar Robert Alter explains the full meaning of the Hebrew word for "helpmate" *(ezer konegdo)* as "sustainer beside him."[4] Every other time this word is used in the Hebrew scriptures it refers to God as our savior. God is revealing himself through the woman as the

---

3. Saint Catherine of Genoa, *The Life and Doctrine of St. Catherine of Genoa*, http://www.saintsbooks.net/books/St.%20Catherine%20of%20Genoa%20-%20Life%20and%20Doctrine.pdf, p. 41.

4. Robert Alter, in Eldridge, *Captivating*, 31.

sustainer and help in time of need.[5] Eve failed in her role to be a nurturing advocate to Adam. As the new Eve, Mary fulfills her saving and sustaining role throughout the New Testament—in her visit to Elizabeth in need, as she intercedes for the couple at Cana, and when she stands by Jesus as a consoling presence during his crucifixion. Through Mary, we discover the presence and love of God which is "strong as death" (Song 8:6).

Luca Di Tolve was a homosexual activist in Italy who at twenty years of age exchanged his Christian values for pleasure and wealth. Just when many of his friends were dying of AIDS, Luca was diagnosed as HIV positive. He became ill and weak and his world seemed to collapse. He felt as if no one truly loved him. Luca felt the spirit of death torment him within. His mother had given him some beautiful icons of the Virgin Mary, which he hung in the hallway of his house. Luca started to believe that Mary was not just an image or a tale, but that she really existed. It was then that he asked for help, clutching a rosary to pray, even though he didn't remember the mysteries. Luca began to feel a warmth and serenity to the point of seeing Mary in the heart of his conscience. He knelt in a kind of cardiac arrest of love, his heart enfolded by a loving maternal presence. Mary extended her hands and told him to move forward. With compassion for his suffering she told him to keep moving like a child making his first steps. Luca realized he could keep moving, confident that even if he fell that Jesus would raise him up. He overcame his phobia of leaving the house and went to Mass. He confessed his sins and, like Saint Paul, experienced the scales of his blindness falling from his eyes. He ultimately felt lively and

---

5. See Robert Alter, Gen 2:16 in *Genesis: Translation and Commentary* (New York: W.W. Norton and Co., 1996).

robust in his conversion.[6] Mary's love brought him from the verge of fatality to healing and a new life in Christ.

Mary's love is strong as death and helps to preserve us from death as the wages of sin. Saint Bernard of Clairvaux speaks of the saving help of Mary, Star of the Sea, in the midst of trials and temptations:

> O you who find yourself tossed about by the storms of life, turn not your eyes from the brightness of this Star, if you would not be overwhelmed by its boisterous waves. If the winds of temptations rise, if you fall among the rocks of tribulations, look up at the Star, call on Mary. If anger, covetousness, or other passions beat on the vessel of your soul, look up to Mary. If you begin to sink in the gulf of melancholy and despair, think on Mary. In dangers, in distress, in perplexities, think on Mary, call on Mary. Let her not depart from your lips, let her not depart from your heart, and, that you may win the suffrage of her prayers, never depart from the example of her life. Following her, you will never go astray; when you implore her aid, you will never yield to despair; thinking on her, you will not err; under her patronage you will never wander; beneath her protection you will not fear; she being your guide, you will not weary; if she be your propitious Star, you will arrive safely in the port, and experience for yourself the truth of the words, "And the virgin's name was Mary."[7]

Mary is like the bride of the Song, who is the seal set on her Bridegroom's heart and arm. The Bridegroom never ceases to

---

6. See "Former Activist Helps Others with Same Sex Attraction, Blessed Mother Showed Luca Di Tolve the Way to Christ," Luca Di Tolve, Interview with Roxanne King, *National Catholic Register*, August 4, 2019.

7. Saint Bernard of Clairvaux, *Sermons of St. Bernard on Advent and Christmas* (New York: Benzinger, 1909), 47. https://archive.org/details/sermonsofstberna00bernuoft/page/46.

think of her on his heart. She accompanies him wherever he goes in whatever he does, holding on to his arm. Everything that she does will be an extension of his arm and done by his power. Blaise Arminjon explains: "And because she will be his seal, all that he will do in the world throughout the creation and history of men she will also do with him. She will participate in all his works. Without her, he will not do anything anymore. They can work only together. They can be committed only together."[8] So too, Mary as the special possession of the Holy Spirit is a seal on his heart. She acts on our behalf as a seal on God's mighty arm. She represents God to us and brings us the Holy Spirit. In our work as priests at the Lanteri Center for Ignatian Spirituality, I feel the support and enjoy the collaboration of many women staff members and volunteers. Our women share in the leadership, planning, and execution of our mission. They bring a Marian dimension—personal, compassionate, caring—to our ministry of spiritual direction and training of spiritual directors. They are wise and competent professionals as teachers, and often "lifesavers" when it comes to taking responsibility for persons, situations, and events. When I must be away to offer retreats, seminars, and parish missions, I trust our Center is in their good hands as our representatives.

Mary Leads Us into a Closer Relationship with God

Through Mary, God reveals his desire for relationship. Eve was created for relationship because it was "not good that the man should be alone" (Gen 2:18). Woman, who is relational to

---

8. Arminjon, 345.

her core, reflects God who is relational to his core.[9] God is fundamentally relational, intrinsically in the persons of the Holy Trinity, and extrinsically in his relationship with angels, human beings, and all of creation. Women tend to characterize themselves by their relationships as mother, daughter, sister, or friend, which is a glory that reflects the glory of God.[10] Our thirst for God is a pale reflection of God's infinite thirst and yearning for relationship with us. Jesus said, "And this is eternal life, that they may know you, the only true God, and Jesus Christ whom you have sent" (Jn 17:3). Jesus reveals his desire for relationship with us, inviting us to come to him. He extols Mary of Bethany for choosing the better part in remaining at his feet in relationship to him, communicating with him. He is vulnerable in being lifted up during his crucifixion, desiring to draw all people to himself. Jesus even commands that we love him with our whole heart, mind, soul, and strength, since it is what he desires for himself and knows will make us truly fulfilled.

Mary has shown total love to her son and is now given a share in the Holy Spirit's mission of inviting others into their relationship of love: "The Spirit and the bride say 'come'" (Rev 22:17). The bride begins the Song with her desire for relationship in the form of a kiss from her Beloved. The entire Song is about their deepening fascination and concludes with a union of profound love, which "many waters cannot quench" (Song 8:7). John Eldredge notes that the realization that life is a wondrous love story renews our lives. God, who passionately and forever loves us, engages us with beauty, familiarity and adventure. All of

---

9. See John and Stasi Eldredge, *Captivating: Unveiling the Mystery of a Woman's Soul* (Nashville: Nelson Books, 2005), 26–27.

10. Ibid., 27–28.

creation, rivers and mountains, fields and beaches, is meant to draw us into this friendship. This entire world was made for romance—the waterways and the glens, the knolls and shorelines. We become dull to God's alluring when we become absorbed in work and stress.[11] Through a woman, God invites us into the passion of divine relationship. Mary reveals the Holy Spirit's intense fire of love for us. The very flashes of love in the relationship between the Bridegroom and bride are the flashes of the Lord himself (Song 8:6). The fire of the Holy Spirit enflames the heart of Mary, his bride, making it a great furnace of motherly love for the whole Church.

The Lord's love in the Song is revealed as a passionate, jealous love (Song 8:6). In the Old Testament, God's jealousy, his zeal for our welfare, was manifest to purify his people from their idolatry, so that they would seek him alone. The Bridegroom's jealousy in the Song is a more positive jealousy that is meant to preserve the bride in their love. Jesus used a maternal image of jealousy in his love for his people: "Jerusalem, Jerusalem, the city that kills the prophets and stones those who are sent to it! How often have I desired to gather your children together as a hen gathers her brood under her wings" (Mt 23:37). With this metaphor, Christ reveals his motherly care and protection of his children, shared by Mary.

Saint Francis de Sales comments on this passage:

> Remember our Lord's own illustration of the hen's jealous care of her young. No animal is more timid till she is mother; but once she has her brood to guard, she becomes bold as a lion, with watchful eye and alert step mounting guard over

---

11. Ibid, 29–30.

them, and ready to fly at the most unequally-matched foe if they are in peril. Such is the jealous zeal of parent for child."[12]

The Role of Beauty

One of God's essential attributes is beauty. God is transcendental beauty that reveals his unity, truth, and goodness, which attract us to him. His beauty is reflected in the beauty of his creation, especially the creation of woman, God's masterpiece. John Saward notes that God elevated human *nature* in the male gender when the Eternal Word took human flesh in Jesus Christ. However, God elevated the human *person* to its zenith in the female gender in the Virgin Mary. As Mother of God she has an incomparable dignity greater than the angels.[13] Woman is a reminder of the primacy of beauty before function, and contemplation before action. Woman gives us a sense of well-being at rest. She is a reminder of our fundamental receptivity to reality in our minds and hearts. Women tend to behold others with their hearts and acknowledge their dignity, with little moral or conceptual bias. They affirm the goodness of others while having mercy on their shortcomings and rendering assistance. John and Stasi Eldredge comment on how the experience of the beauty of a woman, beyond the merely physical, draws us to God: "Her eyes, her form, her voice, her heart, her spirit, her life. She speaks all of this far more profoundly than anything else in all creation, because she is

---

12. Saint Francis de Sales, *Treatise on the Love of God*, X:14, trans. H. L. Sidney Lear (London: Rivingtons, 1888), 346–347. https://archive.org/details/OfTheLoveOfGod/page/n369.

13. See John Saward, *The Beauty of Holiness and the Holiness of Beauty: Art, Sanctity, and the Truth of Catholicism* (San Francisco: Ignatius Press, 1997), 151.

incarnate, she is personal. It flows to us from an immortal being."[14] Woman, made in the image of God and sharing in his likeness, speaks to us of God's beauty unveiled, his plan taking flesh in human history. As we seek the Lord in prayer and study, he unveils the endless beauty of his hidden mysteries. The truth and goodness of God is attractive and meant to be explored and savored. C. S. Lewis notes that we are not satisfied with merely beholding beauty with our sight, but that we desire to be united with beauty, to enter into it and drink it unto ourselves.[15] The bride of the Song is enamored of the beauty of her lover, and he in turn desires to drink in her beauty like wine (7:9). In the Incarnation, God unites with the magnificence of his human creation and experiences beauty. God created holy Mary with the greatest delight, admiring her virtues, especially her humility and her fidelity to grace. Saint Louis de Montfort exclaims that "her purity, so otherworldly, drew him down to her. He found her lively faith and her ceaseless entreaties of love so irresistible that he was lovingly conquered by her appeals of love."[16] God allows himself to be conquered by pristine beauty! As we behold our mother (see Jn 19:27), contemplating Mary's lovable beauty, we, like the Lord, take delight in it and desire to share in it.

We delight in beauty by immersing ourselves in it. Jesus Christ is revealed as beautiful in the book of Revelation: "There in heaven stood a throne, with one seated on the throne! And the one seated there looks like jasper and carnelian, and around the throne is a rainbow that looks like an emerald . . . and in front of

---

14. John and Stasi Eldredge, 40.

15. See C. S. Lewis, *The Weight of Glory* (New York: HarperCollins, 2009), 42.

16. Saint Louis de Montfort, *Love of Eternal Wisdom*, 105, 107, in *Jesus Living in Mary*, 75.

the throne there is something like a sea of glass, like crystal" (Rev 4:2–3, 6). John describes the beauty of Jesus in terms of precious gems, surrounded by heavenly colors and a crystal sea. Mary is then revealed as beautiful as the heavenly woman clothed with the sun, with the moon under her feet, and on her head a crown of twelve stars. She is clothed with the very beauty of God and manifests his glory. The glory of God is a human being fully alive, and Mary is completely animated by the Spirit. She is vivacious in bearing the life of her son and her children in Christ. Finally, the Church is described as the heavenly bride, the New Jerusalem coming down from heaven (see Rev 21:9–18). Mary is the eminent member of the Church as her mother and as spouse of the Holy Spirit. The beauty of the bride stands out. She shines with the glory of God, and her brilliance is like that of a very precious jewel, clear as crystal. As a city she is pure gold, clear as glass, with walls of jasper. The foundations of the city are adorned with precious gems. So much beauty speaks of God's loveliness, bestowed upon the bride. The beauty of God invites, and "the Spirit and the bride say, 'Come!'" (Rev 22:17). God desires us to partake of his beauty and to make us like him in beauty. Mary's splendor invites us to enter into the same beauty of God, which has so transfigured her being: "In every age Mary is and remains the supreme ideal, the most sublime representative of the longing of human beings for goodness and beauty, a longing which they carry within them, like a divine seed, in the recesses of their hearts. . . . It urges the visual power of the spirit to an ecstatic, transcending leap of ineffable joy."[17]

Mary teaches us contemplation of beauty in her son and receptivity to the grace of God. In her contemplation of God's

17. Paul VI, *Insegnamenti* II, in Lombardi, 294.

Word, she conceives Christ in her heart and womb, giving flesh to the Word. The center of the human mind is openness, receptivity to reality and the capacity to admit into oneself all forms of things.[18] It is not only by their active mental processes that human beings comprehend reality, but also by leisurely contemplation. Von Balthasar contends that when imitation of our Lady wanes, the womanly contemplative heart of human culture is lost. Then male activism and utilitarianism will dominate: "Without Mariology, Christianity threatens imperceptibly to become inhuman. The Church becomes functionalistic, soulless, a hectic enterprise without any point of rest, estranged from its true nature by the planners. And, because in this manly-masculine world, all that we have is one ideology replacing another, everything becomes polemical, critical, bitter, humorless, and ultimately boring, and people in their masses run away from such a Church."[19] When the Church is separated from Mary, she is no longer seen as a person, a woman, the bride of Christ and our Mother, but instead as a cold and controlling bureaucracy.

Mary's ability to touch hearts is seen in the life of Fulton Oursler. He was the publishing supervisor of a popular magazine who told an intriguing account of his search for God. As a correspondent for the *Baltimore American*, Oursler had reported on Methodist assemblies, Baptist rallies, and open-air revivals. He had even observed people calling upon spirits of the dead in candlelit séances. He reported that out of all this he evolved at the age of thirty into a self-styled skeptic. But rather than finding

---

18. See Saint Thomas Aquinas, *Disputed Questions on the Soul,* I,3, sed contra, in Thomas Dubay, *The Evidential Power of Beauty.*

19. Von Balthasar, "The Marian Principle," *Elucidations,* trans. John Riches (San Francisco: Ignatius Press, 1998), 112–113.

harmony, his incredulity left him with an interior void. It also made him despondent. Pretty soon, the hollowness and despondency changed to a depression that ate away at him. Eventually his family developed some grim problems. Fulton knew he needed help beyond what mere friends could offer. He had no one to turn to, not even God, for he had no faith. Oursler was strolling down Fifth Avenue in New York City on a blustery day when he happened upon Saint Patrick's Cathedral. Stopping, he looked up at the magnificent structure. Feeling desperate, he decided to climb the steps and go in. He sat down, gathered his thoughts, and bowed his head in prayer, asking for the gift of belief in God. Then he rose and strode over to the cathedral's Chapel of Our Lady. He entered, knelt down, and offered a petition in words like this: "In ten minutes or less I may change my mind. I may scoff at all this and love error again. Pay no attention to me then. For this little time I am in my right mind and heart. This is my best—take it and forget the rest, and if you are really there, help me."[20] At that moment, he said, a remarkable transformation began in his life. The transformation ended in his becoming a deeply committed Christian.

The Marian Dimension of Life in Christ

Women in our contemporary culture are more and more viewed sensually by men and exploited for pleasure. Mary's pristine beauty and holiness invite men to love and behold women with respect. Devotion to Mary instructs a man in gallantry, bringing about mental, emotional, and spiritual refinement.

20. Mark Link, *Illustrated Sunday Homilies*, Years A, B, C, Year B, Mother of God, 15.

Marian devotion is a Christ-given remedy against the threefold inclination to sin with the lust of the flesh, the lust of the eyes and the pride of life (see 1 Jn 2:16).[21] John Saward speaks of devotion to her as "an instrument of the cauterizing fire of the Holy Spirit, purging away the dross of male pride and lust."[22] Facing Mary, men are encouraged to remain humble like her, while experiencing power like her in the Spirit. Just before the passing of Fra Angelico, Francois Villon graduated as a Master of Arts of the University of Paris. He was a man driven to excess, altogether different from the peaceful Dominican painter. Villon was a lush, a brigand, and a criminal who spent much time in prison or in exile from medieval Paris. He is likewise one of France's most prominent medieval artists and lyric poets who composed one of the world's tenderest sonnets, *The Ballade of Our Lady*. Villon composed this from the perspective of his own pitiful mother. In it he conveys the genuine confidence which he needs to live, and he throws himself in complete assurance on the compassionate Virgin. Villon shows us the peaceful energy of dedication to Our Lady, the impact of the Mother of God to move the hearts of the most miserable of men. For him, the pure excellence of the Virgin did not dampen his spirits, but inspired him with hope.[23] Our Lady is the most wholesome and attractive of human beings and accordingly the most caring and modest of all. We rely on her magnificence in order to restore within our hearts and in our actions a sense of joy in what is truly beautiful.

The Marian dimension of life in Christ also has implications for the situation of women today. In the Incarnation, Christ

---

21. See Saint John Paul II, *Mulieris Dignitatem*, no. 10.

22. Saward, 155. www.ignatius.com. Used with permission.

23. Ibid., 157–158.

entrusted himself to the action of a woman. In Mary, women find the secret of their femininity and dignity. Saint John Paul II relates: "In the light of Mary, the Church sees in the face of women the reflection of a beauty which mirrors the loftiest sentiments of which the human heart is capable: the self-offering totality of love; the strength that is capable of bearing the greatest sorrows; limitless fidelity and tireless devotion to work; the ability to combine penetrating intuition with words of support and encouragement."[24] For all of us Mary is a model who shows us how to imitate Christ in trust, humility, obedience, and all virtue. As we contemplate her sublime beauty we are inspired to live according to authentic spiritual values. Her beauty helps to purify our hearts of the false and deceptive values of this world and conform our minds to Christ. Mary encourages us in our weakness to imitate her perfection and find the richness of God's grace in the midst of our poverty of spirit. Contemplating her magnificence, we are filled with noble thoughts and great desires to serve God in purity of heart.

The Irish historian William Lecky, though not a Christian, nevertheless acknowledged the enormously positive effect of Mary on Western moral and spiritual tradition: "The world is governed by its ideals and perhaps never has there been one which has been more influential than the medieval idea of the Virgin."[25] Because of Mary, woman was finally elevated to her legitimate status. The sacredness of vulnerability and sorrow in

---

24. Pope John Paul II, *Mother of the Redeemer*, no. 46.

25.William Edward Hartpole Lecky, *History of the Rise and Influence of the Spirit of Rationalism in Europe, vol. 1* [1865], Chapter III : Aesthetic, Scientific and Moral Developments of Rationalism, 202–234, https://oll.libertyfund.org/titles/lecky-history-of-the-rise-and-influence-of-the-spirit-of-rationalism-in-europe-vol-1/simple.

human experience were acknowledged. Woman would no more remain the slave, plaything, or object of erotic debasement. She ascended in Mary to a new realm, unknown to prior ages, where she was revered for her dignity. Mary embodied another sort of character and encouraged another sort of deference. She instilled a tenderness and purity into an unforgiving and insensible age.[26] Lecky continues: "In the pages of living tenderness, which many a monkish writer has left in honor of his celestial patron; in the millions who, in many lands and in many ages, have sought to mold their characters into her image; in those holy maidens, who, for love of Mary, have separated themselves from all glories and pleasures of the world, to seek in fastings and vigils and humble charity to render themselves worthy of her benedictions; in the new sense of honor, in the chivalrous respect, in the softening of manners, in the refinement of tastes displayed in all walks of society; in these and in many other ways we detect the influence of the Virgin."[27] All that was finest in Europe gathered around it, and it is the beginning of many of the purest components of our society. Marian devotion can help to restore that lost sense of women's dignity in our contemporary culture.

In conclusion, we can approach Mary with affectionate trust and experience her beauty and holiness shining upon us. Mary taught us to follow her son, saying "Do whatever he tells you" (Jn 2:5). Jesus in turn tells us "Behold your Mother" (see Jn 19:27), which means that we ought to contemplate Mary and, like the disciple John, take her into our hearts and homes. The greatest way to honor someone we love is to imitate her. As we imitate the heroic virtue and devotion of her heart, we set her as a seal

26. Ibid.

27. Ibid.

on our hearts (Song 8:5). Saint Bonaventure testifies to the value of contemplating and imitating Mary:

> The Holy Spirit came upon her like a divine fire, inflaming her soul and sanctifying her flesh in perfect purity. But the power of the Most High overshadowed her so that she could endure such fire. By the action of that power, instantly Christ's body was formed, his soul created and, at once both were united to the divinity in the person of the Son, so that the same person was God and man, with the properties of each nature maintained. Oh, if you could feel in some way the quality and intensity of that fire sent from heaven, the refreshing coolness that accompanied it, the consolation it imparted; if you could realize the great exaltation of the Virgin Mother, the ennobling of the human race, the condescension of the divine majesty; if you could hear the Virgin singing with joy; if you could see the sweet embrace of the Virgin and the woman who had been sterile and hear the greeting in which the tiny servant recognized his Lord, the herald his judge and the voice his Word, then I am sure you would sing in sweet tones with the Blessed Virgin that sacred hymn: "My soul magnifies the Lord . . ." and with the tiny prophet you would exalt, rejoice, and adore the marvelous virginal conception.[28]

Fulfilling the image of the bride, Mary has experienced the kiss of the divine fire of the Holy Spirit in the depths of her heart, transforming her into a pure flame of love for her Lord and Savior. As we behold her beauty, we are drawn to imitate her experience of contemplative union with God and so be transfigured in Christ's glory, pouring out our whole being to him in

28. Saint Bonaventure, *The Tree of Life*, 1, 3 in *Bonaventure: The Soul's Journey into God, The Tree of Life, The Life of St. Francis*, Translation and Introduction by Ewert Cousins (Mahwah, NJ: Paulist Press, 1978), 127–128.

love. Like Mary the bride, we experience the flashes of love that are the presence of God himself in the depths of our souls and in all that surrounds us.

Questions for Reflection and Discussion

1. How has our Lady been good to you? Have you ever begged or commanded her to be your advocate? Do you sense that she desires what is good for you?
2. Are you aware of Mary as a representative of the Holy Spirit, who mediates his presence and acts on his behalf?
3. How do you experience God's desire for relationship revealed through women in general, and Mary in particular? How do you see your life in terms of romance and relationship with God?
4. How much do you seek beauty in nature and in God? How do you see beauty revealed in Jesus and in Mary? Do you perceive the beauty of women, especially Mary's beauty, as revealing the beauty of God?
5. How has Marian devotion made you a better man and one more appreciative of women? How has Marian devotion helped you to realize your dignity and vocation as a woman? How do you see the importance of Marian devotion for our spiritual formation in the Church and for our culture?

Prayer Exercises

1. Contemplate Mary as the New Eve and advocate for human beings (p. 257). Pray with Genesis 2:18–25 and ask for the grace to know Mary's help.

2. Ponder Saint Bernard's exhortation to call upon Mary (p. 258). Pray with 1 Corinthians 10:1–12 and ask to know Mary's help especially in time of danger.
3. Reflect on God's desire for relationship as revealed through women, especially Mary (pp. 259–260). Pray with Revelation 21:2, 9–11; 22:3–5, 17 and ask for a closer relationship with God through Mary.
4. Consider women, especially Mary, as the revelation of God's beauty (pp. 262–263). Pray with Song 8:6–7 and ask for a greater appreciation of the beauty of the Lord and his Mother.
5. Ponder Saint Bonaventure's quote about contemplating Mary (p. 270). Pray with Luke 1:46–56 and ask for the grace to rejoice for what God has done for us in Mary.

Acknowledgments

The Scripture quotations contained herein are from the *New Revised Standard Version Bible: Catholic Edition,* copyright © 1989, 1993, Division of Christian Education of the National Council of the Churches of Christ in the United States of America. Used by permission. All rights reserved.

Excerpts from the English translation of the *Catechism of the Catholic Church* for use in the United States of America, copyright © 1994, United States Catholic Conference, Inc. — Libreria Editrice Vaticana. Used with permission.

Excerpts from papal and magisterium texts copyright © Libreria Editrice Vaticana. All rights reserved. Used with permission.

Excerpt(s) from *Conjectures of a Guilty Bystander* by Thomas Merton, copyright © 1965, 1966 by The Abbey of Gethsemani. Used by permission of Doubleday, an imprint of the Knopf Doubleday Publishing Group, a division of Penguin Random House LLC. All rights reserved.

Excerpt(s) from *The Life of Christ* by Fulton J. Sheen, copyright © 1958 by Fulton J. Sheen. Used by permission of Doubleday, an imprint of the Knopf Doubleday Publishing Group, a division of Penguin Random House LLC. All rights reserved.

Excerpt(s) from *Walking with Mary: A Biblical Journey from Nazareth to the Cross* by Edward Sri, copyright © 2013 by Edward Sri. Used by permission of Image Books, an imprint of the Random House, a division of Penguin Random House LLC.

Excerpted from *Letters of St. Ignatius of Loyola*, by Saint Ignatius of Loyola, translated by William J. Young, SJ (Loyola Press 1959). Reprinted with permission of Loyola Press, www.loyolapress.com.

Taken from *Captivating: Unveiling the Mystery of a Woman's Soul*, by John and Stasi Eldredge. Copyright © 2005 by John and Stasi Eldredge. Used by permission of Thomas Nelson. www.thomasnelson.com.

Brief quote from p. 70 from *Care of Mind/Care of Spirit* by Gerald G. May. Copyright © 1982 by Gerald G. May. Used by permission of HarperCollins Publishers.

Brief quote from p. 76 from *The Day Christ Died* by Jim Bishop. Copyright © 1957 by Jim Bishop. Used by permission of HarperCollins Publishers.

Timothy N. Gallagher O.M.V., excerpts from *Meditation and Contemplation: An Ignatian Guide to Praying with Scripture*. Copyright © by Timothy N. Gallagher. Reprinted with permission of The Permissions Company, LLC on behalf of The Crossroad Publishing Company, Inc., crossroadpublishing.com.